The Political Economy of Space in the Americas

```
I0130572
```

This book presents a novel and cutting-edge interpretation of the evolving political economy of the Americas. Through a combination of qualitative research and theory, it considers the reconstruction of American-led hegemony in the Americas since the 1982 debt crisis and presents an examination of the New *Pax Americana*.

Drawing on the Gramscian concept of hegemony as understood by Robert Cox and Henri Lefebvre, this book argues that since the 1982 debt crisis there has been a reconstruction of American-led hegemony under the signature of neo-liberalism and that it has taken place in the last four ten-year developmental planning stages: "market reforms" in the 1980s, "good governance" in the 1990s, "poverty reduction" in the new millennium and, currently, the "disembedding of security." Each "evolutionary stage" was constructed to secure the continuing motion of capitalist accumulation on a world scale. Moving from the global to the local scale, the book includes two detailed case studies on mining extraction in Bolivia to show how subaltern groups actually experienced and negotiated the transition from the Old to the New *Pax Americanas* at the level of everyday life and what conflicts arose. The book ends with a chapter on President Evo Morales and the re-foundation of Bolivia as an indigenous nation.

The Political Economy of Space in the Americas will be of interest to students and scholars of political economy and Latin American politics.

Alejandra Roncallo is Assistant Professor of International Relations at Bucknell University, USA.

Routledge advances in international political economy

The Political Economy of Space in the Americas

in the Americas

The New *Pax Americana*

Alejandra Roncallo

Routledge
Taylor & Francis Group

LONDON AND NEW YORK

First published 2014
by Routledge
2 Park Square, Milton Park, Abingdon, Oxon OX14 4RN

Simultaneously published in the USA and Canada
by Routledge
711 Third Avenue, New York, NY 10017

First issued in paperback 2017

*Routledge is an imprint of the Taylor & Francis Group, an informa
business*

British Library Cataloguing in Publication Data
A catalogue record for this book is available from the British Library

Library of Congress Cataloging-in-Publication Data
Roncallo, Alejandra.
The political economy of space in the Americas: the New Pax Americana /
Alejandra Roncallo. – 1 Edition.
     pages cm. – (Routledge advances in international political economy; 20)
     Includes bibliographical references and index.
     1. Latin America–Economic policy–20th century. 2. Latin America–
     Economic policy–21st century. 3. Latin America–Politics and
     government. I. Title.
     HC125.R66 2013
     330.98–dc23   2013005374

ISBN 13: 978-1-138-49630-9 (pbk)
ISBN 13: 978-0-415-67154-5 (hbk)

Typeset in Times New Roman
by Wearset Ltd, Boldon, Tyne and Wear

To my students, friends and family
my pillar

Contents

Acknowledgments

Writing a book is an isolating experience and it would not be possible to go through this process without the encouragement of colleagues, editors, students, friends and family. Because this book started as a doctoral dissertation, I want to first thank those who supported me from the beginning: my supervisor Isabella Bakker, as well as Stephen Gill and Alan Simmons, the other two members of my committee. I am also thankful to my defense committee members, Jorge Nef, Shannon Bell and Lisa Phillips, for their diligence in their reading of the manuscript and for their constructive comments that allowed me to improve the writing. I am extremely grateful to Robert Cox, whose legacy, particularly the method of historical structures, allowed me to understand the transition from the Old to the New *Pax Americanas* and the social construction of the mechanisms of hegemony. I treasure the moments we have talked about this manuscript, and his insight and advice are present all through the text.

What gave shape to the topics in this book was the fieldwork I conducted in Bolivia in 2000. I therefore want to give special thanks to the *Programa de Investigación Estratégica en Bolivia* (PIEB) where I held a visiting research position, and to Godofredo Sandoval for his invaluable guidance. I am also indebted to a number of people who provided the information and connections that facilitated my research in that southern country: Hermano Gilberto Pauwells from the *Centro de Estudios de Ecología y Pueblos Andinos* (CEPA); Pedro Gómez Rocabado, Cecilia Molina and Mario from the *Centro de Promoción Minera* (CEPROMIN); Julieta Rodríguez de Antonio from the *Comité Nacional de Amas de Casa Mineras*; Sacha Llorente and Víctor Vacaflores Pereira from the *Asamblea Permanente de Derechos Humanos de Bolivia* (APDHB), and Asencio Lazo from the *Confederación de Maestros Rurales*. I also wish to thank the *Centro de Documentación e Información de Bolivia* (CEDIB); the *Centro de Estudios para el Desarrollo Laboral y Agrario* (CEDLA); *Andean Silver Corporation Bolivia LDC*, and all those who asked to remain anonymous. Special thanks go to Wendy McFarren and Juan Arbona for their heartfelt support during my research trip to Bolivia. I am also indebted to the community members of San Cristóbal who taught me so much about their livelihoods and traditions. I hope their story will encourage others to continue research on this topic, and that it inspires policy makers to find solutions to the injustices suffered by them and so many people in the South since the looting of natural resources under the neo-liberal moment emerged.

The writing process took place in Toronto, Canada; Bariloche, Argentina and in Lewisburg, the United States. I am greatly indebted to those "Spanglish-to-English" "translators" who edited sections of the first draft of the incipient book: Dennis Pilon, Matina Karvellas, Liisa North, Jamie McLennan, Nigmendra Narain and Elaine Brown. I am also grateful to some special people at York and Bucknell Universities, namely Marlene Quesenberry, Josephine Campanelli, Donna Dalton, Bakham Hensberger, Chantal Lishingman, Lila Manseur and Kim DiRocco, for solving every single problem along the way. I extend my thanks to Claire Lyons for her caring and helpful advice. I want to thank those departamental chairs at diverse universities that allowed me to teach courses which strengthened and expanded the ideas presented in this book. These are Don Abelson from The University of Western Ontario, Neil Thomlinson from Ryerson University, Amrita Daniere from the University of Toronto, David McNally, Elisabeth Abergel, Stan Kirschbaum and Principal Kenneth McRoberts from York University, and Emek Uçarer, Hilbourne Watson and David Mitchell from Bucknell University. I extend my thanks to Associate Dean Abe Feuerstein, to Dean George Shields and to all the members of "the Hall" for their collegiality, and for transforming the workplace into a paradise where it is a delight to debate ideas; these are Zhiqun Zhu, Jason Cons, Karen Morin, Paul Susman, Adrian Mulligan, Kim DiRocco, Amanda Wooden, Peter Wilshusen, Richard Waller, Duane Griffin, Bernhard Kuhn and Ben Marsh; to those special people who have not so long left "the Hall," Steve Stamos, Bonnie Poteet and John Peeler; to the i-tech and library support, Aaron Deibler-Gorman, Jey Bailey, Debra Sarlin, Brody Selleck, Debra Balducci; also to those who helped me along the way: Slava Yastremski, Peter Jansson, Ned Searles, Geoff Schneider, David Kristjanson-Gural, Erdogan Bakir, the faculty and staff of the Teaching and Learning Center, the board of the CSREG, the Spanish Department, the Latin American Studies Program and the Environmental Studies Program.

I wish to acknowledge the financial support of two institutions, the Centre for Refugee Studies (CRS) at York University which funded my research trip to Bolivia through their Social Sciences and Humanities Research Council project entitled "The Ethics of Development-Induced Displacement" and to the Centre for the Study of Race, Ethnicity & Gender (CSREG) at Bucknell University for funding the wrap-up of this book. At CSREG special thanks go to Nina Banks, Martha Shaunessy and Susan Reed.

I also wish to extend my gratitude to all those academic associations and universities in which I had the opportunity to present sections of earlier drafts of this book and where I have received invaluable feedback from peers; these are the Centre for Research on Latin America and the Caribbean (CERLAC), Mining Watch Canada, the Canadian Association for Latin American Studies (CALACS), the International Studies Association (ISA), the Canadian Association for the Study of International Development (CASID), the Latin American Studies Association (LASA), the Canadian Political Science Association xiv *Acknowledgments*

(CPSA), the Karl Polanyi Institute of Political Economy, the European Research Network (EMES), Guelph University, Glendon College-York University, the Sir Wilfred Grenfell College-Memorial University of Newfoundland and Bucknell University.

I wish to thank Amanda Crocker, the editorial coordinator at Between the Lines, who allowed me to include in this book a chapter entitled "The Amaya-pampa and Capasirca Gold Mines: Double Movement and State Repression" that was previously published by her editorial in the volume *Community Rights and Corporate Responsibility. Canadian Mining and Oil Companies in Latin America*, edited by Liisa North, Timothy Clark and Viviana Patroni, and published in 2006. Special thanks go to the Routledge/Taylor and Francis Group team, Heidi Bagtazo, Hannah Shakespeare, Alexander Quayle, Lucy Dunne and Harriet Frammingham, for all their magnificent editorial and administrative work around this book. I also wish to thank the three anonymous reviewers for their time reading the manuscript and for their constructive comments. I am also grateful to those "invisible people" who moved underground to make this book happen.

Finally, I wish to thank my students, friends and family for being the pillar that sustained me all these years. Thanks to Jamie McLennan, Alexandre Brassard, Susan James and Jorge Nef: without you this project would have not been possible. I cannot express with words the gratitude I felt and will eternally feel for your encouragement and unconditional support. To my family, Hilda, Adrián, Silvia, Luciana, Malén, Manuela and Juan, thank you from the bottom of my heart. I dedicate this book to all of you.

Acronyms

A–B–C Alliance	America, Britain, Canada
ACN	Andean Community of Nations
AFL-CIO	American Federation of Labor/The American Federation of Labor and Congress of Industrial Organizations
AFN	Assembly of First Nations of Canada
AFP	*Agence France-Presse*
ALBA	Bolivarian Alliance for the Peoples of Our America
AP	Andean Pact
APDHB	Bolivian Permanent Assembly for Human Rights (*Asamblea Permanente de Derechos Humanos de Bolivia)*
ASC Bolivia LDC	Andean Silver Corporation
ATF	Bureau of Alcohol, Tobacco, Firearms, and Explosives
ATTAC	Association for the Taxation of Financial Transactions and for Citizens' Action (*Association pour la taxation des transactions financières et pour l'action citoyenne*)
AUC	United Self-defense Forces of Colombia (*Autodefensas Unidas de Colombia*)
BBC	British Broadcasting Corporation
BINLEA	Bureau of International Narcotics and Law Enforcement Affairs
BITs	Bilateral Investment Treaties
BG	British Gas
BP	British Petroleum
BRICS	Brazil, Russia, India, China, South Africa
CA4FTA	Canada–Central America Four Free Trade Agreement
CACM	Central American Common Market
CAF	Andean Corporation for Promotion (*Corporación Andina de Fomento*)
CAFTA	Central American Free Trade Agreement
CALACS	Canadian Association for Latin American Studies
CAN	Andean Community of Nations (*Comunidad Andina de Naciones*)
CARICOM	Caribbean Community

CARIFTA	Caribbean Free Trade Association
CASID	Canadian Association for the Study of International Development
CBI	Caribbean Basin Initiative
CBOs	Community-based Organizations
CBSI	Caribbean Basin Security Initiative
CDM	Clean Development Mechanism
CEDIB	Bolivia's Center for Documentation and Information (*Centro de Documentación e Información de Bolivia*)
CEDLA	Center for the Study of Labor and Agricultural Development (*Centro de Estudios para el Desarrollo Laboral y Agrario)*
CELAC	Community of Latin American and Caribbean States
CEPA	Center for the Study of Ecology and Andean Peoples (*Centro de Estudios de Ecología y Pueblos Andinos*)
CEPROMIN	Center for Mining Promotion (*Centro de Promoción Minera)*
CERLAC	Centre for Research on Latin America and the Caribbean, York University
CFTA	Caribbean Free Trade Association
CIA	Central Intelligence Agency
CIS	Council for Inter-American Security
CJIRA	Indigenous Juridical Commission of the Argentine Republic (*Comisión Jurídica Indígena de la República Argentina*)
CKP	Kuna Congress of Panama (*Congreso Kuna de Panamá)*
CMN	Mapuche Confederation of Neuquén (*Confederación Mapuche de Neuquén*)
COB	Bolivian Workers' Council (*Central Obrera Boliviana*)
CODDIA-PB	Council for the Defense of the Dignity and Interests of the *Ayllus* of the Province of Bustillos (*Consejo por la Defensa y Dignidad de los Intereses de los Ayllus de la Provincia de Bustillos*)
CODHES	The Consultancy for Human Rights and Displacement (*La Consultoría para los Derechos Humanos y el Desplazamiento*)
COMIBOL	Bolivian Mining Corporation (*Corporación Minera de Bolivia*)
COMSUR	Southern Mining Corporation (*Compañía Minera del Sur)*
CONAIE	Confederation of Indigenous Nationalities of Ecuador (*Confederación de Naciones Indígenas de Ecuador*)
CPE	Complex Political Emergency
CPSA	Canadian Political Science Association
CRS	Centre for Refugee Studies, York University
CSREG	Centre for the Study of Race, Ethnicity & Gender, Bucknell University

CSUTBC	Union Confederation of Peasant Workers of Bolivia (*Confederación Sindical Única de Trabajadores Campesinos de Bolivia*)
DDs	Delegative Democracies
DEA	Drug Enforcement Agency
DHS	Department of Homeland Security
DID	Development-induced Displacement
DOJ	US Department of Justice
ECLAC	United Nations Economic Commission for Latin America and the Caribbean
EEC	European Economic Community
ELN	National Liberation Army (*Ejército de Liberación Nacional*)
EMASA	Mining Enterprise of Amayapampa, Anonymous Society (*Empresa Minera de Amayapampa Sociedad Anónima*)
EMES	European Research Network
ENARSA	Argentine Energy, Anonymous Society (*Energía Argentina Sociedad Anónima*)
EOI	Export-oriented Industrialization
ESAF	Enhanced Structural Adjustment Facility
EZLN	Zapatista National Liberation Army (*Ejército Zapatista de Liberación Nacional*)
FACAT	Federation of Christians for the Abolition of Torture
FARC	Colombian Revolutionary Armed Forces *(Fuerzas Armadas Revolucionarias de Colombia)*
FDI	Foreign Direct Investment
FMLN	Farabundo Martí Liberation Front (*Frente de Liberación Farabundo Martí*)
FREPASO	Front for a Country in Solidarity (*Frente del País Solidario*)
FSLN	Sandinista National Liberation Front (*Frente Sandinista de Liberación Nacional*)
FSTMB	Federation of Mine Workers of Bolivia (*Federación Sindical de Trabajadores de Bolivia*)
FTA	Free Trade Agreement
FTAA	Free Trade Area of the Americas
GATT	General Agreement on Trade and Tariffs
G-7	Group of Seven
G-8	Group of Eight
G-20	Group of Twenty
GDP	Gross Domestic Product
GHGs	Green House Gases
GJM	Global Justice Movements
GPE	Global Political Economy
GPS	Global Positioning System

HIPCs	Heavily Indebted Poor Countries Initiative
HIV/AIDS	Human Immunodeficiency Virus Infection/Acquired Immunodeficiency Syndrome
IADB	Inter-American Development Bank
IBM	International Business Machines Corporation
IBSA	India–Brazil–South Africa Dialogue Forum India, Brazil, South Africa
ICSID	International Center for Settlement Related to Investments Disputes
IFC	International Finance Corporation
IFIs	International Financial Institutions
ILO	International Labour Organization
IPE	International Political Economy
IPSPs	Interim Poverty Reduction Strategy Papers
IRC	Inter-hemispheric Resource Center
IRLR	Impoverishment Risk and Livelihood Reconstruction Model
ISA	International Studies Association
ISI	Import-substitution Industrialization
LAFTA	Latin American Free Trade Association
LASA	Latin American Studies Association
LICs	Low Intensity Conflicts
MAS	Movement towards Socialism (*Movimiento al Socialismo*)
MDGs	Millennium Development Goals
MERCOSUR	Southern Cone Common Market
MFN	Most Favoured Nation
MIGA	Multilateral Investment Guarantee Agency
MINUSTAH	United Nations Stabilization Mission in Haiti
MNR	Nationalist Revolutionary Movement (*Movimiento Nacionalista Revolucionario*)
MNV	Nueva Vista Mining Corporation, Anonymous Society (*Minera Nueva Vista S.A.*)
MST	Brazilian Landless Movement (*Movimento Sem Terra*)
NAFTA	North American Free Trade Agreement
NEP	New Economic Plan
NGOs	Non-Governmental Organizations
NICs	Newly Industrialized Countries
NIDL	New International Division of Labour
NRA	National Rifle Association
NSC	National Security Council
OAS	Organization of American States
OECD	Organisation for Economic Co-operation and Development
ONIC	National Indigenous Organization of Colombia (*Organización Nacional Indígena de Colombia*)
ONPIA	Organization of Indigenous Peoples of Argentina (*Organización de Pueblos Indígenas de Argentina*)

OPEC	Organization of the Petroleum Exporting Countries
OPIC	Overseas Private Investment Corporation
ORIT	Inter-American Regional Organization of Workers (*Organización Inter-Americana del Trabajo*)
PAN	National Action Party (*Partido de Acción Nacional*)
PDVSA	Petroleum of Venezuela, Anonymous Society (*Petróleos de Venezuela, Sociedad Anónima*)
PEMEX	Petroleum of Mexico (*Petróleos Mexicanos*)
PETROBRAS	Petroleum of Brasil, Anonymous Society (*Petróleo Brasileiro S.A.)*
PIEB	Program for Strategic Research of Bolivia (*Programa de Investigación Estratégica de Bolivia*)
PLRA	Authentic Liberal Radical Party *(Partido Liberal Radical Auténtico*)
PRD	Party of the Democratic Revolution (*Partido de la Revolución Democrática*)
PRGF	Poverty Reduction Growth Facility
PRS	Poverty Reduction Sourcebook
PRSPs	Poverty Reduction Strategy Papers
Repsol	Escombreras Petroleum Refinery (*Refinería de Petróleos de Escombreras*)
RHASA	Argentine Rutilex Hydrocarbons, Anonymous Society (*Rutilex Hidrocarburos Argentinos Sociedad Anónima)*
SACN	South American Community of Nations
SALs	Structural Adjustment Loans
SAPs	Structural Adjustment Policies
SIEs	Small Island Economies
TJN	Tax Justice Network
TMCs	Transnational Mining Corporations
TNCs	Transnational Corporations
TRIPS	Trade-related Aspects of Intellectual Property Rights
UK	United Kingdom
UNASUR	Union of South American Nations
UNFED	United Nations Financing for Development
URNG	Guatemalan National Revolutionary Union (*Unidad Revolucionaria Nacional Guatemalteca*)
USAID	United States Agency for International Development
USIA	United States Information Agency
WACL	World Anti-Communist League
WEF	World Economic Forum
WOLA	Washington Office on Latin America
WSF	World Social Forum
WTO	World Trade Organization
YPFB	Bolivia's National Oil Company (*Yacimientos Petrolíferos Fiscales Bolivianos*)

Introduction

This book presents a novel and cutting-edge interpretation of the evolving political economy of the Americas from a southern perspective. It is argued that a New *Pax Americana* has emerged since the 1982 debt crisis and that this reconstruction of American-led hegemony under the signature of neo-liberalism has taken place along four ten-year security and developmental planning stages: "market reforms" in the 1980s, "good governance" in the 1990s, "poverty reduction" in the first decade of the new millennium and, currently, it has shifted to a "green growth" mechanism. Each "evolutionary stage" was constructed to secure the continuing motion of capitalist accumulation on a world scale. In other words, if the "debt crisis" was the Gordian knot that harnessed and maintained hostage the debtor countries; the neo-liberal policies, designed by the International Financial Institutions (IFIs) and implemented coercively in the South, led to the enclosure of new spaces and the appropriation of resources that intensified the accumulation of capital by dispossession and the crisis of social reproduction. In fact, those formerly favored by the social cushion of the Keynesian model – women, the elderly, children and the youth – and those that lived in areas rich in natural resources – indigenous peoples and Afro-descendants – became the targets of a project centered in the commodification and capitalization of livelihood.

This coercive economy was coupled with a very effective search for consensus at the ideological level, a consensus that captured the most urgent popular desire in each decade and utilized it to mask the economic coercion that accompanied it. What strongest desire than *democratization* for those who have been submerged in dictatorships for about twenty years? What strongest desire for ending *corruption* for those who lived through the privatization or looting of the welfare model? What strongest desire for *poverty reduction* and *debt reduction* for those who, decade after decade, became poorer and poorer? What strongest desire for *combating climate change* for those being affected by natural disasters and new epidemic outbreaks? Although, at first, the ideological consensus worked well in hiding the layout of an economic, juridical, social and environmental global architecture that favored the dominant groups, in the long run the disillusions and the visible gap between unmet promises and the lived reality started to break the ideological consensus with the neo-liberal model. In fact, a wide array of social movements emerged dialectically all along the continent and in every single scale to counteract the genocidal model, from the body, to the household, the municipal, the national, the subregional, the regional and the global scales. Soon, the voices of the marginalized fused through the formation of transnational networks, though maintaining their particularities in time and space, into what became known as the Global Justice Movements (GJMs). These counter-hegemonic movements met, since the new millennium, in a dialogical arena,[1] the World Social Forum, which, under the banner of "Another World is Possible" searched for fresh ideas to reverse the neo-liberal World Order.

In the past three decades, the dominant mode of production in the continent has penetrated the periphery – of both North and South – in a multi-scalar manner. In fact, the implementation of neo-liberal multi-level governance has opened up a wide array of new spaces of negotiation, contestation and rebellion, outcomes that differed according to time and space; that is why it is necessary to link the global to the particular in a relational manner. Thus, the objective of this book is to focus on both the structure of World Orders and also on its impact in a specific country, Bolivia. Bolivia is a key country to study the shift in World Orders because it has been the arena of experimentation of neo-liberal policies – the site which the international financial institutions and donors have utilized to implement the above-named new policy models that later on were exported to other countries in the world (see Kohl 2003: 317) – it is also the country where neo-liberal policies were most clearly delineated. Hence, it becomes the most important socio-political landscape to generate ideas about how to create alternative models of governance.

In fact, it was in the 1980s in Bolivia where Jeffrey Sachs became advisor to President Paz Estenssoro in the implementation of structural adjustment policies (SAPs). In the 1990s, his friend and colleague Gonzalo Sánchez de Lozada modified Bolivia's superstructure, which included a neo-liberal national constitution and myriad laws that allowed for the entry of transnational corporations into the country. In the new millennium, Bolivia became one of the two South American countries – together with Guyana – to be considered under the Heavily Indebted Poor Countries (HIPCs) Initiative and, as such, it had to accept the conditionalities that accompanied the HIPCs: the Poverty Reduction Strategy Papers (PRSPs). The PRSPs included the commodification of natural resources and, since Bolivia has many of those natural resources, fueling the post-Cold War conflicts, also called "new civil wars" – those involving the control of oil, gas, mining, water, food, logging, biodiversity and coca. This advance of neo-liberalism started to be turned upside down in January 2006, when Evo Morales Ayma became the first indigenous President of Bolivia – and, until now, the second indigenous President of the Americas – a country where indigenous peoples encompass 71 percent of the population. Morales started to untie the neo-liberal Gordian knot, first at the local scale, by nationalizing the natural resources and modifying the national constitution to create a plurinational state; then joining counter-hegemonic subregional formations such as *The Peoples' Trade Treaty, The Bolivarian Alliance for the Peoples of Our America* (ALBA) and the *Union of South American Nations* (UNASUR) and, finally, struggling at the global scale. In fact, in April 2010, Morales called for a *World People's Conference on Climate Change and the Rights of Mother Earth*, a very successful conference that launched the *Cochabamba Peoples Accord* to respond to the failure of the United Nations *Copenhagen Accord*, proposing substantive solutions to the climate change *problematique*. Morales put into practice the Zapatistas' slogan by creating "another world in which many worlds fit," and it is for this reason that he has been nominated for the Nobel Peace Prize. The future will say if the Nobel Peace Prize Jury will this time be just or if it will continue to utilize the Prize to legitimize Cold Warriors and agents that perpetuate the neo-liberal World Order.

In sum, the main purpose of this book is to rethink and de-construct the neo-liberal World Order and re-imagine how, following the steps of Morales, to construct a "pluriversal"[2] and ethical World Order that puts human beings and non-human communities, rather than the market, at the center of the scenario. The role of organic intellectuals is to demolish the Ivory Tower, to act in the scale in which each one belongs, allowing people at more micro scales to construct and be the agents of their own destinies. Dialogue and the implementation of humane policies rather than the violence of wars should be the "weapon" used to construct a new "Pluriversal" World Order. Because women and indigenous peoples' spaces have been the target of neo-liberal restructuring, this book aims to bring these social forces more to the forefront.

A relational research methodology: everyday life, historical structures and scaling. Putting the pieces of the puzzle together

In order to be able to conduct a research agenda on the Americas in the context of globalization, it is necessary, due to the scope of the subject matter, to combine a series of disciplines and methodological techniques. These will vary depending on the research topic, the purpose and cultural background of the researcher, and the culture, the geographical scale and the specific moment under analysis. The methodology utilized in this book is qualitative and based on "grounded theory" (see Charmaz 2005). In fact, the research started from *place*, from the ground up, with the Bolivian mining case studies.

The objective of the case studies was to analyze, at the body, household, ethnic, subnational and national scales, how ordinary people have experienced their relationship with transnational mining corporations – negotiations, agreements, disagreements and/or rebellion – when these new actors penetrated their territories and livelihood. However, a focus on everyday life in the context of globalization cannot be fully understood if it is not relationally connected to other, more broader *spaces*: subregional, regional and global. Spaces from where conflicts at the local scale are largely generated and, also, from where a dialectical response to this intrusion will emerge. In other words, the objective is to analyze a specific issue, "from below," "from above" and "from the middle," the articulation, the negotiation process between local and global forces, in a holistic and non-deterministic manner.

Place and everyday life

The field research was conducted in the summer of 2000 and the two case studies selected were from the Northern Potosí region in Bolivia. The purpose in selecting this region was because, according to Xavier Albó (1990), in Northern Potosí the *ayllus*[3] continued practicing what John Murra (1980) called the *vertical control of multiple ecological zones*, a specific subsistence economy of the Andes, of which, although it disappeared in the 1970s, it is still possible to find minor enclaves. This allowed for the analysis of the transition from what Olivia Harris (2000) called the *ethnic economy* – vertical control but with sporadic relations to the market – to the neo-liberal economy. Thus, the main concern was about how subaltern groups actually experienced and negotiated the transition at the level of everyday life and what conflicts arose.

For the case study on *Amayapampa and Capasirca Gold Mines: Double Movement and State Repression*, history was the methodological technique chosen because the conflict in these mines took place in 1996, four years before the field research was conducted. Therefore, the sources selected were written documents and the approach interpretive. The places from where the material was collected included various government agencies, documentation centers, non-governmental organizations, mining corporations, human rights organizations, a women's mining union and a rural teacher's confederation. Four sets of historical sources were gathered to reconstruct the story. First, the specific documentation from the trial regarding the "Christmas Massacre" was found in the archive of the *Centro de Promoción Minera* (CEPROMIN) in La Paz. This package of juridical documentation contained letters from all the actors involved in the process: the manager of the TMC, the national and regional governments, unions, miners and *pueblos originarios* – originary people – and also documents pertaining to the company, including the public deed of the concession of the mines extended by the "Special notary in mines and oil" and the Bolivian Judicial Power. Documentation from trials[4] is the richest source to understand the confrontation, position and demands of different actors regarding a specific issue, in this case the privatization of two mines to a foreign company. It is the best source because it reflects the confrontation of opinions and perspectives with regard to the core issues that underpin conflict that arises in a specific issue; it is a documentary "gold-mine."

Second, written sources that dealt with the articulation of global and local mining interests and the internationalization of the conflict: the 1997 Mining Code, newspapers, the International Labour Organization's Convention N.169 – which deals with the right of local people to be consulted when development projects affect them directly – as well as two human rights reports regarding the conflict in the mines, one prepared by the Organization of American States and the other by the Bolivian Permanent Assembly for Human Rights. Third, these two sets of written documents were complemented by personal interviews with researchers at NGOs and a union leader whom I especially asked about the characteristics of what was called the "old" and the "new" mining. This information, together with the 1997 Mining Code, was utilized to reconstruct the transition between the two phases of mining extraction in Bolivia – which are part of the transition from the Old to the New *Pax Americana*, but at the local scale. Finally, the last set of documents were a series of letters, newspapers and legal documentation that some miners from Amayampa, through an intermediary, sent to me in March 2003, when they were about to occupy the mine once more. In sum, the significance of document analysis is that it brings to the fore the strong relationship between history and law; as Ginzburg acknowledged, "historiography, when it is based on documents, can rise above all disagreements and become an established court of law" (2002: 12–13). In fact, what links historians and judges is the search for proof through documents: documents become a very powerful tool for those organic intellectuals who aim to change the structures of World Orders because they provide legitimization and guidance regarding what rules and policies to change. However, because documents do not speak by themselves it is necessary to interrogate them, as historian Lucien Febvre has argued:

> The essence of his [i.e., the historian's] work consists of creating, as it were, the subjects that he observes, often with the assistance of exceedingly complex techniques; and then, once he has acquired these subjects, "reading" them, "reading" his prepared specimens. A daunting task, in truth. Because to describe what one sees is one thing; to see that which must be described, that is the hard part.[5]

Thus, a *textual interrogation* was developed to facilitate the organization of the material collected and to reconstruct the conflict of Amayapampa and Capasirca in the context of the global political economy. These questions were also present in my mind a few days later when conducting field research in San Cristóbal, a town located in the Bolivian *Altiplano* – highlands – yet, in the latter case, the interrogation was adapted to the specific group in question.

The case study on *Multilateralism, Population Displacement and Resettlement in San Cristóbal Silver Mines* was instead based on ethnographic research. This research technique was selected because the community of San Cristóbal was displaced from the old to the new town just a year before my field research trip to Bolivia; therefore the experience and feelings regarding the displacement were fresh in people's minds. Although this chapter was especially based on interviews, it was also backed by newspaper articles and agreements related to Apex Silver Mines and the community of San Cristóbal. The difference between interrogating written documents and human beings is that you can ask technical and theoretical questions of a text, but when questioning human beings you have to avoid all types of discriminatory technicality. Instead, what is needed is to be knowledgeable about the culture of the informants, to respect each human being's position in society, worldviews and beliefs, gender and age, and to adapt the questions to their own epistemology and ontology, to their own language. Hence, when the interviews in Bolivia were conducted, I knew what to ask each informant according to her or his background but to give priority to what each person wanted to tell me and, in the middle of open and friendly conversations – in which I was also interrogated by my informants regarding who I was and what was the objective of my research – I inserted my own questions. The methodology was based on semi-structured and unstructured interrogation where the guiding thread was designed by the informant and not the "detective."[6] It is only in the analysis of the information and writing of the story where the researcher has the right to freedom of expression.

Thirty-two interviews were conducted and each interview had a duration of about one to two hours; however, in many cases they went beyond that timeline. The interviews were carried out with two sets of people: those who belonged to a Western culture and those who belonged to an Andean one. The first group included a total of seventeen key informants, members of the church, the transnational mining corporation, researchers, union leaders, rural teachers, NGOs and human rights organizations from La Paz, Oruro and Uyuni. Because of their westernized knowledge, the focus of their explanation/story was on the global, national and subnational context of the mining industry, on the transition from the old to the new mining, on the history of San Cristóbal and how the rich silver deposits were discovered. Then the focus shifted to the company, Apex Silver Mines and its subsidiary in Bolivia, the amount and types of investments, infrastructure, new technology, the creation of the Foundation *Llama de Plata* and the legal aspects involved in the transnationalization of mining extraction. The more critical informants focused on the Quechua population, on the impact on human beings such as the reasons why the indigenous population agreed to negotiate, the contradictions in the negotiation process, the displacement of the population from the old to the new town, how the company circumvented the ILO Convention 169 and, finally, the encounter between two different cultural knowledges.

The second group included fifteen Quechua – *ayllu Lípez* – informants from San Cristóbal including women, men, young people and children who had been displaced by the TMC from an old to a new modern town built by the company. The conceptualization of old and new town came from the same community members. Having undergone previous training on the Andes at the University of Buenos Aires in Argentina through the fascinating classes of Professor Enrique Tandeter, I was familiar with the Andean epistemology and ontology, with their cosmovision, their subsistence economy based on the *vertical control of multiple ecological zones*, on the *ayllu* and the social relations based on reciprocity such as the *ayni* and *mink'a* systems. Therefore, I knew that the displacement from one town to another conducted by the TMC also meant the transition from an "ethnic economy" to a fully marketized one through the creation of micro enterprises. I also knew from interviews, conducted some days before in La Paz, that there was conflict within the community regarding their decision to move to a new town; this is why I have selected informants from different genders and generations. The objective was to focus on how the transition from one mode of production to another affected different groups.

I spent ten days in San Cristóbal, living in one of the new houses built by the company and participating in community life, such as the sacrifice of two llamas,[7] processions, the *San Juan* bonfire[8] and games that the children played, which facilitated the openness and confidence of the community towards me, a foreigner. Only three broad questions were posed, questions that could lead the informants to tell their own experience: first, to describe one day of their life in the old town; second, why they decided to move and how the negotiations with the TMC were conducted; and third, how their life had changed in the new town. Along the narrative, special attention was paid to details on what issues people felt more affected by the transition and then more questions were asked regarding that specific conflict. Through this unstructured method, a wide array of issues that I would have never have touched upon came to the fore. For example, the importance of the symbolic values of the stones: the sentinel, the frog, the tree giants and the *achupalla*. By rereading the chapter and my notes I am extremely surprised about how rich the data can be when not forcing questions formulated in a foreign mind. In fact, the key is to listen to what the interviewees have to say, not the other way around.

In sum, the richness of personal interviews and ethnographic research over textual interrogation is that the researcher transforms her or his living experience into written documents, re-creating them based on the informants' worldview – the real authors. However, in both case studies, the concepts arising from written documents and interviews to explain community–TMCs–state relations were interwoven with subregional, regional and global ones; therefore it was necessary to think relationally from *place* to *space*. In fact, to uncover from what scale or constellation of scales local mining conflicts were emerging, it was necessary to understand how power or the mechanisms of hegemony worked, and what policies allowed corporations to move to the South and extract the mineral from foreign soil.

From place to space and back to place: hegemony, historical structures and scaling

When the analysis moves from *place* to *space*, from local to global, other, more abstract, interpretive and theoretical techniques need to be utilized, central to which is the concept of hegemony and how it works in time and space. Both Robert Cox and Henri Lefebvre understood hegemony in Gramscian terms, as a dominant mode of production that penetrates the periphery, and also both put emphasis on the temporal and spatial connotation of the concept; however, while the former put more emphasis on movement, the latter did so on space. Cox advanced the method of historical structures to explain how hegemony changes in a diachronic manner. For him, structures are socially constructed, they exist in the "intersubjectivity of relevant groups" and become part of the "objective world of institutions"; it is about ideas, institutions and material conditions (Cox

[1992]1996: 149–50). According to Cox, a historical structure is "a picture of a particular configuration of forces. This configuration does not determine actions in any direct mechanical way but imposes pressures and constraints. Individuals and groups may move with the pressures or resist and oppose them, but they cannot ignore them. To the extent that they do successfully resist a prevailing historical structure, they buttress their actions with an alternative, emerging configuration of forces, a rival structure (Cox [1981]1996: 97–98).

For Cox, the latest historical structure that he studied, *Pax Americana* (1945–1964), was followed by a *period of non-hegemonic conditions*. Writing thirty years after Cox wrote his method of historical structures and, following his insight, this book aims to analyze the reconstruction of American hegemony and therefore, retrospectively, three modifications have been introduced. The first was the addition of a new structure; this required the renaming of his *Pax Americana* as Old *Pax Americana* (1947–1965), the period of non-hegemonic conditions, *Impasse* (1965–1982) and the current historical structure New *Pax Americana* (1982–). The second modification of the Coxian method was the analytical disaggregation of the concept of "social forces" into class, gender and ethnicity. Although Cox did consider these categories under the concept of social forces,[9] he did not include their specific struggles and demands in the analysis. Lastly, his three levels of analysis, "World Orders, States and Social Forces" were modified to better understand the impact of neo-liberal multi-level governance in the Americas. It is here where Henri Lefebvre's concept of "production of space" and critical geographers' (e.g., Sheppard, Sziarto, Smith, Swyngedouw, Peck, Leitner, Brenner) concepts of "scales" were needed.

For Henri Lefebvre, "any activity developed over (historical) time engenders (produces) a space, and can only attain practical 'reality' or concrete existence within that space" (2008: 115). According to Lefebvre, the "production of space" starts with the conquest of the land and natural resources in the periphery but also includes the "juridical and legal fiction of ownership of things" – or private property – and spatial planning as, for example, it was done through "modernization" (2008: 349–350). However, the fact that today neo-liberalism has implemented a multi-level governance structure on a wide array of spatial scales, it was necessary to conduct research on the struggles emerging in each of those points of interaction or governance arrangements. As Leitner, Sheppard and Sziarto have sustained, "Scale is conceptualised as a relational, power-laden and contested construction that actors strategically engage with" (2008: 159). Thus, it may be said that the agency–structure debate in international relations does not capture the various scales and actors in different geo-historical contexts. This book tries to bridge that gap by focusing on the changing geographies and structure of multiple governance spaces in the Americas and, towards that end, it concentrates on the following eight scales, from the global to the body.

At the *global scale*, the shift from the Old to the New *Pax Americana* involved the passage from the consensus of the Keynesian economy, the social contract embedded in it and the coercion of the Cold War; towards a coercive neo-liberal economy, characterized by the disembedding and commodification of the social contract and the search for a political consensus built around the idea of "democratization." Through this shift of historical structures initiated in 1982, following the debt crisis, which also entailed the deterritorialization of the state towards the global institutions, Latin America entered the global political economy (GPE) in a subordinate manner. The interpretive method is the most adequate one to analyze this scale and the main themes to analyze are international institutions (e.g., the United Nations, World Bank, International Monetary Fund (IMF), World Trade Organization (WTO), World Economic Forum (WEF), Inter-American Development Bank (IADB), the Organization of American States (OAS), the "G-8 nexus," the G-20 nexus, tax havens, stock markets, private elite organizations or think-tanks) and the rules and policies that emanate from them. However, it is crucial to also pay attention to the dialectical response to the mechanisms of hegemony, such as the global justice movements and their meeting space, the World Social Forum (WSF) and their demands. It is this tension between opposing forces and, especially, the negotiation process among them that becomes the key arena for research on this scale.

In the conundrum of globalization, the *regional and subregional scales* were modified from closed to open regionalism, from protectionist economic blocs that followed the import substitution industrialization (ISI) model created in the 1960s, towards a frenzied creation, since the 1990s, of subregional free trade agreements (e.g., the North American Free Trade Agreement (NAFTA), the Central American Free Trade Agreement (CAFTA), the Caribbean Community and Common Market (CARICOM), among others) that aimed to build a Free Trade Area of the Americas (FTAA) from Alaska to Tierra del Fuego. This led to the reconfiguration of space from Latin America and the Caribbean, one of the three "Third World" regions constructed by modernization theorists as a Cold War tool for American foreign policy; towards the construction of the "Americas," as a conservative American-Canadian design to break down the barriers to trade and foreign direct investment to their corporations. Counter-hegemonic regionalism includes ALBA, the People's Trade Treaty and the indigenous peoples' of Abya Yala's[10] continentalism built around ties of solidarity. In addition, there is UNASUR which, instead, searches for an autonomous integration into the GPE. Thus, the methodologies used to analyze regionalism and counter-regionalism are interpretive and mixed methods, analyses of old and new trade agreements, transnational lawmaking, transnational corporations, foreign direct investments, the different understandings of trade – free and fair – property rights and human and non-human communities, and material and spiritual demands.

The shift from the Old to the New *Pax Americana* has also led to changes at the *national scale*. The old, inner-oriented and strong developmental states were based on a tripartite alliance together with capital and labor and on a social contract as a tool for consensus building. The latter, together with the design of people-centered national constitutions, gave rise to social citizenship. The role of the developmental state was to manage foreign assistance funds, plan the internal economy and encourage industrialization and urbanization (McMichael 1996).

In contrast, the new "competition state" (Cerny 1997) was outward-oriented, based on a state–corporation alliance, privatized the social contract, which gave rise to a market citizenship, and, built its consensus in the politico-ideological arena – e.g. giving civil rights to women and indigenous peoples while curtailing their economic space. Thus, the spatial action of the state shifted from being geared towards the internal market to one that regulated the economy towards the outside, towards the external market. Moreover, the new managerial public administration was modified in order to allow the open doors economy to unfold – e.g. independent central banks, judiciary, police, health, education. As a dialectical response from below, there was the emergence of transnational networks contesting and operating at multi-layered spaces (Radcliffe 2001: 24) and the creation of plurinational states – Bolivia and Ecuador. Hence, the research methods to better assess the impact of the shift in World Orders at the national scale are interpretive of constitutional changes and legal codes, policy and discourse analysis, case studies, comparative studies and mixed methods. Meanwhile, the sources to search for and analyze include government documents, state reform documents, data for changes in political representation, old and new constitutions and legal reforms.

At the *sub-national scale* the change in historical structures meant a movement away from an urban scale defined by developmental planning, industrialization and urbanization towards one based on neo-liberal decentralization from states to the provincial and municipal levels. Hence, states were weakened from both, the global and the sub-national scales and, according to Ryan, the economic, political and socio-infrastructural decentralization was promoted in the 1990s by multilateral lending agencies with the objective to generate a more favourable environment for private capital (Ryan 2004: 81). The main intermediary agents in this process of re-articulation of power between the national and sub-national scales were the neo-liberal NGOs. The transition at this scale led to a party-system fragmentation and inter-municipal conflict, a conflict between large and small municipalities – the former better positioned to secure funding (see Ryan 2004: 86–90). The most adequate research methods include comparative, interviews, mixed methods, and interpretive and; the main sources, decentralization laws and policies, fiscal and social data, analysis of TNCs and NGOs, political parties and voting systems.

The passage from the old to the new structure of World Orders at the *ethnic-community scale* involved the shift from a semi-subsistence or subsistence economy to a market one through the creation of micro-enterprises and, the main aim was the appropriation of land and natural resources. The coercion of dispossession and displacement was coupled with a consensual element, the incorporation of ethnic groups into politics, particularly in legislatures. The methods include interviews, oral history, ethnographies, comparative, case studies, mixed methods and participatory observation and; the sources, interviews, analysis of trials, a diversity of newspaper articles and written documents.

At the *household scale*, the incorporation of women into the labour market – the service sector in the north and maquiladora industry in the south – led to the "feminization of labour," adding a "double-burden" for women, and, producing the marginalization of men. In fact, the objective of structural adjustment policies was to "shift all responsibility for survival from the state to the individual and the family, forcing families to absorb a greater share of the cost of living by reducing government policies aimed at redistribution" (Safa 1995: 33). In this movement in place from the private to the public sphere, women shifted from being supplementary wage earners to primary breadwinners. Thus, the nuclear family centered on the male breadwinner model of the Keynesian World Order begun to crack; in some cases, the fact that women also became wage earners led to more egalitarian relationships within the household; however, in other cases, the shift in gender authority and the pressure of the "double-burden" led to marital instability, divorces and the increase of female headed households and violence against women. In other words, the subordination of women shifted from the home to the workplace and the polity (Safa 1995: 41–47). Very different is the case of indigenous gender relations, which shifted from the gender equilibrium in the subsistence economy to the subordination of women when incorporated into the capitalist economy. Research methods in this scale involve oral history, ethnographic research and policy analysis; meanwhile, the main sources are the raw data that comes from the interview process.

The most intimate scale, *the body*, is the site where the violence of policies decided at broader scales is most dramatically felt. However, it is also the less addressed in academic literature and it is urgent, following the path of pioneer feminist and ethnic studies scholars, that social justice analysis based fill this vacuum. In the neo-liberal world order the violence against women, children and the ethnic "other" has dramatically intensified. In fact, rapes, sex trade, slavery in assembly lines, trafficking in human beings and organs, sex tourism, population displacement, torture and genocide are strongly linked to natural resource corporations and haute finance (see Appadurai 1998; Baines 2003; Eriksson-Baaz 2009; Le Billon 2001; Ong 1989; Pettman 1997; Swords and Mize 2008). Yet, as Elisabeth Grosz has argued, the body is also "the site of contestation, in a series of economic, political, sexual and intellectual struggles" (quoted in Pettman 1997: 100). Methods that can capture the everyday of bodily harm are ethnographies, oral history, interviews and sources include human rights reports, newspapers, testimonies and documentary videos.

In sum, the research that started in Bolivia ended with too many questions that could not be resolved at the local scale and the search for answers moved the analysis upwards to broader spaces and then downwards to find an explanation for the reconstruction of hegemony "in practice." The outline of the above eight scales aimed at introducing a holistic methodology that could explain the multi-scalar struggles for power in the Americas in the context of globalization. Of course, the complexity and scope of the subject matter cannot be grasped by one single discipline and therefore it is necessary to borrow from history, geography, international political economy, law, public administration, anthropology, feminism and ethics. In other words, it fuses the old fictitious disciplinary boundaries, it renders them obsolete. Thus, the role of the researcher is what

Denzin and Lincoln (2003, 2005) described as a "bricoleur," someone that puts the pieces of the puzzle together and utilizes critical empirical and theoretical analysis at the service of ethical practice – policy design and implementation. Because the objective of the book is to uncover how American hegemony was re-constructed at the continental scale, the *structure of the book* starts in opposite direction in which the research was conducted, from the top-down and then, shifts the analysis from the bottom-up, to the Bolivian case studies and to Evo Morales' re-founding of Bolivia as an indigenous nation, what Karl Polanyi called the "double-movement."

Structure of the book

Chapter 1, "The 1980s: development as 'free markets,' the demolition of the old and the rise of the new," argues that the Latin American external debt was the Gordian knot that tied the region to the new "global managerial infrastructure."[11] At that time, development was defined as "free markets" and the external debt became the tool to demolish the remains of the Old *Pax Americana* and to forge the rise of the New. While the Southern Cone was experiencing the transition from military authoritarianism to market dictatorships, Central America was battling the last of the "old wars"[12] in the continent – characterized by the Cold War containment to communism and, the Caribbean was being transformed into a site for *maquiladoras*, tax havens and tourism. A new form of state, the "competition state" (Cerny 1997), facilitated the internalization of structural adjustment programs (SAPs), which, because it hit women hardest, led to the intensification of women's movements, which set the tone of the so-called "lost decade."

In Chapter 2, "The 1990s: development as 'good governance' and the consolidation of hegemony," in contrast to the mainstream literature that saw the 1990s as a period of democratic consolidation, it is contended that the 1990s was a period of hegemonic consolidation. During this period, development was re-defined as "good governance." The end of the Cold War was followed by the creation of transnational legal regimes or "new constitutionalism" (Gill 2003) aimed at sustaining the structural reforms that took place in the former decade. This ensemble of juridical reforms at different scales consolidated the American-led hegemony in the hemisphere and accelerated the construction of a Free Trade Area of the Americas (FTAA). It also led to the formation of a new patriarchal order through the incorporation of women into politics – gender quotas – (Waylen 1998; Htun 2004, 2006) and promoted – through the creation of natural resource regimes and the harmonization of national constitutions – the entry of transnational corporations into the region, which led to the rise of indigenous peoples' movements in defense of their livelihoods. The chapter ends with four case studies: "peacebuilding" in "post-conflict" Central America, NAFTA and the Zapatista uprising, displacement of Afro-descendants in Colombia and, finally, haute finance, tourism and displacement in the Caribbean.

Chapter 3, "The new millennium: development as 'poverty reduction' and the commodification of livelihood," examines how in the new millennium the meaning of development shifted once more, this time to "poverty reduction." It is argued that September 11, 2001 was the trigger that expanded and legitimized the "end of poverty" discourse as an antidote to terrorism. Yet, it was not until the United Nations Financing for Development (FED) summit in Monterrey, in March 2002, that a private sector development agenda to "reduce" poverty was officially launched. The Monterrey consensus seemed to represent the sealing of the ensemble of structural, superstructural and social top-down reforms that were planned respectively in the 1980s, 1990s and 2000s. As such, these latter policies have elements of the former and are deepening the hegemonic project led by the United States. Their cornerstone is the strengthening of an authoritarian social contract through the commodification of livelihood, particularly the appropriation of land, natural resources and welfare – indigenous peoples' and women's terrains. The chapter focuses on the analysis of the infrastructure section of the World Bank's Poverty Reduction Strategy Papers (PRSPs) – particularly the privatization of energy, water and mining – and then addresses the critiques to continentalism posed at the II Indigenous Peoples Summit and the IV Americas Summit in 2005, both in Argentina. In fact, during that encounter, five Latin American presidents declined to sign the Free Trade Areas of the Americas (FTAA), considering it detrimental to their countries. This was the pivot towards the rise of "New Left" governments and the intensification of South–South cooperation. Meanwhile, the impact of the 2008 global financial meltdown led to the search for new alternatives to neo-liberalism. The victory of Barack Obama in the American elections was seen, at the beginning, as the shift towards social justice emerging at the heart of the hegemon.

Chapter 4, "Obama, 'change' and the disembedding of security in Latin America: the tension between polyarchy and democracy," describes how, after a year in power, it became clear that the Obama Administration could not put into practice its many promises. This disjuncture between the high expectations raised and the actual results brought enormous frustration to those who believed in "change." Thus, this chapter argues that the Obama Administration represents the continuity of the system, "more of the same" rather than "change," a fourth moment of the New *Pax Americana*, centered on the shift to a clean market economy. The chapter is especially anchored in Obama's Four Freedoms in "A New Partnership for the Americas" and its confrontation with the actual implementation of the policies in Latin America. The document draws on Roosevelt, Truman and Kennedy, and the Four Freedoms include *Political Freedom/Democracy* which targets Cuba and Venezuela; the *Freedom from Fear/Security* that centers on Central America, Mexico and Colombia; the *Freedom from Want/Opportunity* focuses on Haiti, and the *Working Towards Energy Security* section addresses Brazil and the region as a whole. This strongly ethnocentric and interventionist document – which seems to be a continuation of the Santa Fe documents – is carefully confronted with the history of Obama's first Administration.

Chapter 5, "The Amayapampa and the Capasirca gold-mines: double movement and state repression," aims to explain the articulation of global and local mining interests in historical perspective. It introduces the shift from the old, nationally oriented mining system based on tin extraction, to the new, outward-oriented system that prioritizes the extraction of gold. It then addresses the encounter between a Canadian gold company and the mining towns of Amaya-pampa and Capasirca, the formation of a progressive countermovement estab-lished by the miners and *pueblos originarios* (original people); the repression and massacre conducted by the competition state in defense of the transnational mining corporation; and the emergence of a two-tier human rights system – the Organization of American States' Inter-American Commission for Human Rights, which sided with the transnational mining corporation and the "competition state"; and the Bolivian Permanent Assembly for Human Rights which defended the rights of the miners and *pueblos originarios*.

In contrast, Chapter 6, "Multilateralism, population displacement and resettle-ment in San Cristóbal silver mines," is based on ethnographic research con-ducted in the summer of 2000 and explores the peaceful displacement of an indigenous community, whose ties to the market were very slight. It offers a cri-tique to the World Bank's "Impoverishment Risk and Livelihood Reconstruction Model" (IRLR) for development-induced displacement projects. Through a case study, this manuscript analyzes the negotiation process between an American transnational mining corporation with addresses in the Cayman Islands and the Quechua community of San Cristóbal, which was displaced by the transnational mining corporation to a new town because there were silver deposits beneath the old San Cristóbal and the two mountains surrounding the town. In fact, San Cristóbal, located at 4,200 meters above sea level, is one of the three largest open-pit silver mines in the world. Focusing on the everyday life of the com-munity in the old town, it explains the pitfalls of the shift from a subsistence economy, based on the Andean "vertical control of multiple ecological zones" and on reciprocity-based kinship ties and social relations – which meant food sovereignty – towards a neo-liberal model based on micro enterprises in the resettlement site – the new town built by the company – and how this has affected the social reproduction of the group.

Chapter 7, "President Evo Morales Ayma's Pachakutik: re-founding Bolivia as an indigenous nation," argues that President Morales' re-founding of Bolivia as an indigenous nation may be seen as the beginning of the shift towards a more humane World Order. It starts by examining the intensification of conflicts against neo-liberalism, such as mining extraction and the water, gas and tax wars, which ousted two presidents. It goes on to address the origins of the pres-idential triumph of Evo Morales Ayma, the first indigenous president of the Americas in the twenty-first century. Later on, at the national scale, the Presi-dent's particular nationalization of hydrocarbons and the creation of a national constitution that aims to re-found the nation as a plurinational state; at the regional scale, Morales' joining ALBA, the People's Trade Treaty and UNASUR, which replace the greed for free enterprise and "strategic regional-ism" by generating ties of solidarity, fair trade and reciprocity with Latin Amer-ican countries. Meanwhile, at the global scale, I discuss the President's new approach to foreign affairs, the good relations with Europe and his call for a global counter-Copenhagen Climate Change Summit. Particular attention will be paid to the debate that led to the Cochabamba People's Accord, which focuses on the respect for Pachamama or "Mother Earth." This multi-scalar struggle for life "from below" is becoming the strongest opposition to the current neo-liberal hegemonic project.

In sum, the purpose of analyzing the reconstruction of the New *Pax Americana* is to highlight the mechanisms of hegemony implemented for the accumulation of capital at the regional scale and the rise of inequality in Hispanic Americas, two sides of the same coin. This inequality has led in turn to a crisis of governability, widespread corruption and unbearable sorrow for the majority of the population in the periphery – of both South and North. Because Bolivia has been the arena of experimentation of neo-liberal engineering and, today, is the strongest opposition to it, it becomes the key country to study in order to change the current architecture of this psychopathic World Order. There is a long way to go in the transition towards a post-neo-liberal World Order, an order that puts the human and non-human communities, rather than the market, at the center of the scenario. Until the external debt and tax havens are not eliminated, until the structure and superstructure of world orders are not modified and until the social contract is not restored, no alternative projects will ever be able to function, since they will become subsumed under the design of a market fundamentalist project.

Part I

Weaving the Americas together

The four "stages" of a new evolutionary tale

1 The 1980s

Development as "free markets," the demolition of the old and the rise of the new

At the end of the 1970s there was still a widespread belief in Latin America that the revolutionary path offered a real possibility for establishing a just society free from foreign interference. In fact, Central American revolutions were seen as ideal models to follow. In addition, there was not yet any consciousness about the impact of the enormous external debt created in the 1970s and what it would mean in the years to come. Meanwhile, in the United States, as Susan Strange noted, within some academic circles it was believed that the external shocks produced by the oil crisis, coupled with internal issues such as the Watergate scandal and the subsequent election of President Jimmy Carter, had accelerated the decline of American hegemony (Strange 1982: 481). With the election of Ronald Reagan as President of the United States (1981–1989) and Margaret Thatcher as Prime Minister in Britain (1979–1990), a new 'historic bloc' started to emerge. The "New Right" initiated its counter-revolution by re-defining development as "free markets" with Latin America as their center-point for the reconstruction of American hegemony. The following analysis of the Santa Fe documents will demonstrate how this was accomplished.

In this chapter it will be argued that the Latin American external debt was the tool utilized by the "New Right" to demolish the remains of the Old *Pax Americana* and to initiate the rebuilding of a new hegemonic order. The political construction of the Old *Pax Americana* was based on the Westphalian system of states or balance of power and, economically as a Keynesian demand-side, nationally oriented economic model that included a social contract. For the American "New Right," inverting this inward-oriented model towards an outward-oriented one required putting an end to the costly Cold War between the United States and the Soviet Union, and restructuring the economy towards a supply-side neo-liberal model, which resulted in the gradual elimination of the social contract.

These changes were introduced during the past three decades through the enforcement of debt conditionalities. To that end, the hegemonic country designed three four-year planning procedures, or developmental evolutionary stages: "market reforms" in the 1980s, "good governance" in the 1990s, "poverty reduction" in the new millennium and, currently, the "disembedding of security." In short, the social construction of the new structural, superstructural, social and political reforms led to the consolidation of a New *Pax Americana* and its concomitant continental spatial reconfiguration in the Americas.

This chapter will examine the 1980s and will begin with a summary of the ideas behind the continental dream of the "New Right," the construction of new mechanisms of hegemony at the meso-level such as global managerialism and the first generation reforms. It will also examine the Southern Cone's transition from political to market dictatorships, the end of the Cold War in the continent after the Esquipulas peace accords were signed in Central America and the implementation of Reagan's Caribbean Basin Initiative.

Ideas: Santa Fe I, "The Reagan Doctrine"

The Reagan Administration was strongly influenced by the Council for Inter-American Security's "Santa Fe Commission Report," which was written in 1979 by conservative military officers and academics (La Feber 1993: 274).[1] The Council for Inter-American Security, founded in 1976 in Texas, and one of the most prominent think-tanks of the American "New right," formed part of the World Anti-Communist League (WACL). Its objective was to conduct research, produce policy recommendations and also to act as a citizen's lobby regarding national security issues in inter-American relations.[2] The Council for Inter-American Security published three comprehensive documents for inter-American relations: Santa Fe I for the 1980s, Santa Fe II for the 1990s and Santa Fe IV for the first decade of the new millennium. Santa Fe III was never published. Most of the socio-economic policies in these documents are present in the three stages' evolutionary policies advanced through the Bretton Woods Institutions to the region during those same decades –"market reforms," "good governance" and "poverty reduction." The main points of these three documents will be summarized in each of the following three chapters through a careful textual presentation and discursive analysis to avoid distorting the language utilized by the documents' authors. The overall objective – when addressing the three Santa Fe documents in Chapters 1, 2 and 3 respectively – in maintaining the data in its originality is to highlight the tone (with its implied paranoia) and the misconceptions to illustrate the mindsets through which the policies were designed. It should be noted that the language of Obama's "New Partnership for the Americas," the final chapter of Part I, shares enormous resemblances with the Santa Fe documents.

Santa Fe I,[3] originally entitled *Inter-American Relations, Shield of the New Order and Sword of the U.S. Ascent to World Power*, became known as "The Reagan Doctrine." The document starts by declaring that the American continent was under attack and that this aggression was both external and internal, and that the United States was "engaged in World War III." It mentions that the Soviet Union, the "Evil Empire," has been expanding its influence since 1959 and instigating a double strategy – cornering the Popular Republic of China and dominating the Western industrialized nations by controlling their oil and minerals. South East Asia and Latin America and the Caribbean were the regions where that aggression was taking place.

The authors of the document saw the origins of the advance of what they called the "Soviet–Cuban Axis" in the 1960s, with President Kennedy's defeat in the Bay of Pigs, and the Kennedy–Khrushchev agreement that ended the Cuban missile crisis. The situation reached its peak under the Carter Administration (1977–1981) with the President's passive attitude towards "communist expansionism," his position against nuclear proliferation, and his human rights campaign. Carter's human rights policy was criticized for being too soft with the Latin American "extreme left dictatorship" with reference made to President Omar Torrijos from Panama, Castro in Cuba and the Sandinistas in Nicaragua. Carter was also criticized for being too harsh on the "authoritarian non-communist governments" that had been former allies to the United States, namely Argentina, Brazil, Chile, El Salvador, Guatemala, Somoza's Nicaragua and Paraguay.[4]

The principal recommendations of Santa Fe I revolved around three sets of policies: pro-market socio-economic and cultural reforms throughout the region, strong security measures in Central America and the Caribbean, and policies to improve hemispheric relations.

The first set of recommendations related to the socio-economic and cultural reforms included, first, the increase of American foreign direct investment in the region to create an autonomous Latin American capital market that could "help" the region to service its external debt. Second, technology transfer geared towards strengthening the freedom of enterprise and hemispheric relations to facilitate the development of alternative sources of energy such as fusion, geo-thermic, solar and nuclear energy. It also mentioned that four Latin American countries – Mexico, Venezuela, Ecuador and Argentina – were among the world's most important producers of oil and this was the main preoccupation throughout the document. Third, export-oriented agriculture, including "help" to indigenous peoples to facilitate the shift from the "poverty" of subsistence economy towards the creation of "profitable" micro-private enterprises. It also mentioned that food was a "weapon in a world in war" and that the top four world producers of food were located in the Americas – Canada, the United States, Brazil and Argentina. The document stated that the economic reforms should be completed with the creation of a "free" union movement with the participation of the AFL-CIO and the control of the educational system to "win the minds of mankind," because "those that control the education determine the future."

The second set of recommendations focused on the security concerns of Central America and the Caribbean region. There were at that time socialist governments in Guyana, Jamaica, Grenada, Nicaragua and Panama, and it was considered that the "Soviet–Cuban Axis" was expanding its influence into the region. This was understood as a threat to the United States because 52 percent of all the oil imported by the United States from Arabia, Africa and Latin America was transported through the deep waters canal that bordered the island of Grenada to the oil refineries of the Bahamas, the Virgin Islands, Trinidad, Aruba and Curaçao. Once refined, the oil was transported to the United States.

Another oil route to the United States was the Panama Canal, which, according to the document, was under a "leftist military regime." Guatemala was seen as being in a strategic position due to its closeness to the vast Mexican oil camps. In addition to oil, the authors of Santa Fe I were also worried about who had control of minerals. They noted that half of the aluminum that the United States imported from the Caribbean was coming through Jamaica and argued that since Cuba and the Soviet Union had expanded their influence to Angola, Ethiopia and South Yemen, they could also extend their control to Central and South Africa, which were rich in minerals, and the Persian Gulf, which was rich in oil.

Given the above circumstances, it was crucial to improve hemispheric relations. To face the challenges of the next twenty years, the authors recommended that the American continent should start – depending on its own vast natural resources, especially those related to energy – to create an intra-hemispheric market for oil and gas. To this end, they proposed the revitalization of the Organization of the American States, the Monroe Doctrine, which opposed extra-continental colonization of the Americas and the Río Treaty with its focus on hemispheric security, bilateral agreements and military training, particularly technical and psychological training to fight against "terrorism" (note that this is the first time that the concept "subversion" is replaced by "terrorism"). The document ended with a call to Canada to assume more responsibilities in defense of the continent and to revitalize the old A–B–C Alliance (America–Britain–Canada) by extending its influence in the old British colonies in the Caribbean.

In sum, Santa Fe I represented the origins of the "New Right's" social construction of threats and terrorism on the American continent. It was a prelude to the appropriation of the region's resources; however, for that to happen, a new organizational structure of global scope needed to be created in order to transform those ideas into policies and to have the power to implement such policies at the local scale.

The new mechanisms of hegemony: a global managerial role for the international financial institutions

"Global managerialism"[5] may be defined as the deterritorialization of power relations, a shift in place from the nation-states to multilateral agencies (not only limited to southern states), and from the domestic to the systemic level. The common justification for the social construction of this supra-state architecture was that states were "overbureaucratic," "inefficient" and "corrupt," and that the centralization of economic decision making under the global managers would correct those anomalies. Hence, global managerialism represented the institutionalization of disciplinary neo-liberalism and new constitutionalism, and was strongly militaristic, gendered and embedded in masculinist values. A number of critiques of the managerialist approach have been developed from different conceptual frameworks.

From a neo-Gramscian critical strategic management approach, Levy, Alvesson and Willmott, in *Studying Management Critically*, argued that the mainstream strategic managerialist perspective was rooted in the "managerial functionalist paradigm." According to these authors, this is characterized as a pragmatic and technocratic process of decision making that was based on instrumental rationality to detect the most efficient and competitive means that could improve specific ends. In the context of a global market economy, the emphasis was on the goals, and those ends referred to economic growth, the maximization of wealth and the increase of corporate profitability. Therefore, it served the interests of "specific elites" (Levy *et al.* 2003).

The discourse on strategic management was based on game theory, and a linear and evolutionary understanding of institutions and enterprises (Levy *et al.* 2003). Moreover, for strategic management, "organizations evolve to match the environment through a process of natural selection" and therefore, for those who professed this ideology, it was crucial to plan the evolution of institutions or enterprises (Levy *et al.* 2003). Levy, Alvesson and Willmott concluded that the "planning-implementation" sequence was a ahistorical and "unsustainable" hegemonic strategic project based on a totalitarian ideology (Levy *et al.* 2003). This point is echoed by a growing number of academics who refer to globalization as a "global fascist" project (Mushakoji 2004; Patel and McMichael 2004).

Socialist feminists working on organizational theory have instead emphasized the strong parallels that exist between the discourses on militarism and managerialism, and have highlighted where the hyper-masculinist values were always present (Hopton 1999: 72). Hopton argues that since the 1980s, managerialism has started to replace militarism as an ideological mechanism for social control and, as such, it brought to light the strong links between patriarchal power and the logic of capitalism. Moreover, it represented a "fusion of free-market liberalism, authoritarianism and masculinism" (Hopton 1999: 71–78).[6]

A notable component of new managerialism, according to Hopton, was the manipulation of women in the context of a "new form of patriarchy." Women no longer faced obstacles when entering senior management positions. However, this was only the case if they conformed to the masculinist values identified above. The author concluded that the entry of women into men's world represented a "smokescreen" to neutralize the critiques of feminists regarding gender discrimination, particularly the critiques of the elimination of the social contract through structural adjustment programs (Hopton 1999: 75–80).

First-generation reforms

"Global managerialism" emerged in the 1980s and was based on "market reforms" or "first-generation reforms," as it was also called. Notwithstanding the fact that 60 percent of the Third World debt was with private banks,[7] the Bretton Woods Institutions were given the role of managers of the private lenders.

The "debt regime," a rule-based procedure, was the first new constitutionalist reform of quasi-global scope that the global managers had to coordinate. McMichael argued that although the debt crisis was driven by a combination of international problems, namely the oil shocks and increase in the price of oil, higher interest rates due to the United States shift to monetary policy, the early 1980s credit crunch and the recession in the First World that led to the cutting of imports from the Third World, the World Bank blamed the Latin American and African countries. The World Bank justified its accusation by comparing the situations of the Latin American and African countries to the success of the NICs. All these issues led to the breakup of the Third World as a "collective entity." From then on, the World Bank's role was to manage the structural adjustment loans (SAL) and the IMF's role was to add restructuring conditionalities to them (McMichael 1996: 126–131).

The debt regime took two forms – stabilization measures or cutting imports to solve the balance-of-payments deficit, and structural adjustment programs. The design of structural adjustment programs included the gradual elimination of the former social contract[8] and the privatization of public service enterprises,[9] which increased the vulnerability of the majority of the populations of the debtor countries. According to McMichael, the year 1984 was a "turning point" because the direction of capital flows reversed. The outflow of capital from the South was much larger than the inflow, eventually reaching a maximum of US$400 billion in the 1980s. By 1990, the debtor countries owed 61 percent more debt than in 1982 (McMichael 1996: 132–134). These data reveal that "global managerialism" not only shifted power but also led to a massive transference of resources from South to North, and it can probably be said that from 1984 onward the South started to "develop" the North.

In short, the design of the first-generation reforms was the prelude of the 1980s evolutionary appropriation of the region's resources, either through the implementation of gendered market-oriented policies in the new "democracies," as was the case of the Southern Cone countries, through military intervention, as in Central America and Grenada, or through a new constitutionalist agreement in the Caribbean, namely the Caribbean Basin Initiative (CBI).

The Southern Cone: transition from authoritarianism to disciplinary neo-liberalism and the strengthening of women's movements

In the Southern Cone countries, although the 1980s started with great euphoria and enthusiasm due to the return to democratic rule, by the end of the decade the initial optimism had vanished and the period became known as "the lost decade." This deception requires an analysis of what type of democracy was being implemented in the region.

The majority of the studies on the transition from authoritarianism to democracy focused their analyses at the national or meso level[10] and utilized a top-down approach. O'Donnell argued that while the old "representative democracies" were based on accountability to the voters and institutions (for example, Congress and political parties), the new democracies, or "delegative democracies" (DDs), lacked both "vertical" and "horizontal" accountability. DDs were characterized by the centrality given to the figure of the President and the technocrats, especially economists, who surrounded him (O'Donnell 1994: 9).

Although the power of the President was "delegated" by the voters and the Congress and political parties became active again (after many years of dictatorship when they were banned), the President had strong *caudillista* – the Spanish term for what Gramsci called Caesarism – defined as individualist, populist and paternalist "*macho*" tendencies (O'Donnell 1994: 11–13). In fact, the President made extensive use of governing by decree, bypassing the Congress and Senate and protecting the *técnicos* from public resistance by just ignoring their demands, and making "the voters/delegators ... return to the condition of passive" (O'Donnell 1994: 9). As such, DDs bore strong resemblances to the previous bureaucratic-authoritarian regimes, with the only difference being that the President was elected by the public. Delegative democracies were a hybrid and, because of this, O'Donnell argued that DDs were not consolidated democracies. Instead, they were "enduring" as there was no threat of a return to dictatorial rule. They were also not representative democracies but were "incomplete democracies" (O'Donnell 1994: 11). O'Donnell ended his analysis with the claim that "even if DDs belong to the democratic genre, it would be hard to find something that is more uncongenial to the building and strengthening of democratic political institutions" (O'Donnell 1994: 11).

The new social movements literature utilizes a bottom-up approach in its analysis and has strongly criticized the notion of a "passive public," which echoes Gramsci's concept of "passive revolution." Evidence of this is the myriad grassroots movements that have emerged since the mid-1970s and that played a crucial role in bringing down the military dictatorships.[11] Women's movements were particularly active during this period, which coincided with the UN Decade for Women (1975–1985). They maintained a diverse array of women's organizations – human rights groups, grassroots feminisms, Catholic, rural, urban working-class and middle-class women – and gave the impression of a multi-class and multi-ethnic women's movement, which for the first time achieved political visibility and legitimization (Jaquette 2000). The common objectives of the women's movements were to see the return to democratic rule. Yet, even if social movements in the Southern Cone had a crucial role in bringing back democracy, the transition to democracy was crystallized through negotiated pacts between the elite and the military (Waylen 1998: 202). In fact, in the 1980s former military dictators and torturers entered the political arena transformed into "civilians" and, by doing so, they militarized the political arena. This point is crucial in explaining the relevance for the analysis of the 1980s decade and of what Gramsci called "passive revolution."

"Passive revolution" does not mean the absence of social movements or that people are "dupes," as many authors have understood the concept (e.g., Schild 1998; Sklair 1995). Instead, what Gramsci meant was that change was brought from the "top-down" rather than from the "bottom-up." As in the case of Gramsci, what O'Donnell meant by "passive voters" was that resistance did exist but that the demands from civil society were absolutely ignored by the authoritarian "*caudillo*" and therefore, civil society movements were not able to produce change "from below." Missing from both O'Donnell's and the new social movements literatures is the external geo-economic constraints that do not allow representative democracies to unfold[12] and that gave rise instead to what Stephen Gill calls "disciplinary neo-liberalism" (2003).

Disciplinary neo-liberalism, the competition state and structural adjustment programs

Due to the nationalization of the external debt and the coercive measures put into place for its repayment, developmentalist governments began to be more accountable to global managers and market forces. The global interventionism into national affairs generated new elite/military negotiated democracies, which responded to the interests of the international financial institutions rather than to the voters within the national borders. William Robinson refers to this group as a transnational capitalist class which implemented a polyarchy, something that was neither a dictatorship nor a popular democracy but which maintained the elite in power. The mechanisms put into place to effect this change were the disciplinary stabilization measures and structural adjustment programs (SAPs), which demolished the remains of the old corporatist state model and gave rise to the "competition state."

Cerny defined the "competition state" as a "quasi-market actor'; a strongly interventionist state that abandoned the former "social embeddedness" of the Keynesian state by re-regulating the economy in favor of market forces and also became a "commodifying agent" itself.[13] This neo-liberal state, by privatizing and deregulating national economies, increased the "interweaving of the domestic economy and the global economy"[14] and states became "splintered states increasingly intertwined with transgovernmental networks."[15] As such, Cerny asserts, the competition state shared enormous resemblances with the American state governments whose role was to promote market activities (Cerny 1997: 272). This market-oriented state was the engine that implemented the international financial institutions' structural adjustment programs, which at the same time reshaped the role of the state from a public to a private function, and from an inwardly to an outwardly oriented institution.

Structural adjustment programs were the policy tools or the mechanisms of disciplinary neo-liberalism that, as mentioned previously, produced the shift from the former Keynesian nationally oriented economy towards a neo-liberal global interventionism into the national affairs of Latin American countries with a focus on the protection of transnational corporations or market forces. Structural adjustment programs involved austerity measures, the privatization of public enterprises, the reduction of the social contract, the liberalization of trade and exchange rate policies (McMichael 1996).

Austerity measures such as the reduction of wages and export prices were the mechanisms designed to attract foreign investors interested in "buying" public service industries. The privatization of public service enterprises such as gas, water, communications, media, transport and electricity weakened the state both in geo-political and socio-economic terms and resulted in the loss of national control over basic needs for human survival. The prices of resources were now set according to the international market. States had less income to maintain their social infrastructure (public health, education and pensions) and to service their debts. The liberalization of trade and exchange rate policies guaranteed a structure favorable to capital and the control of local central banks secured the servicing of the external debt. In sum, by privatizing the public arena to trans-national corporations, structural adjustment programs incremented the dependency of Latin America from the G-7 countries. Although structural adjustment programs had a negative impact on both men and women, they affected them in different ways depending on their class and ethnic status, and modified the previous gender relations that existed in "embbeded liberalism." The privatization of public enterprises led to the creation of a "new bourgeoisie," which was initially integrated by men who were the populist administrators of the former developmental states.[16] They were empowered by becoming property owners of public enterprises, either by forming joint ventures with foreign enterprises, by becoming members of their board of directors or, in many cases, sole owners. Thus the basis of the fusion of this local and global bourgeoisie in a "trans-national capitalist class"[17] was the appropriation of public goods in each country of the region with, of course, the contextual differences taken into account. Austerity measures included the reduction of wages of working-class men; work was flexibilized in favor of capital, and unemployment, as well as riots, became widespread. Both middle-class and poorer women were severely affected by the structural adjustment programs (Waylen 1998: 200–203). The shrinking of the public services led to the unemployment of middle-class professional women who previously worked as social workers, teachers and nurses. The reduction of welfare provision and state subsidies mainly affected those women whose primary roles were as household managers (Waylen 1998: 201).[18] Children and the elderly were also hit hard by the reduction of public social services, particularly in education, health and pensions. Waylen, analyzing the women's movements in Argentina, Brazil, Chile and Peru, demonstrated that women organized kitchens to provide one meal a day as well as health services and artisanal workshops (Waylen 1998: 203–204).

Transnational corporations, particularly in the textile, electronic and agricultural sectors, started employing young women, whom they preferred due to their "nimble fingers," "passivity" or being less prone to organizing in unions; most of all, women made cheaper workers (Fernández-Kelly 1984; Tiano 1994). Hence, the "feminization of survival" and the "feminization of the labor force" implied that women became tied up in new ways to the reproductive and productive economy, which intensified their exploitation (Sassen 2000).

Capitalist accumulation now had two new sources of revenue – debt servicing and the privatized returns from the regions' public service enterprises (gas, water, communications, media, transport and electricity), which shifted from belonging to the "local commons" towards the "global commons."

Central America: civil wars and the end of containment[19]

The Central American region also became the epicenter of the Council for Inter-American Security and the Reagan Administration's paranoia with the "Soviet–Cuban Axis," an imaginary threat that not even American businessmen operating in the region believed in. As La Feber demonstrated, sixty-seven of the top 100 American corporations were operating at that time in Central America, including nine of the largest ten petroleum companies, which felt secure and managed to deal with any government that held power, whether capitalists or socialists (La Feber 1993: 274). Moreover, the rebel movements could not even be labeled "Marxist-Leninists" as the White House tended to define them. The Guatemalan National Revolutionary Union (URNG), formed in 1981 to 1982 with the unification of four revolutionary guerrilla groups, as well as the Salvadoran Farabundo Martí Liberation Front (FMLN), were mainly integrated by indigenous peasants. Meanwhile, in Nicaragua, the Sandinista National Liberation Front (FSLN), in power after defeating the Somoza regime in 1979, defined its government as pluralist, and proclaimed the creation of a mixed economy and a non-aligned position in foreign affairs (La Feber 1993: 310; Smith 1996: 182). To this end, the Sandinista National Liberation Front sought economic assistance from various countries, receiving between 1979 and 1982 about 20 percent from countries of the Soviet bloc, 40 percent from Mexico and over 30 percent from the rest of Latin America (Smith 1996: 182).

Notwithstanding, the Reagan Administration insisted that an external communist threat existed in the region, particularly in Nicaragua, and authorized the CIA to organize covert operations. This gave rise to the paramilitary force known as the *Contras*, the shortened name for *contrarevolucionarios* or counter-revolutionaries (La Feber 1993: 300). The CIA hired Argentine militaries, trained at the US School of the Americas in Panama, to train the *Contras* in Honduras, a US military enclave (La Feber 1993: 283). The Argentines remained in the region until the 1982 Islas Malvinas War (La Feber 1993: 277). In 1983 the CIA recruited Miskito indigenous peoples from the Atlantic Coast on the side of the *Contras* (La Feber 1993: 307).

Parallel to the militarization of the region, Reagan launched the Caribbean Basin Initiative (CBI) with the objective of increasing US direct investment in manufactured goods or *maquiladoras*, and to profit from low wages and low environmental legislation, and later, to export those goods to the United States (La Feber 1993: 285–287).

The opposition to this geo-economic strategy mounted, both within the United States and abroad. In the United States, the strongest opposition came from the Democrats, especially from the Chair of the House Select Committee on Intelligence, Edward Boland. In 1982, Boland sponsored an amendment that later on became known as Boland I, and which prohibited the use of American funds to overthrow the Sandinistas in Nicaragua (La Feber 1993: 296; Smith 1996: 183). Abroad, the Contadora Group, formed by Colombia, Mexico, Panama and Venezuela, together with the support group formed by Argentina, Brazil, Peru and

Uruguay, created a peace plan, which the Reagan administration declined to sign (La Feber 1993: 297).

Instead, Reagan took three aggressive measures. First, he launched the invasion of Grenada – a Caribbean island that is strategically located on a petroleum pipeline route through which half of the petroleum imported by the United States has to pass to be refined at various Caribbean islands before being sent to the United States.[20] Second, he appointed a commission chaired by the Nobel "Peace" Laureate Henry Kissinger to study the Central American situation. The "Kissinger Report" recommended a large program of economic assistance and more arms to the *Contras*, Honduras, Guatemala and El Salvador (La Feber 1993: 298–299; Smith 1996: 184). Third, the CIA was ordered to bomb Managua and to mine the harbors (La Feber 1993: 301; Smith 1996: 185). In the face of these measures the opposition intensified, and a Boland II agreement stipulated the termination of all lethal aid to the *Contras* (La Feber 1993: 302; Smith 1996: 185).

However, after his re-election in 1985, President Reagan found a way to circumvent Boland II by initiating a covert operation by diverting funds from selling arms to fundamentalist groups in Iran, resulting in the "Iran–Contra Scandal," which finally ended President Reagan's eight-year aggression in Central America (Smith 1996: 185). The Esquipulas Accords, proposed by President Arias from Costa Rica, advanced the peace plan that ended the Cold War in Latin America (for which he received the Nobel Peace Prize). Yet, peace was far from being reached (Smith 1996: 186). In the 1990 elections, Violeta Barrios de Chamorro, a conservative, won the elections and in effect destroyed the Sandinistas in Nicaragua. It may therefore be said that although Reagan did not win the war, he indirectly won at the polls (Smith 1996: 186; see also Dunkerley 1990; Vanden 1997).

The Caribbean: the Caribbean Basin Initiative and the heyday of the tax havens

The Caribbean countries, which had acquired their independence in the 1960s and 1970s after 300 years under European colonialism, found themselves in a very weak position when the 1980s economic crisis hit the region. The crisis was due to the increase of prices of imports (e.g., oil), the decline of the price of exports (e.g., bauxite and nickel), and the high rise in interest rates on the foreign debt, which totaled US$410 billion in 1987 (Safa 1995: 33). On February 24, 1982, President Reagan, in a speech at the Organization of American States (OAS), announced the creation of the Caribbean Basin Initiative (CBI),[21] which, for him, was seen to be a way out of the crisis. However, the CBI, which entered into effect in January 1984, was instead an effort to reassert the New *Pax Americana* in the region through structural adjustment programs (SAPs) and the new gendered international division of labor (NIDL). The introduction of *maquiladoras* entailed the reconfiguration of gender relations and, as Watson (1985: 27) asserted, the deepening of white economic power and growth of black poverty.[22] Kari Polanyi-Levitt defined the CBI in the following terms:

President Reagan's CBI is a lineal descendant of President Kennedy's Alliance for Progress and is similarly inspired by Washington's pathological fear of popular social forces in the hemisphere. The Alliance for Progress was a response to the Cuban revolution. The CBI is a response to the Farabundo Martí in El Salvador, the victory of the Sandinistas in Nicaragua, democratic socialism in Manley's Jamaica, and the Grenada revolution of 1979. Its economic component is secondary to United States politico-strategic objectives in the Caribbean Basin and is carefully targeted to maximize United States leverage by assisting overseas political and private sector allies in the region.

(Polanyi-Levitt 1985: 237)

In fact, as a hegemonic project, the Caribbean Basin Initiative had an economic, a political and a military component. The *economic component* was characterized by a strong belief in market fundamentalism, and was designed as a "one-way free trade area" that aggressively promoted private businesses by providing them with resources and tax incentives to invest in the region. Indeed, the US$350 million provided through the initiative were to be utilized by the private sector, whose products were guaranteed to receive duty-free treatment to enter the United States for a period of twelve years, the time required to pay off their investment; therefore it was a risk-free enterprise (Polanyi-Levitt 1985: 232–235). The commodities excepted from duty-free access were textiles, apparel, footwear, handbags, luggage, flat goods, work gloves, tinned tuna, watches, petroleum, petroleum products and sugar by-products (Polanyi-Levitt 1985: 235–236; Watson 1985: 19). All these commodities were to be produced in the foreign-owned *maquiladoras*, and, because the CBI was not a treaty between sovereign states, it gave the US the power to impose uncertainty and insecurity upon the Caribbean beneficiaries while also keeping female and male workers on edge; in effect, the CBI was decidedly a market-driven strategy to deepen the integration of the Caribbean into the US sphere of influence. Moreover, the CBI, as well as the 1975 European Economic Community's (EEC) Lomé Convention, dealt with the contradictions arising from the transition from the Old to the New *Pax Americanas*, and was an attack on the 1973 progressive social construction of the Caribbean Community (CARICOM).[23] Although the tax incentives for United States enterprises investing in the CBI found strong opposition in Congress and were eventually dropped (Polanyi-Levitt 1985: 232–233), the tax incentives were very possibly introduced through the Caribbean tax havens. It is therefore necessary to deepen research into the role played by tax havens in the 1980s, when the liberalization of finances took place and the CBI was created. Palan refers to tax havens as the:

jurisdictions that deliberately create legislation to ease transactions undertaken by people who are not resident in their domain. Those international transactions are subject to little or no regulation, and the havens usually offer considerable, legally protected secrecy to ensure that such transactions are not linked to those who are undertaking them. Such transactions are "offshore" – that is, they take place in legal spaces that decouple the real location of the economic transactions from the legal location, and hence remove the tax liability of the transaction from the place where it actually occurred.

(Palan 2010: 4)

The Caribbean tax havens originated in the late 1950s following the creation of the London-based Euromarket and provided the "basis for the emergence of transnationalism" (Christensen 2011: 177). Moreover, they became the engine of the neo-liberal agenda, of tax evasion, capital flight and the globalization of corruption. Yet, those that park their money in tax havens are not only the wealthy elite but all types of criminals, those involved in activities such as theft, fraud, piracy, terrorism, narco-trafficking, human trafficking, extortion and the "secrecy world" of money laundering (Murphy 2011: 57). The growth of offshore finance is astonishing: from US$11 billion in 1968 it increased to US$385 billion in 1978 and, in the 1980s, the deposits held in the Caribbean alone amounted to over US$400 billion – the same amount of the region's external debt. In the 1990s, in all offshore havens, it reached US$6 trillion (Hampton and Christensen 2002: 1658). More recently, on July 2, 2012, the *Guardian* reported that the amount of money passing through tax havens amounted to US$21 trillion. In sum, to analyze the Caribbean Basin Initiative it is necessary to link it to the internationalization of finances, the neo-liberal globalization project, the new international division of labor and the heydays of the Caribbean tax havens.

The *political component* of the Caribbean Basin Initiative was the counterpart of "private sector expansion" and was characterized by "state sector contraction" (Watson 1985: 21). The space reduced in the latter was occupied by the former. This shift in the role of the state, from a developmental to a competition state, was promoted by the Reagan Administration, which considered that large states were the cause of the 1970s economic crisis, and the objective was to eliminate the remains of the Keynesian social contract. As Ramsaran sustains, the new role of the state was to assist the private sector to develop an export-led economy, through "investment promotion, export marketing, technology transfer and facilitate adjustments to greater competition and production in agriculture and industry" (Ramsaran 1982: 431).

Central to this modification in the state is "the tightening of the relationship between the Caribbean bourgeoisie, managerial and technical personnel, and the U.S. state and foreign capital" (Watson 1985: 22). This is key to understanding the formation of a white transnational capitalist class in the Caribbean, which was especially linked to agro-commercial capital and the deepening of black poverty (Watson 1985: 27). In the case of the industrial sector it was a similar situation, characterized by "import intensity" in manufacturing production, manufacturing that was limited to "mixing, blending, assembly, packaging and other final stage processes" (Girvan, quoted in Watson 1985: 26). This type of export-led production had negative outcomes for the Caribbean population: first, because production was for the external market rather than for the internal market, and very little income remained in the local economy. Second, labor-saving technologies increased the "labor absorption problem," and finally, because those who provided the technology were foreigners who did not have any obligation to reinvest their profits in the Caribbean (Watson 1985: 25).

Writing ten years after the Caribbean Basin Initiative entered into effect, Helen Safa studied the shift in the gendered composition of the industrial labor force in two members of the CBI: Puerto Rico and the Dominican Republic. Indeed, as in other parts of the world, the export-led industry in the Caribbean preferred to employ women because wages paid to them were lower, they were generally not unionized, and they were considered to be more resilient than men when doing tedious, repetitive work. At the same time, men, who used to work in the domestic economy, an economy that was disintegrating due to the pressure of export-led industrialization, started to lose their jobs. This situation in the workplace had an impact at both the household scale and the individual. Men were no more the breadwinners, in some cases there were two wage earners in the family and in some other cases just one: the wife. Therefore, male authority in the household started to erode while women gained more negotiating power in it (Safa 1995).[24] This reconfiguration of gender relations, which is about power relations between men and women, threatened men's masculinity, who feared that women would begin to occupy decision-making positions in society. It was men's patriarchal privilege that was threatened and their response was sexual harassment and violence against women (Lewis 2007). In sum, the shift in the role of the state under the CBI as a promoter of the private sector had reconfigured gender relations in the workplace and the household.

Finally, the *military component* of the CBI or the coercive element secured private sector expansion in the Basin. Military aid assistance to the region increased from US$50.5 million in 1981 to US$112.1 million in 1982. President Reagan justified the massive increase of military expenditure by stating that it was needed to meet "the growing threat of Cuban and Soviet subversion in the Caribbean Basin" (Ramsaran 1982: 431–435). The President even added that the communists wanted to take advantage of the economic crisis in the Caribbean to undermine the United States' "legitimate interests in the region" (Watson 1985: 32). The military, as Vaughan Lewis argued, believed that they were "the savior and protector of the status quo of directed social changes in these countries" and that this created a favorable climate for the "coup and countercoup syndrome" (quoted in Watson 1985: 32). Hence, the Caribbean Basin Initiative was one of the many sites where the New *Pax Americana* unraveled immediately after the 1980s debt crisis; yet what was characteristic of this region was that because most of these small island economies (SIEs) were tax havens, they became one of the most important engines of the New *Pax Americana*.

In sum, the "lost decade" meant the demolition of the "old" bipolar order represented by the East–West conflict and the division of the globe into First, Second and Third Worlds. It was the end of what the American hardliners called "static containment" and the rise of the "new" represented by polyarchical democracies and the gender-biased pro-market structural reforms. While the Southern Cone was ending the transition from the "dirty wars" towards the first-generation reforms, Central America was ending its "civil wars," which retro-spectively may be called the "old civil wars," and which were both class- and ethnic-based. At the same time, in the Caribbean, the Caribbean Basin Initiative was being implemented while tax havens were gaining momentum in the region. The "Three Worlds division" was replaced by a new division, referred to as "North/South," and which opened up a new dichotomy. This new dichotomy was deepened in the 1990s by the so-called second-generation reforms or "good governance," which intensified the crisis of social reproduction. This will be addressed in the following chapter.

2　The 1990s

Development as "good governance" and the consolidation of hegemony

The mainstream literature on democratization saw the decade of the 1990s as a period of democratic consolidation, as a second moment that followed the 1980s transition from authoritarianism to democracy. This assertion is based on the existence of consecutive elections held without the interruption of military coups. In contrast to this view, it will be argued that the 1990s was a period of hegemonic consolidation. In other words, the 1980s strengthened the formation of the dictatorship of the market. It did so by expanding what Stephen Gill called a "new constitutionalism for disciplinary neo-liberalism," or the creation of transnational legal regimes on different scales with the objective of consolidating a new geo-economic and political space: the Americas.

In fact, when George H.W. Bush assumed the Presidency of the United States in 1989, he announced the creation of a New World Order, free of the Soviet Union. A center-piece of the New World Order was the formation of a Free Trade Area of the Americas (FTAA) that would extend from the Arctic to Tierra del Fuego – the southern territory of Argentina. This formation would bridge the Northern and Southern Poles – as was already announced in the Santa Fe I document written in 1979. Towards this end, in 1990, Canada became a member of the Organization of American States. By doing so, it seems that the A–B–C Alliance (America, Britain, Canada) that was previously formed in the Caribbean[1] expanded towards the South through the creation of transnational economic rules as a mechanism for opening borders to trade (also called "good governance"). The North American Free Trade Agreement was the first expression of the American and Canadian alliance.

This chapter examines: (1) the "New Right"'s Santa Fe II document, particularly its frontal attack on Gramscian thought and its juridico-political and cultural approach; (2) at the meso level, the World Bank's law-bound second-generation reforms; (3) the harmonization of supra-national, regional and national constitutionalisms that are binding on the Americas; (4) the institutionalization of a local new managerialism that fragmented the competition state into a variety of service providers – the process of NGOization – and allowed the entrance of women into politics; and finally (5) the relationship between the creation of natural resources regimes and the so-called "new civil wars" or "low-intensity conflicts" of the post-Cold War period, which led to the deepening and internationalization of the indigenous and Afro-descendants' movements and the struggle between global and local constitutionalisms.

Ideas: Santa Fe II, *trasformismo* and the reversal of Gramscian thought

In August 1988, the Council for Inter-American Security launched Santa Fe II, *A Strategy for Latin America for the 1990s*,[2] as a guide for the new American President to be elected. This document was still framed in a strong East–West conflict discourse.

First, in geo-political terms, the document enshrined President Reagan's success in returning democratic rule to Latin America. Yet, it asserted that democracies based only on elections were not sufficient to create "permanent" governments. The authors distinguished between the notion of "temporal" and "permanent" governments. The former referred to the elected officials and the latter to the non-elected, such as the Armed Forces, the Judicial Power, the civil bureaucracy, the democratic organizations – such as unions, business groups, commercial associations and educational organizations – and the political culture. It was these "permanent" organisms that were the essence of what the authors of Santa Fe II called "democratic regimes," which they presented as opposed to "statism" or centralization of cultural and economic control promoted by what they considered as the "marriage of Latin American nationalism and communism."

The authors asserted that Gramscian Marxist intellectuals would dominate the culture of nations, by creating common values to be diffused through religion, media and new curricula in schools and universities. It is in this context that they saw liberation theology as a dangerous "Marxist political doctrine disguised as a religious belief that was against the freedom of enterprise and it was also anti-Papal." They also interpreted the increase of Soviet fellowships awarded to Latin American students as Soviet penetration into the statist Latin American regimes with the goal of destroying democracy. To combat this urgent problem they recommended increasing the budget of the United States Information Agency (USIA) to initiate a "cultural war" against "Gramscian Marxism."

To face the threat caused by a "subversive and terrorist network operating from Chiapas in Mexico to Chile in the South" and narcotraffic in Nicaragua, Cuba, and especially in Colombia, the authors of Santa Fe II recommended that the United States help strengthen the other two principal "permanent organisms" in Latin American governments, namely the Armed Forces and the Judicial Power. To strengthen the Armed Forces, in 1986 the Congress had already approved the Goldwater-Nichols Law to reorganize the US Defense Department, which included an amendment that created a Special Operations Commando Unit to deal with special operations and low-intensity conflicts (LICs). In accordance with the changes in the US military, it was necessary to reform the Organization of American States to face the new low-intensity conflicts. To strengthen Judicial Power, the authors suggested its independence and new constitutions to promote human rights in favor of what they called "democratic" regimes.

Second, Santa Fe II sought to establish an economic system independent from government interference. To this end, it highlighted (1) the need to reduce the external debt of Latin America by exchanging debt for equity. The document suggested that national and foreign investors together (to avoid the surge of nationalism) should buy the external debt of creditors in dollars and then exchange it with local money to buy productive enterprises; (2) the acceleration of the privatization of national industries; (3) the revitalization and extension of the Caribbean Basin Initiative until 2007 and to move the *maquiladoras* out from the US–Mexican border towards the interior of Mexico. The objective was to stop the migration of Mexican men into the United States (since *maquiladoras* only employed female workers) and to avoid the dislocation of families; (4) profiting from comparative advantage, the document recommended that the United States should export cereals, beans and corn to Mexico, Central America and the Caribbean, and to import melons, asparagus and raspberries from them. This would incorporate indigenous peoples, who were living on a subsistence economy based on the same staple foods that the United States wanted to sell, into the market economy; (5) the document suggested the elimination of the protectionist quota for Central American sugar; and finally; (6) ecological policies for the "conservation and protection" of tropical forests within the framework of the OAS and in cooperation with private groups.

In sum, Santa Fe II represented a new evolutionist ten-year plan for the expansion of American interests towards Latin America and the Caribbean based on the appropriation of land and natural resources. Meanwhile, the recommendations sought to consolidate the institutions that would give permanency to a New World Order. The pillars for the consolidation of the New *Pax Americana* were the juridical, cultural, military and civil liberal organizations, or what Santa Fe II referred to as "democratic regimes."

Second-generation reforms

A second "evolutionary stage" of the New *Pax Americana* was therefore initiated during the 1990s. In security terms, a New World Order was born with the demise of the Soviet Union. The substitution of a bipolar to a multipolar world was now anchored in the G-8 nexus, which included Russia. In political-economic terms, the 1989 Washington Consensus for Latin America added a new component to the 1980s focus on "market reforms": "good governance," also known as "second-generation reforms." While the "first-generation reforms" sought to restore the world's financial system by restructuring the external debt through structural adjustment programs, the "second-generation reforms" emphasized the strengthening of institutions to facilitate trade and foreign direct investment (FDI). The international financial institutions adopted the "good governance" framework, which the World Bank defined as follows:

> Governance refers broadly to the exercise of power through a country's economic, social, and political institutions in which institutions represent the

organizational rules and routines, formal laws, and informal norms that together shape the incentives of public policymakers, overseers, and providers of public services. This is often referred to as "the rules of the game." Three key dimensions are (a) the process by which governments are selected, held accountable, monitored, and replaced; (b) the capacity of governments to manage resources efficiently and to formulate, implement, and enforce sound policies and regulations; and (c) respect for institutions that govern economic and social interactions.[3]

Thus, governance represented the expansion of the transnational juridical regimes or new constitutionalism that forced national institutions to "manage" their economies according to the disciplinary laws of the market. Although it was a framework favorable to the G-8 nexus as a whole, its primary beneficiary was the United States, because new constitutionalism represented an extension of its domestic law to the systemic level.

The "Ten Commandments" of the Washington Consensus (good governance) included: fiscal discipline; the reordering of public expenditures – especially health and education; tax reform; a competitive exchange rate; privatization; deregulation; property rights and liberalization of interest rates; trade, and inward foreign direct investment.[4] All of these regimes crystallized in the creation of the WTO in 1995 and, according to Desai and Imrie, the new managerialist agenda was expanded to southern countries through foreign aid policies of northern governments. This occurred mainly through multilateral and bilateral aid mechanisms, remodeling nation-states according to market-centric instead of people-centric needs, yet within the specific characteristics of each country's context (Desai and Imrie 1998).

If the explicit objective of "good governance" was to put an end to southern governments' "corruption," the meaning of "corruption" needed to be further explored. The main architect of the policies included in the Washington Consensus, John Williamson, defined corruption as a "global apartheid" against the United States. In his own words:

> The three big ideas here are macroeconomic discipline, a market economy, and openness to the world (at least in respect to trade and FDI). These are ideas that had long been regarded as orthodox so far as the OECD countries are concerned, but there used to be a sort of global apartheid which claimed that developing countries came from a different universe which enabled them to benefit from (a) inflation (so as to reap the inflation tax and boost investment); (b) a leading role for the state in initiating industrialization; and (c) import substitution. The Washington Consensus said that this era of apartheid was over.
>
> The basic ideas that I attempted to summarize in the Washington Consensus have continued to gain wider acceptance over the past decade, to the point where Lula has had to endorse most of them in order to be electable.
>
> (Williamson 2002: 1–2)

The fact that Lula "has had to endorse" the Washington Consensus "in order to be electable" reflects how the debt trap and the "new constitutionalism for disciplinary neo-liberalism" was used to tie the hands of local governments, forcing them to adhere to policies that were contrary to their own political beliefs and directed against the population that voted for them. If a government did not conform to these global rules, capital flight towards tax havens and unstoppable inflation would bring them down; thus the possibilities for maneuvering for local governments were reduced to a minimum.

Yet, this situation was not only limited to southern states. Although the other members of the G-8 are also currently benefiting from globalization, they are caught in the new constitutionalist web that has been designed in the mirror image of the American legal system. It is very possible that in the long run, this may become what Arthurs calls a "new lex mercatoria" "whose texts are written in a kind of juridical *Esperanto*" (2001: 17), and will eventually turn against them too.

Forms of new constitutionalism: building gateways for the continental FTAA

Economist Jeffrey Sachs, who has been one of the most important promoters of structural adjustment programs in the 1980s all around the world, argued that the demise of the Soviet Union had created an "unprecedented opportunity to create a law-bound and prosperous international system" in order to consolidate capitalism (Sachs 1995: 50). According to his analysis:

> The cement that will ultimately hold the world system together is not markets per se, but the international rule of law. The world has already had one brief episode of global market integration at the end of the nineteenth century, under the domination of Western powers, but it collapsed in an orgy of imperialism, lawlessness, and, eventually, war among the leading states of Europe. The weaker countries are now signing on the world system and joining the global institutions, not only because they recognize the advantages of capitalism, but because they see the hope of joining a system that protects their national sovereignty while operating on the basis of an agreed upon international rule of law.
>
> (Sachs 1995: 64)

In fact, in the 1990s the "New Right"'s focus was on the social construction of a supra-national juridical system which had the objective of giving permanence to the structural reforms of the 1980s. In the American continent, this transnational constitutional text was written at a range of spatial scales and, step by step, it started to weave together the "Americas." David Schneiderman (2000) has pointed out the convergence between the transnational, regional and national regimes of legal ordering in shifting their focus from the public to the private spheres, from state to markets. He illustrates his arguments by referring to the

Bilateral Investment Treaties (BITs), the North American Free Trade Agreement (NAFTA) and domestic constitutions.

According to Schneiderman, the BITs were juridical tools between two countries that protected and promoted foreign direct investment in various issue areas and gave equal rights to domestic and foreign investors. By doing so, they subverted the old Latin American domestic constitutions, which adhered to the Calvo doctrine, a clause that protected local over foreign investors. By 1998, more than 1,700 BITs were completed in 174 countries. Two-thirds of these were consolidated in the 1990s and, around thirty-seven BITs were agreed between countries of Latin America and the Caribbean. The principal disciplinary measures found in BITs were also present in NAFTA, a trilateral agreement between Canada, Mexico and the United States.[5] These included, besides "national treatment" or equal treatment between local and foreign investors, "most favored nation status" (MFN), protection from expropriation and nationalization, and mechanisms for dispute settlement (international trade tribunals and domestic courts). The latter became a "license for investors to meddle significantly in public policy making within state parties" (Schneiderman 2000: 87).

The "old" regional economic blocs were founded in the 1960s under the auspices of the United Nations Economic Commission for Latin America and the Caribbean (ECLAC). These blocs included the Latin American Free Trade Association (LAFTA/*ALALC*), the Central American Common Market (CACM/*MCCA*), the Caribbean Free Trade Association (CARIFTA), and the Andean Pact (AP/*PA*) – and were created according to the import-substitution industrialization (ISI) framework with the objective to lower tariffs within the country members while maintaining high tariffs for outsiders. In 1982, the first steps towards the creation of the Southern Cone Common Market (SCCM/*MERCOSUR*) also had a protectionist objective, yet this time it was centered on the formation of a lobby for the renegotiation of the external debt on a more humane basis.[6]

This changed by the end of the 1980s and the beginning of the 1990s, when under GATT and later on the WTO, the 'new' Latin American regional economic blocs moved towards trade liberalization and lowered their tariffs to all countries based on the principle of "non-discrimination."[7] In this movement from an inward- towards an outward-oriented economy, the Andean Pact was renamed the Andean Community of Nations (CAN/*ACN*) and the Caribbean Free Trade Association became the Caribbean Community and Common Market (CARICOM), while the other blocs retained their former names. Thus, since the 1990s a web of national, bilateral and regional constitutions started to converge, mimicking the rules set out in the American Constitution.

A new managerialism for new constitutionalism and the fragmentation of the women's movement

A new public administration emerged parallel to the formation of transnational legal regimes which became the domestic organizational setting for "good governance." As Sachs stated, a "capable public administration is surely needed to guide infrastructure, enforce laws, protect the environment, and promote public health and education" (Sachs 1995: 52). The agents of neo-liberalism understood the old bureaucratic-professional public administration based on the welfare model as inefficient and corrupt, and considered that the state was not capable of providing welfare. Therefore, they proposed that the already reduced welfare system (through neo-liberal structural adjustment programs in the 1980s) be privatized, transferred from the public to the private domain and thus com-modified.[8] This required a new form of organization, which became known as "new managerialism."

As Desai and Imrie have asserted,[9] the state under neo-liberalism has been de-centered, fragmented into myriad service providers. Instead of directly pro-viding welfare, the state contracted private agencies to take on that function and, by doing so, reduced its role to a mere regulator of the private sector. In the UK, the USA and New Zealand the re-privatization of welfare took place in the 1980s and gave rise to "quasi-governmental organizations" such as health trusts, educa-tion trusts and urban renewal agencies. New managerialism was expanded to the South in the 1990s through foreign aid policies of northern countries, and non-governmental organizations (NGOs) took on the role that the welfare trusts and agencies had in the North (Desai and Imrie 1998).

While each country had a unique experience, Desai and Imrie have noted the quasi-universal tendency for the emergence of "government-by-contracts," which have created a clientelistic "patronage style of governance," in which a small elite in each country became private providers of welfare without having been elected to do so. This is what the Santa Fe II document called "permanent governments," namely those outside the state. Thus, what is at stake is the de-democratization and lack of accountability of new managerialism. This becomes even clearer with the creation of the "auditing culture" that surrounds this new type of local governance wherein the government auditor controls the output and economic objectives of the "quasi-governmental organizations." The auditor is concerned with assessing the procedural indicators, the accounting and technical measures, rather than the welfare of the population. Moreover, critics of new managerialism argue that the resources that should have been used in service provision were being diverted "towards processes and procedures designed to satisfy the dictates of audit" (Desai and Imrie 1998: 641).

What became a staple of the 1990s was the increasing incorporation of women into the political arena and into this new managerialist structure. This paradox of including women, while at the same time enshrining masculinity, was explained by socialist feminist John Hopton as the moment in which a new form of patriarchy emerged "wherein the perpetuation of traditional masculine values is more important than the gender of the social actors whose actions reflect those values" (Hopton 1999: 75–76); it became a "smokescreen" to neutralize the opposition of women's movements (Hopton 1999). In fact, Latin Americanist feminists have noted this shift in the women's movement. Jane Jaquette (2000), in her studies on democratic transitions and consolidations, argued that during the period of transitions, which took place sometime during the mid-1970s to late 1980s, the women's movement was characterized as a cross-class group that had one common objective in mind: bringing down the military dictatorships. However, during the 1990s, a decade labeled by the democratization literature as a period of "democratic consolidation", the former coalitions broke up and class divisions emerged among women's movements (Jaquette 2000).

According to Jaquette, this fracture was due to a number of reasons such as the changing international norms or second-generation reforms, the reassertion of political parties, and the replacement of women's movements by NGOs (Jaquette 2000). These are key issues to understanding the shift towards a new gender order at the global, national and grassroots levels, and how the progressive women's movements of the past decades were fragmented and their discourses appropriated by neo-liberalism, therefore requiring further analysis.

First, in the 1990s, the international regulatory system incorporated gender into development planning and the political arena, and gave rise to new gender regimes or new gender orders. The old social safety nets of the welfare model were re-privatized and the number of women incorporated into the global political economy increased.[10] As demonstrated above, only those women who conformed to the masculinist values embedded in the neo-liberal model had a place in it. The rest became subordinated to the needs of transnational capital.

Second, at the local level, political parties were modified by the *Ley de Cupos* or electoral quotas,[11] which required that one-third of a party's nominees were women. This pointed to gender equality and the recognition of the importance of women's votes. Yet, Jaquette finds some serious contradictions in the fact that President Menem from Argentina – who, according to her, was far from being a feminist – was the strongest supporter of the *Ley de Cupos*. In Peru popular women's movements were co-opted by an authoritarian President. In Chile the right strongly supported conservative women as a backlash against feminism; and in many other countries women supported "law and order" platforms (Jaquette 2000). These findings were consistent with Verónica Schild's study of the Chilean feminist movement, a movement that in the 1980s had a strong role in undermining authoritarianism. However, in the 1990s, its discourse on "empowerment," "autonomy," "self-development" and "participation" was appropriated by conservative groups to construct a new "gendered market citizenship":

> The latest phase of Chilean state formation … is characterized by renewed attempts by dominant groups to construct a hegemonic project which articulates elements of socio-economic 'modernization' with a particular conception of citizenship – one based on individual subjects as bearers of rights who entrepreneurially fashion their overall personal development through wider relations to the marketplace.… Today the terms of gendered market citizenship and community are being set by some middle-class women in the name of the majority of poor and working-class women.
>
> (Schild 1998: 36–37)

Schild concludes with a plea to examine the social movements more critically. This is precisely the point that Gramsci made regarding how *trasformismo* works; that is, by absorbing the discourse of the opposition with the objective of undermining it. Thus, in the 1990s, the incorporation of conservative women into politics had the objective of capturing women's votes; redefining welfare towards an authoritarian social contract in which only those who could afford to pay for health and education would be able to attain it; and re-defining the meaning of citizenship from a social- towards a market-gendered citizenship. This led to the fragmentation of the feminist movement, and middle-class women were pitted against lower class women (Jaquette 2000).

Third, women's movements were also being divided by the process of "NGO-ization." The decentering of the neo-liberal state was being driven by selective donor financing, and the new NGOs of the 1990s abandoned the activist component and became more technocratic and geared towards gender policy assessment, project execution and social services delivery (e.g., education and health) (Álvarez 1999: 12). The main difference between the old and the new NGOs is that while the old ones' objectives were to empower people within a public collective structure, the new ones promoted people as individuals with an entrepreneurial capacity to compete in the sphere of the free market economy (Álvarez 1999).

This shift in the NGOs tended to "consolidate democracy" in the way the Santa Fe II document promoted through a permanent market-centered civil society and, by doing so, democracy has been dehumanized and commodified. In this transition from political towards market dictatorships the majority of the population will struggle for its own survival, intensifying the crisis of social reproduction.

New civil wars, the quest for land and natural resources, and the rise of ethnic movements[12]

New constitutionalism and neo-liberal citizenship regimes are fueling a new type of civil war. This is partly because the World Bank and IMF are not just designing multi-scale legal rules but are also increasingly financing natural resources mega-development projects. These projects mainly affect those places in the countryside where specific natural resources are located; for example, minerals, hydrocarbons – oil and gas – water, timber, biodiversity and drugs.

The new constitutionalism weaves together and harmonizes rules at the global, national, provincial, municipal and ethnic/community levels with the aim of facilitating the global appropriation of strategic natural resources by transnational corporations. National constitutions and legal codes (e.g., mining codes, hydrocarbon codes) that previously excluded transnational corporations from investing in local natural resources were modified to allow their entrance. Moreover, local taxes were made more "competitive" – either lowered or eliminated – to attract foreign investments, and transnational corporations increasingly had their addresses in tax havens[13] to avoid the payment of taxes in their home countries.[14]

By privatizing and commodifying land and natural resources in the country-side, corporations displaced the indigenous peoples and other ethnic groups living in those territories (Conchiero-Bórquez *et al.* 2000; Escobar 2003; Pearce 1999; Renner 2002). While the former livelihood of indigenous peoples was being undermined, the neo-liberal model included in its repertoire their incorporation into globalization through both production (e.g., crops) and extraction (e.g., minerals).[15] Incorporating them as producers involved the sub-stitution of the subsistence economy by a market one. To that end, land was privatized and there was a shift in the type of food produced. Former locally produced staple foods such as corn, beans and cereals were now being imported from abroad, especially from the United States, and involved ag-biotech prod-ucts. Meanwhile, Latin American indigenous peoples were pushed (as the Santa Fe I and II documents suggested) to produce more expensive and exotic agri-cultural products, such as asparagus, melons, raspberries and so on for export. The privatization of land and the substitution of agricultural products from staple to export-oriented production separated indigenous peoples from nature and represented an attack on their cosmovision – worldview – and traditional organization while it incorporated them into the world market as sellers and buyers.

On the other hand, the case of extractive industries – hydrocarbons, mining – is somewhat different. Extractive industries are capital intensive and therefore do not require a large number of workers. They generally employ few local workers and a larger number of foreign technicians. Other characteristics that distinguish them from productive industries is that they are non-renewable and "spatially fixed" (Le Billon 2001: 569). Indeed, while agricultural products can be produced at different geographical locations that share the same climate and soil quality, extractive resources by definition need to be extracted wherever the minerals or hydrocarbons are found. This means that the population that lives where extractive resources are located are susceptible to displacement, turned into refugees or even murdered, giving rise to a new type of conflict in the post-Cold War era.[16] These conflicts are generally defined as ethnic and/or religious; however, most of them are generated by the quest for land and natural resources.

What distinguishes the new from the old wars is that the progressive counter-movements that emerged during the Cold War were ideologically driven, class-based guerrilla wars that aimed, at the micro level, to overthrow the authoritarian governments and install the dictatorship of the proletariat and, at the macro level, they rejected American imperialism and its penetration into Latin America. In contrast, the new wars reflected the end of a bipolar world order and the reasser-tion of American-led hegemony – which is both structural and superstructural. Renner maintains that with the end of the Cold War a huge number of military became unemployed, and at the same time there was an emergence of private military firms, which attracted many of the unemployed soldiers. It is from these private firms that the majority of oil and mining companies are hiring their private security personnel, forces that are increasingly being charged with human rights violations (Renner 2002: 19–20).

The recruitment of former public military personnel by private military firms gave the new natural resources civil wars a specific tone. In fact, the lootability of natural resources is characterized by being linked to the massive trafficking of small arms, drugs, indiscriminate use of land-mines, the monopoly of trade and widespread corruption (Renner 2002; Robin 2000). The systematic use of violence such as kidnappings, hostage taking, maintenance of a state of siege to induce famine, sexual violence, extortion and exploitation of coerced labor has the aim to terrorize civilians and to turn violence into an extremely profitable source of revenue (Renner 2002).

The beneficiaries form a network that includes warlords, transnational corporations, international organized crime and smuggling groups, leadership of northern countries and also consumers in importing countries (Le Billon 2001: 569–570). As Le Billon has argued, there is a strict relationship between natural resources and conflict: "natural resources both finances and motivates conflicts" (Le Billon 2001: 562); therefore "countries economically dependent on the export of primary commodities are at high risk of political instability and armed conflict" (Le Billon 2001: 562–563). This has given rise to a growing literature that focuses on the "natural resources curse" thesis (e.g., Collier 2000; de Soysa 2000; Le Billon 2001; Ross 1999).

Hence, if the violent shift of development in the 1990s reflected what the Santa Fe II document called "low-intensity conflicts" and "permanent governments" (e.g., armed forces and judicial power as opposed to the less important "temporary governments" or elected officials), the massive rise of indigenous and other ethnic group movements in defense of their autonomy, natural resources and the environment may be understood as their outlet for survival. The internationalization of indigenous movements coincides with the UN Decades of the World's Indigenous Peoples 1995–2004 and its renewal in 2005 (as in the past the emergence of women's movements coincided with the UN International Decade for Women 1975–1985) and with the creation in 1996 of the Heavily Indebted Poor Countries Initiative (HIPC).

All over the world, there is a correlation between those countries considered "heavily indebted" and the foreign investment in natural resources and, therefore, the emergence of violence; this is a link that needs to be urgently researched. The most dramatic examples of natural resources-prone conflicts in Latin America during the 1990s have been the "peacebuilding" efforts in Central America following the civil wars, NAFTA and the Zapatista uprising, the displacement of Afro-descendants in Colombia, and the Bolivian "natural resources wars" around mining, gas and water. It should be noted that the development of tourism as a high finance strategy in the Caribbean has also led to massive displacement of its population, giving rise to the Caribbean diaspora.

"Peacebuilding" in "post-conflict" Central America

In Central America, the peace accords signed by Nicaragua in 1990, El Salvador in 1992 and Guatemala in 1996 signaled the end of the old civil wars of the Cold

War period; yet peace, in spite of post-conflict reconstruction and peacebuilding efforts of the international community (international humanitarian and financial institutions), has not been achieved. This has led Jenny Pearce (1999) to extend the "concept of political emergency" (CPE),[17] which was initially used to classify the post-Cold War situation in African countries, to Central America. To explain this situation she argues that there has been a combination of macro- and micro-level failures.

At the macro level, the complexity emerged when external donors, particularly USAID, shaped the domestic peacebuilding agenda according to the dictate of the global market rather than people's needs at the local scale. There has been a counter-reform that involved the acceleration of capitalist modernization: privatization of land; institutional, state, police, economic and judicial reforms – emphasis on the training of judges – changes in the Constitution, and the reinstallation of power to the elite – who invested in assembly plants; export of non-traditional products such as exotic fruits, vegetables and flowers; and in illegal forms of accumulation such as drug dealing, extortion and kidnapping. This led to an intense political battle with respect to what kind of state and constitution was being implemented, coupled with an enormous growth of corruption and the entering into the violent scenario of the right-wing ex-combatants – which included the Nicaraguan *Contras* (Pearce 1999).

Meanwhile, at the micro level, Pearce argues, the objective of the donors was to promote peace through the "strengthening of civil society" – the hallmark of peacebuilding in the 1990s – or pouring post-conflict international aid into local NGOs. Yet, the old radical grassroots NGOs, which were active during the civil wars, were still very much politicized and distrusted the US interests in "aid." Therefore, at the end, the old NGOs were substituted by the subcontracting of new, more technical (especially with accounting knowledge) and apolitical NGOs integrated by an urban-based educated elite. Hence, the projects designed by these groups became more accountable to the donors rather than to the beneficiaries (Pearce 1999).

Bendaña has called this a situation of "structural violence," part of which included a massive import of small arms into the region. For example, he mentioned that between 1995 and 1999 El Salvador imported 70,889 small arms from the United States, Guatemala 30,326 and Nicaragua 2,750. Indeed, in 2002 2,024 people were killed by small arms in El Salvador alone, averaging 5.5 daily murders. Bendaña, opposing this neo-liberal short-term vision of "peace" promoted from the top down and from the outside, has re-defined "peace." In his terms, the marginalized or southern vision of peace should be a synonym of social justice rather than a pro-market one – built from the bottom up, from within, and geared towards the well-being of every single human being (Bendaña 2004).

NAFTA and the Zapatista *uprising*

In Mexico, the national constitution was modified in 1992, with the most controversial change made to Article 27. This article was introduced by the Mexican revolution in 1917 and referred to the land reform that recognized the existence of *ejidos* or communal lands, which represented half of the country's agricultural land, and was to be held in perpetuity by indigenous communities and therefore could not be sold. In 1992 the neo-liberal government sought to privatize the *ejido* land in an attempt to satisfy a pre-condition of the United States to the implementation of NAFTA. When this regional constitutional text was passed on January 1, 1994, the *Zapatistas* rebelled.[18] On the one hand, the Mexican government, following the World Bank and International Monetary Fund's recommendations, considered the indigenous peasants to be of 'worthless profitability' and implemented reforms geared towards the modernization of the rural sector, the increase of foreign investments in land, and the formation of large-scale and capital-intensive agriculture. These policies pushed Mexican indigenous peasants to either become cheap labor in the maquiladora industry, to migrate to the United States (reaching about four million out-migrants after eighteen years of neo-liberalism) or to rebel (Conchiero-Bórquez *et al.* 2000).

On the other hand, the *Zapatistas* pressured the government to change the constitution once more by incorporating into it indigenous rights and granting them autonomy, something that was accepted with the signing of the San Andrés Accords in 1996. However, the government delayed the implementation of the agreement and, instead, deployed the paramilitary forces that initiated "low-intensity warfare" against civilians with the objective of destabilizing the *Zapatista* Army (EZLN). This situation endured well into the decade. It should be clarified that for the *Zapatistas*, as well as for other indigenous movements, autonomy did not mean secession but the decentralization of power to the community level, where the traditional authorities and customs could be maintained. What was original to the *Zapatistas* was that the notion of self-government being proposed was based on three pillars: (1) indigenous education in both native and Spanish languages; (2) a health care system that combined traditional and Western medicines; and (3) collective and cooperative economic development based especially on organic coffee production and crafts.[19] Hence, the aim was an integration that recognized indigenous control over their territory and cultural identity rather than an integration that appropriated their means of survival and which assimilated and subsumed them into a dominant culture.

Displacement of Afro-descendants in Colombia

The displacement of Afro-descendants in Colombia should also be seen in light of new constitutionalist changes at the macro and micro levels. The Colombian conflict originated in the 1940s and was due to the concentration of wealth in the hands of a small elite. Since the 1960s it has been inscribed within the "old civil wars" of the Cold War period. According to Renner, at that time the Revolutionary Armed Forces of Colombia (FARC, *Fuerzas Armadas Revolucionarias de Colombia*) took control of the coca region in the south of the country. Meanwhile, the National Liberation Army – ELN, *Ejército de Liberación Nacional* – did so over the oil region in the north-east. As a response, the elite and the military created a right-wing paramilitary group (Renner 2002: 35–36). In the 1980s, the conflict for the control over coca and oil intensified; yet this was coupled with a new developmental model implemented with neo-liberalism and its quest for new territories. The peaceful Colombian Pacific region, where Afro-Colombians and indigenous peoples of various ethnic groups co-existed peace-fully, became one of those highly desired territories (Escobar 2003).

According to Escobar, this rainforest region that is rich in biodiversity became the site for mega-development projects financed by multilateral agencies. The projects included, among others, the planning of an inter-oceanic canal, the massive expansion of African palm oil plantations and industrial shrimp cultiva-tion. This region is also rich in timber, gold and, coca plantations, and expands from the south towards the Pacific, resulting in the displacement of the Afro-Colombians and indigenous peoples. In 1991, the national constitution was mod-ified, giving collective territorial rights to those communities. These rights, which intensified the black and indigenous movements, were now empowered to strengthen their demands for the collective titling of their land and the respect for cultural diversity (Escobar 2003: 158–160).

However, since 1996 both the leftist guerrilla groups and the paramilitary forces – which in 1996 joined the drug lords' private militias to create the United Self-Defense Forces of Colombia (*Autodefensas Unidas de Colombia*, AUC) moved into the Pacific, creating instability and intensifying violence and terror. As a result, massacres and massive displacements became the norm. In fact, Escobar mentioned that it is estimated that since 1985 there have been around 2.2 million internally displaced people (IDPs), making Colombia one of the worst cases of development-induced displacement during the period of "consoli-dation of capitalist modernity" (Escobar 2003: 158). This number has since doubled.

What the above examples demonstrate is that since the 1990s there have been a constant struggle between, on the one hand, the Americanization of trans-national law and the intent to reshape and harmonize local constitutions to its image; and, on the other, the resistance of ethnic communities to the removal from domestic constitutions of their right to land and natural resources, which are the basis of the subsistence economy and their own survival. This resistance was contested by an increase of violence by the former Cold War soldiers, who were now integrated into paramilitary forces as well as the state.

Haute finance, tourism and displacement in the Caribbean

Although the case of mass tourism as a development strategy in the Caribbean did not involve a civil war, what it did involve, as in the above addressed cases of Central America, Mexico and Colombia, was the foreign appropriation and consumption of land, the displacement of residents and the exploitation of labor. Since the 1990s tourism in the Caribbean was a high-finance develop-ment strategy linked to tax havens and, as Hampton and Christensen argued, both industries, tourism and offshore finance shared common characteristics, including high mobility, rising global demand, labor-intensive customer serv-ices operations, and the need for an excellent transport and telecommunications infrastructure (Hampton and Christensen 2007: 999). The difference between the old tourism and the post-1990s tourism was that the latter was designed from the "top down"; it was dependent from foreign promotion and manage-ment, it was unregulated, poorly planned and it was vulnerable to market down-turns (Conway and Timms 2010: 329–330). Profit making was at the core of mass tourism; indeed, in 2005 the income generated by international tourism reached US$682 billion, the equivalent of 6 to 30 percent – depending on how it is measured – of the world's exports of goods and services (Swords and Mize 2008: 53). According to Swords and Mize, tourism, as a commodity, transforms both landscapes and social relations of production and consumption.

Landscapes were modified when foreign-owned resorts, high-rise hotels and gated communities were built in the usurped land, and, by doing so, the cost of land increased, making it impossible for residents to maintain their land and homes. Residents have no option than to sell their property to the multinational conglomerates for the development of mass tourism industry, an industry that has a huge environmental cost for the Caribbean. Some of those displaced from their land moved abroad, intensifying the Caribbean diaspora; meanwhile others worked for the tourist industry. The social relations of production and consump-tion introduced by the mass tourism industry was highly asymmetrical: on the one hand, the work done by waiters/waitresses, tour guides, doormen, bartend-ers, showgirls, food service and other type of laborers was highly exploitative in terms of both the intensive amount of work and the low wages paid to them. On the other side of the spectrum, the consumers, the tourists, depended for their leisure time on the exploitation of these workers. The main beneficiaries of both, the classist and racial division of space and the neo-colonial social relations introduced in the islands were the multinational conglomerates (Swords and Mize 2008: 53–56). This situation of exploitation has led tourism scholars to rethink alternative types of tourism.

However, many of the alternative forms of tourism such as environmental, cultural and socio-economic, which have had the objective of improving local conditions, have been co-opted by the mass tourism industry. *Trasformismo*, the appropriation of ideas of alternative movements, as mentioned before, is a con-stant action of those international organizations that promote the neo-liberal model and is one of the main ingredients of hegemony. This is why Conway and Timms (2010) have proposed the idea of "slow tourism" for the Caribbean, a term that draws on the Italian Slow Food Movement, a movement that, as slow tourism, acknowledges the time-space pressures of the New *Pax Americana*. Slow tourism, the antithesis of mass tourism, is a "development-from-below" alternative that puts people at the center; it is participatory and inclusive. Indeed, its objective is that tourism remains in the hands of local entrepreneurs, small businesses and cooperative/communal associations rather than in the hands of multinational conglomerates (Conway and Timms 2010: 335). This local owner-ship would undo the current land tenure system and the social relations between hosts and tourists; it would be more egalitarian, pluralist, respectful of difference and therefore enjoyable for both. Conway and Timms sustain that the engine for slow tourism should be the Caribbean diaspora once they return to the islands. In sum, in the 1990s the connection between mass tourism and offshore finance has been detrimental for both the residents of the Caribbean and the environment, and alternative forms of tourism will only be possible if the structure and super-structure of world orders changes; otherwise it will always be trumped by the latter and, therefore, susceptible to co-option.

To conclude: in the first decade of the post-Cold War period development was re-defined once more, this time as "good governance." New constitutionalist reforms were added to the "market reforms" of the former decade, solidifying the ongoing reconstruction of hegemony and of "the Americas." Towards that end, new constitutionalism was expanded at different geographical scales: at the *global scale*, the role of the international financial institutions as global managers was enhanced with the creation of the World Trade Organization in 1995, and, since then, the "three sisters" became the epicenter for the globalization process, the engine for the construction of transnational legal regimes, and their harmonization at the regional, national and community levels.

At the *regional level*, economic blocs were reshaped from an inward-oriented protectionism based on the import substitution model towards an outward-oriented free trade model. This was the case of the Andean Community of Nations (the former Andean Pact), the Central American Common Market, the Caribbean Community (the former Caribbean Free Trade Association), MER-COSUR, and the newly created NAFTA. Finally, at the *national and community levels*, the construction of a local new managerialism was crucial for the modification of domestic constitutions, with the objective of removing those rules that allowed for the existence of informal and subsistence economies. By doing so it shifted the remains of the public towards the private sphere; yet that private sphere also included rules that facilitated the entrance of transnational corporations into local spaces.

The previous social contract based on the collective goods of each nation (health, education, subsidies, communal lands, natural resources, tourism) became part of the "global commons," or of that powerful northern and southern "transnational capitalist class" that through the design and implementation of macroeconomic policies had the power to commodify them for their own benefit, to the exclusion of the majority of the people in the Americas. Hence, the former social citizenship of embedded liberalism has become a market citizenship under neo-liberalism. It is the vulnerable, the "risk population," especially women, children, the elderly, indigenous peoples and other ethnic groups, who have become the target of the neo-liberal global project and, if they protest, they are labeled as "terrorists" and attacked by those commandos prepared to resolve "low-intensity conflicts." In short, new constitutionalism had a domino effect that produced a shift from the public to the private at different scales and, in doing so, intensified the crisis of social reproduction across the continent. This situation has worsened in the new millennium, as will be demonstrated in the next chapter.

3 The new millennium

Development as "poverty reduction" and the commodification of livelihood[1]

In the new millennium development was re-defined, this time to mean "poverty reduction," and was a definition that echoed the origins of development in the earlier post-World War II period. At that time the World Bank considered those countries with an annual per capita income below US$100 as "poor" and believed that the solution was to design macro-economic policies for economic growth (Escobar 1995: 24). However, more than half a century later it seems that the definition of "poor" was quantitatively downgraded. Jeffrey Sachs noted that today millions of people live on less than US$1 per day and that "more than 8 million people around the world [will] die each year because they are too poor to stay alive" (Sachs 2005: 46). Sachs claims that "it is our task to help them onto the ladder of development, to give them at least a foothold on the bottom rung, from which they can then proceed to climb on their own" (Sachs 2005: 46).

"New Right" think-tanks and the international financial institutions started to design a plethora of "poverty-reduction" policies, with a focus on the Heavily Indebted Poor Countries Initiative (HIPC) and its related conditionalities: the Poverty Reduction Strategy Papers (PRSPs); the Impoverishment Risk and Livelihood Reconstruction Model (IRLR), which sought to solve the displacement of population caused by structural adjustment programs; and the Millennium Development Goals (MDGs).[2] All these policies were put into effect before the September 11, 2001 terrorist attack on the World Trade Center in New York and the Pentagon in Washington.

September 11, 2001 was the trigger that expanded and legitimized the "end of poverty" discourse as an antidote to terrorism. Yet it was not until the United Nations Financing for Development (FED) summit in Monterrey in March 2002 that a private sector development agenda to "reduce" poverty was officially launched. The argument here is that the "Monterrey Consensus" and the praxis of the above policies represented the sealing of the ensemble of structural, super-structural and social top-down reforms that were planned respectively in the 1980s, 1990s and 2000s.

As such, these latter policies have elements of the former and are deepening the hegemonic project led by the United States. Their cornerstone is the strengthening of an authoritarian social contract through the commodification of livelihoods, which include the appropriation of land and natural resources.

Ideas: Santa Fe IV: "The Nine 'Ds' for George W. Bush"

In January 2001, the Council for Inter-American Security (CIS) launched its Santa Fe IV document, *The Future of the Americas: Themes for the New Millennium*.[3] The themes to which the ultra-conservative think-tank of the American military-industrial complex referred were the new threats emerging in Latin America for the achievement of a Free Trade Area of the Americas (FTAA). These threats, "The Nine Ds" designed for George W. Bush, included: defense, drugs, demography, debt, de-industrialization, post-Cold War populist democracies, destabilization, deforestation, and the decline of the United States. These issues will be summarized below as they are presented in the document.

The document noted that the United States under President Clinton's administration has been in decline since 1993. The conservative "New Right" criticized him for focusing on the East–West axis, Europe, China and corruption in Russia, and for his anti-militarist tendency: "switching from the 'green' of the U.S. Army to the 'blue' of the United Nations" was a dangerous move that could only strengthen the power of the enemies of the United States. Thus, the authors of the document suggested that the new administration should reverse this situation by strengthening the links between North and South America, extending the militarization of the area and extending the Monroe Doctrine from the nineteenth century to the new millennium.

Defense, the first "D," highlighted the primary importance that Latin America represented for the United States in terms of availability of natural resources, its strategic location and human potential, and focused on two main issues: the principal geo-strategic elements in the South for the security of the United States, and the new enemies that were emerging in the region. The main geo-strategic issues included control of the Atlantic Ocean's straits, the use of the Panama Canal, the south route through the *Cabo de Hornos* – the intersection of the Atlantic and Pacific Oceans south of Argentina and Chile – and the reassurance that the "natural resources of the hemisphere be available to respond to *our* national priorities."[4]

The list of enemies included people and movements in Latin America, within the United States and in a new extra-continental power. Fidel Castro who, following the demise of the Soviet Union, and who, according to Santa Fe IV, was being backed by Colombian narcoterrorists, headed the Latin American list as the principal threat in the region. President Hugo Chávez from Venezuela, referred to as a "Castrist," was presented as a third danger. In particular, the Bolivarian movement was interpreted as the intent of "communists and socialists" to "extend [their] influence over all the hemisphere, including Canada and Mexico" and, by doing so, would undermine the Monroe Doctrine.[5]

The "Gramscian Left" were considered the biggest challenge within the United States. According to the document, their objective was to expand communism to the hemisphere using liberation theology, the press, universities – more broadly, educational institutions – and the juridical system as dissemination channels. However, the biggest threat was seen as the increasing economic penetration of China – both communist and Taiwanese – into the continent. The document refers to it as the "Chinese problem," which included: China's potential control over the Panama Canal – the western hemisphere's and the world's most important strategic point; its advance into the Caribbean where the Chinese had solid links with Fidel Castro; their help in de-stabilizing the Andean bloc, especially Colombia; and their increasing connections to President Chávez from Venezuela. In sum, according to Santa Fe IV, China and the "Gramscian Marxists" were behind all the threats that were emerging in the Americas.

The concern related to *drugs* referred to the expansion of narcoterrorism into Colombia and the international movement that favored the legalization of drugs. The concept "narcoterrorism" is presented as the juxtaposition of terrorism, drug-trafficking and organized crime (that is, arms trafficking and money laundering), and it replaced the danger that the Soviet Union represented before its demise. According to the document, drugs, particularly cocaine and heroine, have been one of the principal causes of death amongst Americans during the past decades, bringing with it a series of threats. The identified threats included the spread of HIV/AIDS, the moral degeneration of millions of Americans, de-stabilization and corruption of the international financial system and the undermining of democracy. Although President Nixon initiated the 'war on drugs' in the 1970s and President Clinton had continued it during his presidency, their efforts were not considered sufficient.

The "New Right"'s authors recommended that the new administration should attack the source of the drug problem, which they identified as the two "Marxist" Colombian guerrilla movements: the *Fuerzas Armadas Revolucionarias de Colombia* (FARC – Colombian Revolutionary Armed Forces) and the *Ejército de Liberación Nacional* (ELN – National Liberation Army), whose final objective, it was argued, was to take over the states and install totalitarian governments. They also criticized President Andrés Pastrana from Colombia, who denied that the Colombian Revolutionary Armed Forces and the National Liberation Army had links with narcotrafficking. An even stronger critique was directed at George Soros' international movement, which favored the legalization of drugs and focused on "treatment" rather than on the "war on drugs." This focus was considered short-sighted insofar as it was thought to be blind towards the possible "Colombianization" of the neighboring countries.

The *demographic* threat, the third "D," analyzed the asymmetric population growth in the Americas during the past 200 years, the shift in the ethnic composition of the population in the United States and linked migration to drug trafficking. In 1850, the United States had a similar number of inhabitants as Hispanic America as a whole. However, since 1950, the Latin American population started to increase at a higher rate, reaching 497 million inhabitants in the year 2000, while the United States population accounted for only 273 million. The document recognized that when the natural increase of population due to birth rates was in decline, it is important to increase the number of people in a country through the promotion of immigration, a necessary influx for sustaining the economy and the provision of tax income to maintain a welfare system.

However, according to the document, migration also posed a threat, since it promoted a change in the ethnic composition of the receiving countries. For example, Muslim migration into Europe was seen in comparative perspective to Hispanic (mainly Mexican) migration to the United States. Hispanic migration to the United States had many causes, such as extreme poverty, high inflation and unequal distribution of wealth in the country of origin. In addition, NAFTA, which was supposed to stop migration, only increased it. To this should be added that the fertility rate of Hispanic women in the United States tended to double that of American-born women. Projections showed that by the year 2010 the number of the Hispanic population in the United States would surpass the black population by one million, reaching a total of thirty-nine million Hispanics. Moreover, it was estimated that by the year 2100 the United States would have 571 million inhabitants, of which 377 million would be immigrants. The document also noted that migrants were linked to drug trafficking, especially to the Colombian cartels in Mexico.

The authors considered the fourth "D," the external *debt* of both Latin America and the United States, as a threat to security. Between 1980 and 1990 Latin America had paid US$418,000 million in interest over a total debt of US$80.000,00 million [*sic*]. By the new millennium, Latin America owed a total of US$665.951,00 million [*sic*] to foreign creditors of which US$11.192,26 million [*sic*] were owed to the United States. The fact that Spanish banks flooded the continent, supposedly financed by the narcodollars of the Russian mafia, was considered to have the potential of leading to a return to colonialism. In fact, the "New Right" authors called this process the Spanish "Re-conquest of the Americas." Meanwhile, it recognized that the United States was also experiencing deep financial problems: in the year 2000 it had a public debt of US$5,646,486–626,691 [*sic*] and a trade deficit of US$300,000 million. Thus, both Latin America and the US were in the hands of external creditors, although with very different relations to them.

De-industrialization, the fifth "D," is defined in the document as the transfer of factories to other nations where wages and taxes were lower and environmental laws were more "flexible." This process, as was claimed in the document, had accelerated in the Americas in the 1990s and the losers were Argentina, the countries that were integrated into the Caribbean Basin Initiative (CBI) and, the United States. With the creation of MERCOSUR in 1991, Argentina, a country that had a strong industrial base, lost its auto and textile industries to Brazil where wages were lower. Similarly, the creation of NAFTA in 1994 produced the de-industrialization of the Central American countries that had been integrated through the Caribbean Basin Initiative (CBI), a free trade area formed in 1982 under President Reagan's Administration. According to Santa Fe IV, textiles and assembly plants moved from the CBI countries to the Mexican–American border, which by the year 2000 accounted for about 4,000 *maquiladoras* that employed around one million workers. The authors claimed that the United States also accelerated its process of de-industrialization due to NAFTA (in the United States the process of de-industrialization was initiated in the 1960s due to its competition with Asia). While in the 1960s the US transferred textile and computer assembly plants to southern nations; in the 1990s it also transferred auto, steel, railway equipment, plane and microchip industries to Mexico.

The process of de-industrialization produced the re-emergence of *populist democracies* in Latin America, the sixth "D." According to Santa Fe IV, these post-Cold War populist democracies deferred from those that existed during the Cold War period. While the populist democracies of Argentina and Mexico followed a similar path, Venezuela's took a different route. The old populist democracies (in Argentina the *Partido Justicialista* and in Mexico the *Partido Revolucionario Institucional*) favored state capitalism by implementing policies that promoted the internal market, the nationalization of industries, discouraged foreign investments and created full employment, which tended to favor working class-interests. Meanwhile, the same parties in the 1990s reversed the former social and economic policies by favoring globalization, the privatization of national enterprises, the promotion of foreign direct investment and were less favorable to the working class. The increase in unemployment and disappointment with populism led to the re-emergence of old parties and the creation of new ones – in Argentina the *Frente del País Solidario* (FREPASO) and, in Mexico, the *Partido de la Revolución Democrática* (PRD) and the *Partido de Acción Nacional* (PAN).

It is the different path which Venezuela followed that was considered a challenge to the authors of Santa Fe IV. President Hugo Chávez won the elections in 1998 with the promise to utilize Venezuela's oil revenues to reduce poverty in his country. To this end he made drastic changes to the state-owned oil company and increased Venezuela's role within the OPEC countries. Other red flags for the American new right in the continent were: the take-over of farms by the movement *Obreros Rurales Sin Tierra* [sic] in Brazil; the Bolivian opposition to the privatization of water in Cochabamba; the fact that the indigenous peoples of Ecuador brought down a neo-liberal government and, as always, Fidel Castro. In sum, notwithstanding some shifts in populist democracies towards the right, there was a notorious emergence of progressive populist movements.

The seventh "D" refers to the *de-stabilization* of the continent due to President Clinton's disregard for Latin America, particularly the lack of a project to build a post-Castro Cuban nation. Clinton's reliance on scientific knowledge rather than on traditional values embedded in Latin America and his failure to understand that the problems of Latin America are mainly economic all added to the disregard paid to Latin America.

The eighth "D" refers to the process of *deforestation* as a result of the cutting and burning of trees to be used as wood supply in the chemical and paper industries, and ultimately the danger resulting from the loss of biodiversity. This could lead to desertification, population displacement and illnesses.

Finally, the ninth "D" posited that, because of all the above points ("D"1 through "D"8), the *decline* of the United States would be inevitable, it would lead to the cultural destruction of the US as a nation.

Third-generation reforms[6]

In 1996 the World Bank and the International Monetary Fund proposed the Heavily Indebted Poor Countries (HIPCs) initiative,[7] which was passed after a major review in 1999. The creditors, the Paris Club, the World Bank and the International Monetary Fund, agreed to reduce the total external debt of US$90 billion of the thirty-three poorest countries in the world. In Latin America only four countries fell into this category – Bolivia, Guyana, Honduras and Nicaragua.[8] Initially, to qualify for debt reduction, a country's debt should have been one-and-a-half times higher than the total value of its exports (Greenhill 2002).[9] However, the Heavily Indebted Poor Countries initiative was later extended to more than seventy low-income countries in need of soft loans to service their debts.

However, this "generosity" came with a new package of conditionalities attached to it: the Poverty Reduction Strategy Paper (PRSPs).[10] "Poverty reduction" became the objective of the new millennium and the third "evolutionary stage" in the New *Pax Americana's* continuum. As such, the basic policy matrix contained elements of the former SAPs and also of the "good governance" approach. This has led activists and academics to denounce the Poverty Reduction Strategy Papers as "SAPs in disguise" and even as the "reinforcement of SAPs."[11] Since the 2002 United Nations Financing for Development Summit in Monterrey (also known as Monterrey Consensus), the Poverty Reduction Strategy Papers became the basis for the international financial institution's lending to all countries and were adopted by all northern development agencies.

The Poverty Reduction Strategy Papers stipulated[12] that the resources released from debt servicing should be utilized into those issue areas that led to poverty reduction, such as health, education, living standards and water (here they are linked to the Millennium Development Goals). Therefore, the government of a country in need of soft loans would have to present a "paper" or Interim Poverty Reduction Strategy Papers (IPRSPs) specifying who were the "target beneficiaries," where the policies were to be applied to, the costs, how it would alleviate poverty and how the results would be monitored. Crucial to the Interim Poverty Reduction Strategy Papers was that civil society and the "target beneficiaries" should have participated in the debates and formulation of the "nationally owned" document. Thus, the Interim Poverty Reduction Strategy Papers were to be the outcome of joint work among a wide range of actors, which included the target population, non-governmental organizations, academia, think-tanks, churches, the private sector, women and international organizations. However, coordination of the Poverty Reduction Strategy Papers would be undertaken by the western donors: the World Bank, the International Monetary Fund, the World Trade Organization, other international organizations and the development agencies of the G-8 countries.[13]

The "nationally owned" and "participatory" characteristics were pure rhetoric when it became clear that the Interim Poverty Reduction Strategy Papers were to be designed according to the World Bank's "Poverty Reduction Sourcebook"

(PRS), which set out the main guidelines for poverty alleviation. The Source-book was divided into six main parts: (1) the explanation of the technical methodology; (2) the pro-market cross-cutting issues – which included governance/new constitutionalism, gender, environment, strategic communication, and the above mentioned rhetoric of participation and community-owned development; (3) macro-economics and trade; (4) rural and urban poverty; human development – market-based social protection, health and education – and finally, (5) the private sector infrastructure – strategic natural resources such as energy, water, mining, transport, information and communication technologies.[14]

The Poverty Reduction Strategy Papers resulted in a more comprehensive set of disciplinary measures than the first- and second-generation reforms proposed by the global managers. This reflects the fact that new constitutionalism has now been expanded to all aspects of human life, intensifying the crisis of what Bakker calls "social reproduction," which includes the reproductive, productive and environmental dimensions (Bakker 2003). Indeed, the re-regulation of welfare in private hands leads to the commodification of basic needs and reduces the accessibility to health and education to the wealthy minority (as demonstrated in Chapter 1). By excluding the vast majority of the population it will reinforce poverty rather than alleviate it, and will have an especially negative impact upon women, children and the elderly. The G-8 nexus' appropriation of Latin American public energy (e.g., electricity, oil and gas) mining resources and land are inducing population displacement (here the Poverty Reduction Strategy Papers are linked to the World Bank's Impoverishment Risk and Livelihood Reconstruction (IRLR) Model,[15] contaminating the environment and fomenting the internationalization of indigenous and Afro-descendants' movements.

As will be demonstrated below, privatized water in Latin America is at least three times more expensive than before, when it was public property, and the most vulnerable of society cannot afford it. Rather than reducing poverty, the Poverty Reduction Strategy Papers are increasing poverty, inequality, violence and the already pervasive dependency of southern with respect to northern countries.

The following analysis will focus on the articulation of power at the local level and will examine the impact of one aspect of the World Bank's third-generation reforms: the Poverty Reduction Strategy Papers.

How the PRSPs actually work in the South: whose development? Whose growth?

This section examines the dialectical relationship between global and local forces regarding the privatization of three strategic natural resources included in the "private sector and infrastructure" section of the Poverty Reduction Strategy Sourcebook: energy, water and mining. Their privatization, particularly to transnational corporations, is considered by the international financial institutions to be the cornerstone for poverty reduction. However, the argument here is that the Sourcebook's assumptions are based on false premises, as the following discussion illustrates.

Energy

According to the Poverty Reduction Sourcebook, energy is presented as the typical tradition–modern dichotomy of modernization theory:

- While poor people may rely in part on self-collected traditional fuels for subsistence cooking and heating needs, they exhibit a strong desire to use more convenient modern energy services and are willing to pay a substantial part of their cash income to obtain it. In doing so they attach a high value to the time saved and the quality of service made available.
- Modern energy services can enable poor households to engage in, and extend, activities that generate income. Electric lighting extends the working day, electric machines (such as sewing machines and looms) increase productivity, and cooking fuels like kerosene and liquefied petroleum gas (LPG) enable households to increase the amount of food for sale.
- No one wants energy for itself; people want it for what it can do – energy is in this sense a "derived demand." People demand energy to cook, provide lighting and refrigeration, drive motor cars, and obtain services like communications (telephones) and entertainment (televisions, radios).[16]

At stake here is the ethnocentric intention to remove the remains of the subsistence economy, in particular its dependency on traditional fuels, such as wood, to light fires. According to this reasoning, the utilization of more modern fuels would free up time, which would become available for commodification through the incorporation of traditional communities into the labor market – mainly in urban areas.

Rather than indigenous peoples being interested in utilizing modern energy, it should be noted that transnational corporations are the ones that want to exploit and commercialize energy resources. Transnational corporations' appetite for energy resources has led to the emergence of violent conflicts all over the continent. Bolivia has sufficient gas reserves for domestic consumption for about 600 years and 87 percent of those reserves are in Tarija, "the Bolivian Kuwait."[17] Pacific LNG (an Anglo-Spanish-Argentine consortium) wanted to exploit Bolivian gas and sell it at a very low price to the United States. The gas was to be exported through a pipeline that would be built by Spanish firms and transported via Chile[18] to Mexico where it would be processed before being sent to California.[19] In sum, all the above-mentioned countries would make enormous profits out of Bolivian gas while the majority of the people of Bolivia themselves were in a paradoxical position of being unable to buy gas owing to its high price. This divided the country between those who wanted to sell the gas – the inhabitants of Tarija – and those who opposed it in a national referendum: the Aymara indigenous peasants organized under the Union Confederation of Peasant Workers of Bolivia (CSUTBC), the Bolivian Workers' Council (COB), the Movement towards Socialism (MAS), the Federations of Coca Producers of El Chapare and the National Coalition of Gas.[20]

President Sánchez de Lozada (1993–1997; 2002–2003) ordered a brutal repression, which was directed by American military personnel and culminated in the death of eighty people and hundreds of wounded. While Sánchez de Lozada asserted that this was an "international conspiracy" to overthrow him and install an "narco-labor dictatorship" in the country, President Bush announced, through the Organization of American States, that no unconstitutional changes would be tolerated.[21] Thus, both were directing their accusations towards Evo Morales, the leader of the Movement towards Socialism (MAS-*Movimiento al Socialismo*) and the Federations of Coca Producers of El Chapare (*Federaciones Cocaleras de El Chapare*), who in the 2002 elections finished only 1 percent below Sánchez de Lozada.

The Bolivian President, Sánchez de Lozada, was obliged to resign and leave the country for Miami on October 17, 2003. Sánchez de Lozada, together with Jeffrey Sachs, were the architects of the Bolivian neo-liberal plan back in 1985. Bolivians constantly repeated words such as the "re-conquest," the "re-foundation" of the country and the "social re-appropriation of hydrocarbons for all Bolivians,"[22] suggesting a search for social justice and a new start without the interference of global generic forces. Bolivians were re-imagining a new national community, and the election in 2006 of Evo Morales as the first indigenous President of Bolivia represented a window for optimism.

Water

Although the planet is made up mainly of water, only 2.5 percent of it is drinkable fresh water. Water is a crucial element for the biological reproduction of society but the new constitutionalist approach of water managerialism sees it as a commodity and as a tool for social control – one that resembles the mechanisms established by the Inca Empire. The Inca elite, who were located in the highlands, controlled the irrigation canals that took the water towards the valleys, where subordinated nations reliant on agriculture lived. By cutting the flow of water the Inca elite were also able to control the production of food, another source of life. In a globalized economy, private ownership replaces the canals, and global, regional and local water management regimes harness that control from above. The International Financial Institutions Sourcebook claimed that:

> [R]ecent evidence strongly indicates that publicly provided water and sanitation services repeatedly fail to provide efficient service or reach the poorest segments of the population. Any water and sanitation strategy will need to recognize and be built around the centrality of private provision .... One important government role may be the establishment of microcredit or other arrangements that avoid unsustainable subsidized services yet facilitate improvements demanded by the poor.[23]

Notwithstanding the international financial institutions' assertion, the mounting evidence of water wars emerging in the hemisphere shows exactly the opposite.

Transnational water corporations, once installed in the South, increase water tariffs according to a price set in the international market; yet wages in the South remain too low and therefore water becomes an extremely unaffordable good. For example, according to the World Development Movement, in 1998, Bolivia received an International Monetary Fund Enhanced Structural Adjustment Facility (ESAF) loan for US$138 million with the condition to accelerate the privatization of public enterprises, including those related to water. In 2000 they also received a Poverty Reduction Growth Facility (PRGF) loan for US$46.1 million and debt relief for US$1.3 billion under the Enhanced Heavily Indebted Poor Countries Initiative. In that same year, the price of water in Cochabamba increased by 200 percent, which represented about 22 percent of the monthly wage of a self-employed man and 27 percent of a woman's.[24] Massive protests developed and were led by new types of organizations, such as neighborhood associations, potable water committees, peasants, indigenous peoples and new ecological movements which arose, displacing the traditional and once strong Central Bolivian Workers Organization (COB – *Central Obrera Boliviana*) (Assies 2003; Farthing and Kohl 2001; Schinke and Strickner 2003). The conflict, as most natural resources wars do, ended with governmental repression and took the lives of eight people.[25]

However, for Andean indigenous communities it was not just the price of water that was at stake but their cosmovision, which is based on the principle of duality (as opposed to western dichotomies) in which everything in the cosmos is considered relational rather than independent. As such, water was seen as the basis for reciprocity and complementarity because it allowed the harmonious articulation between nature and human beings at the family and community levels. Moreover, it represented life, "the blood of the earth and of the Andean universe" and therefore it was sacred.[26]

One of the most important water struggle cases in South America was the World Bank Funded Guaraní Water System – *Sistema Acuífero Guaraní* – located in the Triple Frontier and extending over four of the MERCOSUR countries: Argentina, Brazil, Paraguay and Uruguay. The *Acuífero* is one of the largest underground water reserves in the world; it contains about 50,000 cubic kilometers of liquid which, it is estimated, could provide enough fresh water for the whole planet for two centuries. The United States initiated a campaign under the pretext that an Al Qaeda group was operating in the Triple Frontier, Paraguay, therby allowing US troops, CIA and FBI agents to enter the area. Although it was determined that the alleged terrorists were Lebanese immigrants who did not belong to any terrorist organization, the paramilitaries remained in the region.[27] Nevertheless, on the Uruguayan side, a national referendum called by the National Commission for the Defense of Water and Life sought electoral approval for the modification of the national constitution to prevent the appropriation of water by transnational corporations.

Sixty percent of the population voted for the reform, which declared water a public good and a fundamental human right, and guaranteed the participation of all consumers in decisions regarding the sustainability of water resources and the defense of their sovereignty.[28] In sum, these constitutionalist struggles demonstrate that the privatization of water does not lead to an efficient provision of the service, as the World Bank sustains; rather they put human life in jeopardy.

Mining

The Sourcebook presents mining as a powerful tool for the reduction of poverty, but it recognizes that it could also "heighten risks to the lives of the very poorest of society." Nevertheless, the Poverty Reduction Strategy Paper Sourcebook specifies the steps that governments should take to make mining a successful poverty reduction strategy:

> In developing a section on mining for a Poverty Reduction Strategy Paper (PRSP), policymakers will want to focus on (a) gathering relevant data to understand actual and potential poverty-related impacts, risks, and opportunities of the mining sector in their country ... (b) setting clear objectives and identifying priorities for intervention in a consultative process regarding poverty impacts and the mining sector; (c) identifying the mechanisms to achieve the objectives, including needed changes to policies, laws and regulations; and (d) establishing the necessary institutional arrangements, including authorities, responsibilities, and capabilities, to implement the mechanisms. Depending on a country's civil society, the consultation and priority setting should include local community representatives and community-based organizations (CBOs), local government representatives from respective mining regions, industry associations, trade unions, non-governmental organizations (NGOs), and other relevant parties. In most cases, it would be useful if the process were led by the country's mining ministry or agency.[29]

However, consultation, as in the case of energy and water, never went beyond the global and national scales. Local communities and trade unions were seldom consulted, and non-governmental organizations since the 1990s, as Sonia Álvarez (1999) has argued, have increasingly abandoned the activist component of the 1970s and 1980s and have become more technocratic based on efficiency criteria, a shift produced through the modification of donors' policies and funding.

The general argument is that mining can reduce poverty because it provides jobs and represents an excellent source of income for governments through the taxes collected from transnational mining corporations. However, mining is a capital-intensive industry and therefore does not require a large amount of workers. Generally those few technicians needed are highly trained foreigners. Due to the competition for investments, southern countries are forced to reduce mining taxes to be able to attract foreign direct investment, and besides, most of the time these taxes are not paid. Moreover, transnational mining corporations, which are mainly Canadian, American and British, have their addresses in tax havens, thereby protecting the final destiny of the massive revenues generated through mineral extraction.[30]

Latin America has become the main receiver of mining investments. If in the 1990s only 12 percent of the worldwide investments in mining were located in Latin America, at the beginning of the millennium they increased to 33 percent. In 2004, mineral exports grew an average of 40 percent. In that same year, Chile exported US$16.5 billion in minerals, followed by Peru with US$6.77 billion and Brazil with US$5.2 billion (Remón, Powers and Maurial 2005). By using "growth" based on GDP as a measure, it can be said that mining projects were extremely successful, yet, that income accrued to transnational corporations and, not to the countries they are designed to help. It can therefore be said that Poverty Reduction Strategies increase rather than reduce poverty.

Moreover, the environmental toll left behind with the utilization of cyanide, used for leaching the minerals, and other heavy metals (such as lead, arsenic, mercury, antimony and sulfuric acid), destroy the ecosystems and farmlands by poisoning rivers, streams and underground water. Paradoxically, this happens at the same time as when water is said to be scarce and both industries, mining and water, are being promoted in the same Poverty Reduction Strategy Papers. Another contradiction is between investments in private health systems to reduce poverty, when mining pollution, as Remón and colleagues (2005) argue, increases illnesses such as tuberculosis, skin and respiratory problems (related to breathing aluminum powder) and hypertension (related to bauxite). Moreover, mining was linked to population displacements, violence and massacres, which gave rise, as in the case of the water wars, to the growth of neighborhood associations, "marches for life," "no to mining" campaigns, and referendums for the inclusion of clauses in national constitutions to stop the abuses of transnational mining corporations.

In sum, the Poverty Reduction Strategy Paper is an impositional global constitutional text that undermines sovereignty, and de-democratizes politics because there is no effective wide-based consultation and participation but imposition. It increases inequality, as it represents a massive transfer of resources from South to North, which allows for the development of the North, not the South. The cost of this subsidy to the North is paid by the most vulnerable in society, who are denied access to commodified health and educational systems. The statistical methods utilized for poverty reduction monitoring and evaluation do not capture the marches, referendums and constitutional struggles for "life" that are taking place in the South. The concept of "life" attached to all these struggles denotes the deepness of the crisis of social reproduction, which is a struggle for survival. "Poverty reduction" is an ideological tool that enmasks the fact that the private sector and infrastructure section of the Poverty Reduction Strategy Papers is accelerating the infrastructure process of globalization and the primitive accumulation of capital.

Intensifying the road towards the hemispheric FTAA

The FTAA,[31] which was modeled on the NAFTA agreement, was strongly opposed by Latin American nations and anti-globalization movements in the Miami (1994), Santiago de Chile (1998) and Quebec (2001) Summits.[32] The main controversial issue revolved around the protectionist agricultural subsidies in northern nations, which did not allow southern countries to export their primary production, and the very source of their comparative advantage. This seemed to have called a halt to the continental integration expected to take place by August 2005. However, efforts towards the "evolutionary" integration continued at smaller regional levels, such as "NAFTA Plus," the Canada–Central America Four Free Trade Agreement (CA4FTA), the South American Community of Nations (SACN/*CSN*) and myriad bilateral investment treaties and free trade agreements.

"NAFTA Plus" has also been labeled "deep integration" because it entailed the erasing of borders between Canada, Mexico and the United States, a tri-national merger that step by step is expected to lead to the formation of a "North America bloc."[33] The planned steps include: the integration of a tri-national security perimeter; a customs union; a common market; a monetary union, and finally, a North American identity with a similar discourse, symbols, a tri-national education system and a common mass media (Pickard 2005). Thus, NAFTA Plus aims to produce the convergence of the juridical, economic, security and cultural domains, keeping to the American model.

However, the paradox, as Pickard has argued, is that the intensification of the northern merger was proposed by the Canadian and Mexican elites just before September 11, 2001. In fact, Pickard mentioned that the Canadian elites considered that if the border were to be dismantled, the barriers that the United States had implemented for certain Canadian exports would be eliminated. In turn, they would offer "unrestricted access to Canadian natural resources." Meanwhile, the Mexican President, Vicente Fox, proposed to President Bush that if the free movement of labor was included as part of the merger within the region, in exchange he would push forward *Plan Sur* (the South Plan) which aimed at the militarization and closure of the Mexican southern border to Central American migration. Fox even offered the possibility for the privatization of either PEMEX, the state oil company, or the Federal Electricity Commission. However, after September 11, the idea of "NAFTA Plus" was abandoned and the borders were sealed (Pickard 2005).

On June 27, 2005, the United States agreed to the creation of a North America bloc and the three countries took the first steps towards "deep integration" and signed approximately 300 regulations for the homogenization of security measures for their countries. The meaning of US security was broadened beyond its military aspects to include strategic natural resources, particularly water, oil and gas.[34] The United States proposed two mega projects to transport water from Canada to the Ogalla aquifer in the United States Midwest: the Project Grand Canal in the Great Lakes and the North American Water and Power Authority in the west (Chiapas in Mexico and Central America were also rich in water resources). With respect to oil, since 1994, Canada and Mexico have been the top two suppliers of the United States market and although Mexico's total proven reserves are estimated to last for only another ten to twelve years, Mexico is still rich in gas (Pickard 2005). Thus, it may be said that in the post-9/11 era the social construction of "terrorism" not only led to the brutal military invasion of Afghanistan and Iraq, but also to a "peaceful" militarized unification with the United States' neighbours Canada and Mexico. In all these cases, oil, gas and water were the principal non-renewable resources at stake.

The second new constitutionalist unification which was expected to take place sometime during the Fall of 2005, but which has been delayed,[35] is the Canada–Central America Four Free Trade Agreement (CA4FTA), which is also modeled on NAFTA, particularly on its controversial Chapter 11. According to the Americas Policy Group, CA4FTA will strengthen even more so the power of transnational corporations vis-à-vis local communities and governments, and will facilitate the appropriation of land and strategic natural resources (in the case of Canada's main interests, mining and oil). Central American communities were being displaced from their land, pushed to abandon their subsistence economies while their environment was being polluted with chemical toxics such as cyanide utilized in mining, and oil spills. If people protest and corporations perceive their economic interests to be threatened, corporations have the "right" to sue local governments.[36]

Finally, besides these North and Central American new constitutionalist agreements, there was, at that time, the proposal of a third large merger in the south, the South American Community of Nations (SACN/*CSN*), the first steps towards what later on became UNASUR. The South American Community of Nations was expected to bring together the Andean Community of Nations (CAN: Bolivia, Colombia, Ecuador, Peru and Venezuela) and MERCOSUR (Argentina, Brazil, Paraguay and Uruguay), with the addition of Chile, Guyana and Surinam. The only South American country that would remain outside the community was French Guiana, which was a member of the European Union. The twelve countries mentioned above signed the Cuzco Declaration on December 8, 2004, which stipulated complete integration by 2007 and a gradual elimination of tariffs by 2019. The goal was to move beyond a simple Free Trade Area and towards an economic, social and institutional integration modeled upon the European Union. The negotiations included discussions around harmonizing the legal system and, eventually, to have a common currency, parliament and common passport.[37] In the words of the Andean Community of Nations' Secretary General Allan Wagner, the ultimate goal was to create the "United States of South America."[38]

The Cuzco Declaration announced three pillars: (1) political, social and cultural cooperation, which included the strengthening of democracy, regional security and the fight against drugs and corruption; (2) trade, economic and financial integration, such as the Free Trade Area between the Andean Community of Nations and MERCOSUR, and financial integration in the *Corporación*

Andina de Fomento; and (3) the development of infrastructure, energy and communications, for which ten large axis of South American development and integration have been identified, including 335 infrastructural projects for the following thirty years – bridges, highways, airports, ports, railways and telecommunications – of which thirty-one were considered "anchor projects" and were expected to be concluded in the first five years of the South American Community of Nations.[39]

At that time it was not clear whether the South American Community of Nations reflected an authentic South American search for autonomy and regional protectionism, or if it was one more step towards the continental Free Trade Area of the Americas encouraged by the Bush Administration. The main debate regarding the South American Community of Nations revolved around which was the best way to enter the market in a globalized world and how to attract capital. The obvious path to follow seemed to be to maintain good relations with the United States and, at the same time, to explore new links with emergent blocs.[40] The strong contradictions within the South American Community of Nations emerged in its first meeting held in Brazil on September 30, 2005. One of the main problems seemed to have been the interest of Brazil to become the leader of South America – something that all the other countries have rejected. The fact was that four countries – Colombia, Guyana, Surinam and Uruguay – were absent from the meeting in Brazil and President Kirchner withdrew before the Brasilia Declaration was signed.[41]

Hugo Chávez from Venezuela strongly criticized the Chilean and Brazilian government's drafting of the South American Community of Nations according to a neo-liberal model, and declined to sign the Brasilia Declaration; however, he did not withdraw from the meeting. Chávez was instead very fond of his own integration project, "Alternativa Bolivariana" (ALBA) and very aware that, being the second largest oil producer in the world (Iraq is first, Canada third and Saudi Arabia fourth), Venezuela needed, for security reasons, to move quickly towards a Latin American integration of energy resources. Towards this end, he created *Petroamérica*, whose four pillars were the Venezuelan *PDVSA*, *Petrocaribe*, *Petroandina* and *Petrosur* – MERCOSUR and Chile – and also signed agreements with the Brazilian *Petrobras*, the Uruguayan *Sol*, the Argentinian state company *ENARSA*, the private company *RHASA* and the Spanish company *Repsol* – which controlled, at that time, half of the oil market of Argentina.[42] Notwithstanding the enormous contradictions, three large convergences were discussed in the Americas at the time when the IV Summit of the Americas was going to take place: NAFTA Plus, Canada-4 Free Trade Agreement and the South American Community of Nations. However, something unexpected occurred at that meeting.

A double fissure between South and North: the 2005 hemispheric summits in Argentina

The two summits, the Indigenous Peoples' and the Leaders of the Americas, took place in Argentina at the end of 2005. The former took place on October 27 to 29 in Buenos Aires, preceding the latter in one week, and was financed by the Canadian government. The second took place in Mar del Plata on November 4–5 and was headed by the President of the United States. Both were strongly criticized by parallel anti-summits. While the official, northern-driven summits enshrined the benefits of globalization and hemispheric integration, the parallel anti-summits highlighted the dark reality that globalization and continentalism represented to the South.

The II Indigenous Peoples' Summit (Buenos Aires, October 27–29, 2005)

The second Indigenous Peoples' Summit was organized by the Assembly of First Nations of Canada (AFN) and the Organization of Indigenous Peoples of Argentina (ONPIA – *Organización de Pueblos Indígenas de Argentina*). This meeting was received with anger by independent indigenous groups,[43] who felt deceived by the First Indigenous Peoples' Summit, "Indigenous Peoples: Connecting to the New Economy," which took place in Ottawa in March 2001, and were afraid that this second summit would be a repetition of the former one. At the Ottawa meeting, about 170 indigenous leaders from Latin America participated to debate the impact of the new economy upon indigenous peoples and to draft a declaration. The Assembly of First Nations, according to the independent indigenous group, whitewashed the final document, which was presented to the Presidents of the Americas that met in Québec three weeks later, making it seem that the indigenous leaders were in favor of globalization and the FTAA. The Latin American indigenous delegates felt betrayed and manipulated by the Assembly of First Nations and the Canadian government and could not afford the economic costs to go to Québec to clarify their real position regarding the new economy.[44]

At the Buenos Aires II Indigenous Peoples' Summit, the former declaration of indigenous peoples was to be ratified by indigenous peoples in order to be addressed by the Americas President's Summit in Mar del Plata a week later. The opposition mounted, as reflected by a Mapuche leader:

In our estimation, the Canadian government went a bit far this time in trying to divide the indigenous movements and separate them from many potential allies among genuine and representative civil society organizations who are demanding justice and want to build a more democratic and inclusive society. We agree with the Ecuadorian leader, Luis Macas, who said recently: "It's a hypocrisy that the Canadian government is sponsoring that event [the official indigenous summit] while they are opposing and denying the indigenous rights in all the international conferences, and their oil, mining [uranium], logging, water and other corporations are taking advantage of globalization, plundering natural resources and contaminating the environment."

In the indigenous summit's agenda in Buenos Aires, the AFN features an indigenous business summit.... We indigenous peoples have to build unity between North and South, but paternalism and political manipulation gets in the way of our understanding, even among Indians … the Canadian government has been successful in co-opting the indigenous leadership by creating a well-paid Canadian Aboriginals bureaucracy and is now trying to export a model to Latin America.

The war against terrorism driven by President Bush after 9/11 has been adopted by governments to criminalize the peaceful demands of indigenous peoples, accusing them of terrorist activities against democracy.[45]

It seems that the objective of liberal pluralism was to incorporate the indigenous leadership into the global political economy to silence their opposition to the FTAA and their criticisms regarding the intensification of the appropriation of land and natural resources, human rights abuses and environmental contamination by transnational corporations. This is similar to the mechanism utilized by international organizations in the 1990s to divide the women's movements: by incorporating those middle-class women who shared the masculinist values embedded in the neo-liberal patriarchal model into politics, they tried to neutralize their demands. Hence, de-politicization, domination, re-colonization and exploitation were the real objectives behind this chameleon-like style of politics.

The IV Summit of the Americas (Mar del Plata, November 4–5, 2005)

The second fissure between the Americas was reflected on November 4–5, 2005 at the IV Summit of the Americas: "Creating Jobs to Fight Poverty and Strengthen Democratic Governance." President Bush's objective was to bridge the Americas together with the Free Trade Area of the Americas and towards that end he called for an increase of rules favorable to investments, to fight against corruption and to increase juridical security for American companies so that they could create jobs in the South. This position, endorsed by Prime Minister Martin from Canada, President Fox from Mexico and President Lagos from Chile, was strongly rejected by the Presidents of five Latin American countries: Argentina, Brazil, Venezuela, Paraguay and Uruguay.

In his speech,[46] President Néstor Kirchner from Argentina summarized the main points of the disagreement. Kirchner strongly criticized the Bretton Woods Institutions and their policies, which he considered "detached from spatial and temporal contexts," and made the Bretton Woods Institutions responsible for the external indebtedness of the South as a result of the design of structural adjustment programs, the Washington Consensus, the spill-over effect theory and the conditionalities imposed that did not allow countries to grow. Kirchner argued that these policies were creating deep institutional instabilities and the fall of many democratic governments in the region, and that "in the name of democracy we have less democracy." Using the Argentine crisis of 2001 as an example, Kirchner accused the International Monetary Fund for its "perverse attitude" of not allowing Argentina to re-finance its external debt and by imposing the same conditionalities which led that country to default in its payments. He considered that it was the Bretton Woods Institutions who should take social responsibility for their actions and policies. Instead of debating issues such as representation and voting power, Kirchner sustained that they should be dealing with more substantial topics such as calling closure to contradictory conditionalities that impede the growth of southern countries; he also argued that it is the IFIs who should improve transparency, reduce their administrative costs and improve the capacity of loans. Otherwise, he claimed, "if we are not allowed to grow, we cannot pay."

Kirchner also criticized the unfairness of the international trade system and the northern countries' protectionism, particularly their subsidies to agricultural products, which was affecting the economies of the South. He ended by rejecting the FTAA and every single type of integration that did not consider the asymmetries and differences among the countries in the region, and called instead for an integration that contained mutual benefits and not one designed for the benefit of the North. In sum, Kirchner called for a "more just and equitable continentalism." The Argentine President's words were strongly endorsed by the parallel anti-summit led by President Chávez from Venezuela, whose *Alternativa Bolivariana* (ALBA – Bolivarian Alternative)[47] was increasingly seen by many Latin American and Caribbean countries as the integrationist model to follow.

The "New Left" and South–South cooperation

The IV Summit of the Americas was the turning point in Latin American politics; the joint assertiveness of the five presidents who opposed the FTAA project gave rise to the "New Left" label that grouped them under the same umbrella, even though the shades of their leftist approaches differed, some more radical and others more at the center left. Among the New Left's first generation – those presidents in power at the time of the turning point – Hugo Chávez (1998–present), who spearheaded the Bolivarian dream of a united Latin America and what he called socialism for the twenty-first century, was the most radical of all. Luiz Inácio Lula Da Silva (2003–2010), leader of the Brazilian Workers' Party, did not oppose the neo-liberal model; President Néstor Kirchner (2003–2007) from the Justicialist Party was for a populist nationalist model based on the alliance between the state, capital and labor; and Tabaré Vázquez (2005–2010) represented the Uruguayan leftist broad front.

The second generation of the so-called "New Left" represented the continuity and intensification of the democratic order and progressive politics by broadening the ethnic and gendered diversity of its leaders. Evo Morales (2006–present) of the Movement for Socialism became the first indigenous President of the continent in the twenty-first century, and three women became heads of state. Michelle Bachelet (2006–2010), a social democrat, became the first female president of Chile; Dilma Rousseff (2010–present) from the Brazilian Worker's Party, who succeeded Lula da Silva, also became the first woman president of Brazil. Meanwhile, Cristina Fernández de Kirchner (2007–present) became the second female president of Argentina and her husband, Néstor Kirchner, who preceded her, is a leader of the Justicialist Party. In Ecuador, Rafael Correa (2007–present), representing the País Alliance, leans more to the left, and is closer to Chávez's and Morales' ways of doing politics. Daniel Ortega (1985–1990 and 2008–present), leader of the Sandinista National Liberation Front, assumed for the second time the presidency of Nicaragua, yet this time he was not the revolutionary leader of the past. In Paraguay, Fernando Lugo (2008–2012), a theology liberation priest and head of the Patriotic Alliance for Change, became the first progressive president in the history of that country, yet his hands were tied by the conservative Senate, which in 2012 produced a parliamentary *coup d'état* against Lugo. José Mujica (2010–present) in Uruguay, as was his predecessor Tabaré Vázquez, was a member of the leftist Broad Front. Thus, the "New Left" was quite varied and moderate when compared to the "Old Left"; this was the reason why it was labeled the "pink tide." Nevertheless, both lefts can be defined as counter-hegemonic albeit their differences.

The first difference to consider is the historical conjuncture. The "Old Left," namely the national liberation movements of the 1970s and 1980s, were a response to the Cold War, to the imposition of dictatorships and the Friedmanite economic model, to the beginning of the transition from the Keynesian to the neo-liberal World Order, when the internationalization of the state, production and finances was taking place. Meanwhile, the "New Left" emerged when neo-liberal globalization was consolidated. It was embedded in a neo-liberal structure and superstructure that tied the hands of the heads of state, and which could not be controlled or changed by individual nations because it encompassed broader scales, both regional and global. This is what made the "New Left" a hybrid movement between Left and center Left and neo-liberalism. The second difference was the means of achieving power; for the "Old Left," a product of guerrilla warfare, power needed to be achieved through an armed class struggle against the bourgeoisie, and its aim was the installation of the dictatorship of the proletariat. Instead, for the "New Left," a product of the new social movements, elections were the route to power; this is why Moraña (2008: 34) called it the "institutionalized left," whose aim was the eradication of inequality "from above" and the achievement of social justice. This meant a struggle against the new transnational capitalist class, which had one foot in the local economy and the other in tax havens. This struggle required the strengthening of the state, and the creation of new national constitutions (e.g., in the case of Venezuela, Bolivia and Ecuador) that moved away from neo-liberalism, recognized ethnic diversity and incorporated both individual and collective human rights.

The third difference was the type of regionalism. While the "Old Left" was opposing the transition from closed to open regionalisms – or from import-substitution industrialization to free trade agreements – the "New Left" was not only opposing free trade agreements but at the same time was constructing its own counter-hegemonic regional spaces, such as the *Bolivarian Alliance for the Peoples of Our America* (ALBA: a new name but it maintained the same acronym) and the *Union of South American Nations* (UNASUR), the consolidation of what was previously known as the South American Community of Nations. ALBA was initially a Venezuelan–Cuban alliance signed in 2004 but later on it was joined by the Plurinational State of Bolivia (2006), Nicaragua (2007) and Dominica (2008) and a year later by Ecuador, Honduras, Antigua and Barbuda, Saint Vincent and the Grenadines and, more recently, in 2012 by Suriname and Saint Lucia. ALBA was born in opposition to the Washington proposed Free Trade Area of the Americas (FTAA) and, as Raby has defined it, it is based on an "endogenous development using national and local resources, equitable exchange, social justice and ecological sustainability" (Raby 2008: 3). The main element was the formation of key social programs in health, education, housing, food and joint enterprises in energy – such as *Petrocaribe* and *Petrosur* – in communications, the creation of *Telesur*, a television news program, and, in finances, the creation of the Bank of the South, a regional development bank that aimed at replacing the World Bank and International Monetary Fund in the region (Raby 2008: 4). Instead, UNASUR was a broader union that included all the South American countries apart from French Guiana. Its constitutive treaty was signed in 2008 and entered into effect on March 11, 2011; by this time it was clearly a progressive union. This integration went beyond trade; it was political, cultural, social, economic and financial, and it also included defense, energy, food security and the building of a regional infrastructure. Key to UNASUR is the respect for pluralism and diversity.

Finally, the last difference between the "Old Left" and the "New Left" was that the latter made South–South cooperation a reality. It searched for other trading partners in the South, intensifying relations with China, African countries, India and, in some cases, even Iran (it is worth noting here the case for Brazil's relations with IBSA and the BRICS). By doing so, it eliminated dependency on the North. In sum, by the time the 2008 global economic meltdown took place, the "New Left" had changed its geo-political framework of action. Even if it could not change the global structure and superstructure, it did change the power relations in which it was immersed by constructing its own counter-hegemonic regional spaces, which at the same time strengthened its regional unity.

The 2008 global financial meltdown

In Latin America the period between 2003 and 2007 was a moment of economic expansion, a moment of growth that only paralleled the period between the post-World War II economic boom and the 1970s crisis. The moment in between, namely from the 1970s crisis to 2003, has been a period of economic stagnation (Ocampo 2009: 704). This shows that Latin America's transition from the Old to the New *Pax Americanas* was strongly detrimental to the region, and that the recovery only started to take place when the "New Left" was solidifying its power. According to Ocampo, the 2003 to 2007 economic boom was due to four main factors: a high level of remittances, the growth of international trade, high commodity prices and exceptional financing conditions. Yet, by the mid-September 2008 global economic meltdown, these factors reversed, becoming the main channels of transmission of the crisis. Indeed, remittances shifted from 2 percent of the region's GDP in 2004 to 2006 – a much higher proportion in the smaller economies of Central America and the Caribbean – to stagnation in 2008, and trade and commodity prices, which had been at their highest due to the export-led oriented approach of Latin America, were severely affected. Yet, although the financial situation worsened, the financial shock was less pronounced than the two previous regional crises (Ocampo 2009: 707–722). Ocampo ended by recommending that the economies of the region start to think again about the domestic market, about production as the engine of growth and in regional integration; in other words, a return to the import-substitution model of the past (Ocampo 2009: 703).

Although the official economy was experiencing a recession, the underground economy of the tax havens saw an increase in global financial flows. Tax havens are the site where the power of the transnational capitalist class lies and from where national governments are coerced when implementing progressive policies. When in 2009 the OECD at the G-20 Summit in London launched the black,[48] gray[49] and "other"[50] list of tax havens, many countries on the list reacted, some positively, some with anger for being included in them and others because not all tax havens were included in the list. Two of the four countries on the black list were from Latin America, Costa Rica and Uruguay (*Página 12*, 2009a). It should be noted that from September 2008 until April 2009 the capital flight towards Uruguay increased by 42 percent, most of it from Argentina: about US$200 million left the country on a daily basis. At the time in which Argentina initiated an investigation of its elite, it seems that 63 percent of the 3,442 export enterprises – including the auto industry, cereals, soy, energy, chemical, pharmaceutical, plastics, cooking oil, etc. – sent their revenues *physically in containers* to Europe, particularly to Spain, Belgium and Germany, using three tax havens to do so, namely Uruguay, the Cayman Islands and Luxembourg (*Página 12*, 2009b). Moreover, according to the Central Bank of Uruguay, 90 percent of the US$2,400 million deposited there were from Argentinians, most of it from "ghost enterprises" dedicated to evade taxes (*Página 12*, 2009c). In sum, what this example shows is that more studies are needed and that more pressure should be put on tax havens following the lead of the ATTAC movement and the Tax Justice Network (TJN). Tax havens are the heart of the neo-liberal model, and any change in the model requires the elimination of the tax havens.

As the crisis was hitting hard in Europe, particularly in Ireland, Portugal, Greece and Spain, Latin American heads of state started to debate what measures to take in order to prevent the contagion of the global meltdown. The crisis was perceived in South America as the turning point for the Western Order, as the failure of the neo-liberal model and the opening of new alternatives. At the national scale the crisis strengthened the "New Left" and the state even more, and at the regional scale it strengthened both MERCOSUR and UNASUR and, at the global scale, it tightened relations between South America and China. The South American states took control of the crisis and started to implement counter-cyclical policies, a better redistribution of the national income, the development of the internal market pointing at an industrialization process that added value to local raw materials with the objective of generating employment, social inclusion and reducing poverty (*Página 12*, 2012: 5). These same policies were the ones that were previously implemented in Brazil, which led to impressive growth. As the former President of Brazil Lula Da Silva put it, "the visible hand of the state protected the economic system from the failure created by the invisible hand of the market" (Lula Da Silva, 2010). At the June 2012 meetings of MERCOSUR and UNASUR in Mendoza, Argentina, there was a call to the unity of the region to be "united against the outside and opened towards the inside," to increase by 35 percent the tariffs of about 200 products coming from outside the region and to lower the tariffs within the region in order to intensify intra-regional trade. To this it was added the need to coordinate the implementation of counter-cyclical measures (*Página 12*, 2012: 5). At the MERCOSUR meeting it was decided that Venezuela would become a member on July 31, an incorporation that, according to Brazilian President Dilma Rousseff, would make MERCOSUR the "fifth economy in the world" behind the United States, China, Germany and Japan (Lantos 2012a). Venezuela's delayed entry into MERCOSUR was due to the opposition of the conservative Paraguayan Senate but, because Paraguay went through a parliamentary coup d'état it was suspended from MER-COSUR, opening the doors to Venezuela becoming a member of the common market. At the global scale, both MERCOSUR and UNASUR had strengthened relations with China. MERCOSUR and China have signed agreements on cooperation in nuclear energy, agriculture, the construction of industrial parks, a loan to extend the rail system in Argentina and the intensification of anti-aphtosa vaccines (Delatorre 2012). Meanwhile, UNASUR's agreements with China dealt with food security, a cooperation and investment fund, a student exchange program that would include 5,000 students per year, trade in local currency rather than in dollars, and the installation of Chinese bank subsidiaries in the region (Lantos 2012b). Thus, the 2008 global meltdown has strengthened the independence of the South American nations vis-à-vis the United States. Although at the beginning it was thought that relations with the Obama Administration were going to be positive, relations with his first administration were harsher than expected.

To conclude: in the new millennium the Santa Fe IV document denounced a set of new threats, which were especially linked to the poverty problematique. In fact, "poverty reduction" became the new cornerstone of development and funding was redirected towards strengthening those public services that were re-privatized in the 1990s, deepening even more the crisis of social reproduction. The Heavily Indebted Poor Countries Initiative, the Poverty Reduction Strategy Papers, the Impoverishment Risk and Livelihood Reconstruction model and the Millennium Development Goals represented the praxis of the new authoritarian social contract. By 2005, the fears that the three large economic blocs that were forming could have merged into the Free Trade Area of the Americas had dissipated when, at the IV Summit of the Americas in Mar del Plata, five presidents decided not to sign the FTAA. This was a turning point in Latin American politics; since then the "New Left" has strengthened at the national, regional and global scales. At the regional scale, through the formation of counter-hegemonic spaces (e.g., ALBA, MERCOSUR and UNASUR) and, at the global scale, through the intensification of South–South relations. When the 2008 global meltdown took place, Latin America was in a strong position to face the crisis. Meanwhile, in the United States, Barack Obama became the first African-American President, a fact that was very well received, not just in the United States but all over the world.

4 Obama, "change" and the disembedding of security in Latin America

The tension between polyarchy and democracy[1]

The 2008 to 2009 economic crisis brought people around the world to despair and, when candidate Barack Obama pronounced the magic word "change," he was enshrined, not only in the United States but all over the world, including Latin America. There was a massive multi-class, multinational, multiethnic and multi-age acceptance of Obama as candidate. He became the first black President of the United States and people conferred upon him the power to produce the "change" he had promised. However, after a year in the administration it became clear that Obama could not put into practice its many promises. The disjuncture between the high expectations raised and the actual results brought an enormous frustration to those who believed in "change." This chapter aims to critically analyze why this change in attitude took place, and why Obama lost the acceptance of a specific region, Latin America. It is contended that the Obama Administration represents the continuity of the system, namely "more of the same" rather than "change," a fourth moment of the New *Pax Americana*. The key element of the Obama Administration has been the 'cosmetic hemispheric change' in policy making, a shift away from the controversial FTAA project towards a search for a "Regional Partnership on Crime and Security." The concept of security was anchored in "democracy" promotion, combating drug trafficking, food security and energy independence, and the mode of spreading it was through the formation of "partnerships" with specific Latin American countries. The notion of "shared responsibility" is what allows for interventionism by giving the illusion that there are no power relations involved between the United States and Latin American countries. It gives the illusion of radical change but the neo-liberal matrix of the World Order remains intact. While in the first three decades of neo-liberalism the ideological illusion endured for about ten years (e.g., in the 1980s people did not realize what kind of democracy was being implemented until ten years later and the 1980s became labeled as the "lost decade") Obama's illusion of "change" lasted only a year. This means that neo-liberal ideological creations are being exhausted, that the masses can no longer be co-opted; it is this consciousness that gives the space for the emergence of radical structural change, of moving away from neo-liberalism. In this organic crisis there is indeed a space for "organic intellectuals" to aim for radical change.

This chapter is anchored in Obama's Four Freedoms in "A New Partnership for the Americas" and its confrontation with the actual implementation of the policies in Latin America. The document draws on Roosevelt, Truman and Kennedy, and the Four Freedoms include Political Freedom/Democracy which targets Cuba and Venezuela; the Freedom from Fear/Security that centers on Central America, Mexico and Colombia; the Freedom from Want/Opportunity that focuses on Haiti and the Working Towards Energy Security section which addresses Brazil and the region as a whole. This strongly ethnocentric and interventionist document has been meticulously compared with the actual practice of the Obama Administration.

"A new partnership for the Americas," the Trinidad and Tobago short honeymoon and the question of "change"

In 2008, during his presidential campaign, Obama launched "A New Partnership for the Americas," a document in which he distanced himself from President Bush's policies towards the hemisphere and promised a "new alliance of the Americas." The center-piece of that alliance would be the intensification of diplomatic ties such as the reinstatement of the special envoy for the Americas, the expansion of the Peace Corps and the increase in size of the foreign service, particularly with the incorporation of Latin American immigrants as ambassadors to their own countries of origin (Obama 2008: 1–2). Drawing on Franklin Roosevelt's concept of freedom as "political freedom," "freedom from want" and "freedom from fear," the candidate added the need to work towards energy security. Rather than focusing on the Monrovian ideal of Pan-Americanism – which was present in the regionalist approach of former US administrations and was also strongly rejected by Latin American and Caribbean countries – Obama preferred to deal individually with different clusters of Latin American countries (see Lowenthal 2010: 5, 7) such as Cuba, some Central American countries, Mexico, Colombia, Haiti and Brazil, countries that represented his foreign policy agenda.

On April 2009, just four months after assuming the Presidency of the United States and at the highest point of Obama mania, Obama met for the first time with the Latin American heads of state at the Fifth Summit of the Americas in Trinidad and Tobago. At the Summit, Obama reaffirmed his interest in improving relations with the region; in his speech the President reinstated his Four Freedoms, recognizing the difficult relations that had existed in the past and the need to move forward:

> I pledge to you that we seek an equal partnership, there is no senior partner and junior partner in our relations; there is simply engagement based on mutual respect and common interests and shared values, so I'm here to launch a new chapter of engagement that will be sustained throughout my administration ... I didn't come here to debate the past – I came here to deal with the future ... I think my presence here indicates, the United States has

changed over time. It has not always been easy, but it has changed. And so I think it's important to remind my fellow leaders that it's not just the United States that has to change. All of us have responsibilities to look towards the future ... as neighbors, we have a responsibility to each other and to our citizens. And by working together, we can take important steps forward to advance prosperity and security and liberty. That is the 21st century agenda that we come together to enact. That's the new direction that we can pursue.

(Obama 2008)

The respect that the President showed in his discourse by addressing his Latin American peers as "equals," his incredible charisma and the fact that he was the first Afro-American President of the United States raised enormous expectations for "change." Afro-descendants, women, indigenous peoples and all the marginalized people in the hemisphere welcomed the new president, and when, in October 2009, Obama was awarded the Nobel Peace Prize "for his extraordinary efforts to strengthen international diplomacy and cooperation between peoples,"[2] even Fidel Castro applauded. As Hursthouse and Ayuso have mentioned, a Gallup poll conducted between July and September found that about 51 to 61 percent of Latin Americans approved of Obama's leadership, and the annual Latinobarómetro poll showed that an even higher number, 71 percent, liked Obama (2010: 9). What these data show, in contrast to Obama's misperception, is that there is no anti-Americanism in Latin America. Instead, what exists is a harsh critique of the hegemonic foreign policy historically implemented towards the region. This is exactly what happened after Obama had been in power for a year; when his promises did not match his actions, his image plummeted.

In contrast to the Latin American heads of state, critical scholars, activists and journalists in the North have been very harsh on Obama since the moment when he appointed officials from the Clinton and Bush administrations to key strategic positions and decided, following the financial crisis, to bail out the corporations but not the people. Robert Latham (n.d.), in his "tale of two Obamas," showed the ambiguous feelings: on the one hand, the confusion and disappointment most people were starting to experience at that time and, on the other hand, wishing to be wrong and that Obama's "change" was not just another ideological veil to cover up "more of the same." Latham presented himself as a pessimist-optimist with respect to social and political change. Drawing on Polanyi, he advanced a possible two-step scenario in the Obama Administration and, therefore, the existence of "two Obamas." According to the author, the moment of the first Obama, based on the appointment of team members of the Clinton and Bush administrations, would inevitably lead to failure and deepen the economic crisis because the plans and policies they could recommend responded to a "U.S.–neo-liberal centric framework of world order," a framework that produced the crisis in the first place. This would lead to the increase of international political pressure and the fragmentation of the elite, and it is here where Latham sees the seeds of the emergence of a second moment and, concomitantly, of a second Obama, about whom he is more optimistic.

According to Latham, this second Obama would be surrounded by a new and better team and would be "a leader willing to open the structures of power to many voices, contentions, and frameworks from across the world.... That sort of turn would by its very nature be a success."[3] Latham ended his analysis by suggesting that

> western progressives will have to do their part: they will need to resist their own tendencies to offer solutions and ways forward long before the second Obama gets a chance to help open up spaces of power and usher in not just new policies but systemic change – otherwise we end up with one Obama.
>
> (Latham n.d.)

Although it is important to think about possible future scenarios, it is ahistorical to predict the future; we cannot be certain about what events will unfold and how different social forces will react and utilize those events in their own struggle. The building of crystal castles fossilizes action. This is why in order to exert democracy "from below," it is imperative that constructive critiques constantly emerge to guide the action of our leaders and recall for them who the voters are. This is precisely what Naomi Klein has done.

Klein exerted her democratic rights by demanding action from Obama on behalf of the enormous trust that people all around the world had invested in him. Klein argued that although Obama had a plan to downsize the occupation of Iraq, he did not have a plan to end the war; that although he recognized the broadening of the income inequality gap in the US and the world, he did not have a plan to close that gap; and that even if he shared the idealism of young environmentalists, he did not have a green agenda that matched the dimensions of the current climate crisis (Klein 2008). More demoralized than Klein, activist Vanessa Davis sustained that

> We must understand Obama as a necessity of the US establishment. Obama was the necessary figurehead for the moment in which the US was living, in order to calm the waters and change without really changing. He is a figure who can generate the illusion of change, but without producing that change.
>
> (Vanessa Davis, quoted in Hester Eisenstein 2009: 21)

In the same vein as Davis, John Pilger sees Obama's foreign policy as "continuation as usual" and argues that in order to show that he is serious about change, Obama has to start by dismantling the "war making machine reinforced during Bush" (Pilger 2008a). However, because Obama has in many cases gone even further than Bush, Pilger considers him a "man of the system" and a "truly democratic expansionist" (Pilger 2008b). Noam Chomsky also considers that Obama has recycled Bush's plans, that the Obama-Summers-Geitner programs are not so different from the Bush-Paulson plans, and that their objective is "to preserve the institutions intact, whereas to deal with the problems you have to modify the institutions" (Chomsky 2009). This is precisely the heart of the distortion of World Orders, what Robert Cox calls the "mechanisms of hege-mony." In order to produce change it is necessary not just to reform the architec-ture of the international organizations and their undemocratic system but to turn upside-down all the neo-liberal policies implemented since the 1970s economic crisis, to shift from polyarchy towards popular democracy. To be able to produce radical change history matters and, when Obama told the Latin American heads of state that he did not go to the Trinidad and Tobago Americas Summit to debate the past but to debate the future, he was denying radical "change." Change is about modifying the structure, superstructure and socio-cultural aspects of World Orders in good time; it is about how the interplay of social forces from below and above interact to construct a new global architecture rep-resentative of every single human being on earth, to represent the majority rather than a transnational elite. In sum, despite Obama's promise of "matching rhet-oric with deeds," his foreign policy agenda towards Latin America represented a rupture between rhetoric and praxis. The big question is: freedom for whom and for what purposes?

Freedom for whom and for what purposes? De-constructing the transnationalization of polyarchy and the practice of *trasformismo*

Promoting "democracy": trapped in the contradiction between Cuba and Honduras

The first "freedom" addressed by Obama was Political Freedom/Democracy and its focal point was to "help advance the cause of freedom and democracy in Cuba", to "empower the Cuban people," to "foster the beginnings of grassroots democracy on the island" and "to position the United States to help foster a stable and peaceful transition in Cuba to avoid potential disasters that could result in mass migration, internal violence or the perpetuation of the Cuban dictatorship." His "aggressive and principled democracy" involved lifting travel restrictions for Cuban-Americans and the sending of remittances, "while holding back important incentives such as relaxation of the trade embargo and greater foreign aid so that we can encourage change in a post-Fidel government" (Obama 2008: 3). Obama also pledged to close the US Guantánamo Bay Naval Base in Cuba (Obama 2008: 3), where about 245 suspects of terrorism were tor-tured and held as prisoners.[4]

What Obama's first freedom shows is that he bases his analysis on false assumptions, which demonstrates that he has an absolute misperception about Cuba and Latin America as a whole, his language is embedded in the Cold War era and it is strongly interventionist. This requires clarification of the meaning of "democracy" and "civil society" in the US context and its promotion since the 1980s all over the world, and how Obama is now trying to promote it to Cuba.

"Democracy" in the US and the one that was promoted abroad was not popular democracy but polyarchy. William Robinson made a clear distinction between these two different meanings and types of democracy. Popular democracy refers to the Greek classical definition, in which the power to rule (*cratos*) was in the hands of the people (*demos*); it is about popular sovereignty and human equality. When the balance was broken, revolutions would produce change to rebalance the power of the majority. This was something that the conservatives, such as Huntington, saw as a threat to the social order and the maintenance of stability, and therefore engineered a political system that was neither authoritarianism nor popular democracy, but a polyarchy. Polyarchy is an institutional definition of democracy that has the objective to shift the power from the people to the elite; it does so by disembedding the socio-economic system from the political through privatization, leaving the socio-economic sphere in the hands of the elite, which conservatives equate to "civil society." Because it is in this sphere that the distribution of material resources is determined, the elite secure both their revenue and the control of society (Robinson 1996: 44–52). This type of "civil society" was what the Santa Fe documents called the "permanent government," while elections became a fictitious circus to make people believe that the elected candidate, the "temporary government," was a product of the old and classical "popular democracy." In other words, paraphrasing Abraham Lincoln, who defined popular democracy as the "government of the people, by the people, for the people," it may be said that polyarchy is the government of the people, by the people – because there are elections – but for the benefit of the elite/corporations.

It is in this vein that Robinson argued that the objective of the promotion of polyarchy since the 1980s was to suppress popular democracy at home and, in the case of US–Latin American relations, to produce the transition from backing dictatorships to backing the elite's pseudo-democratic control. By doing so, a transnational capitalist class was created. Robinson states that

> US "democracy promotion", as it actually functions sets about not just to secure and stabilize elite-based polyarchic systems but to have the United States and local elites thoroughly penetrate civil society, and from therein assure control over popular mobilization and mass movements (that is, correct the "flukes", or "dysfunctions", of democracy).... This is a shift from social control "from above" to social control "from below" (and within), for the purpose of managing change and reform so as to pre-empt any elemental challenge to the social order. This explains why the new political intervention does not target governments per se, but groups in civil society itself – trade unions, political parties, the mass media, peasant associations, women's, youth, and other mass organizations.
>
> (Robinson 1996: 69)

Therefore, what Obama really means by "grassroots movements" and by "empower the Cuban people" to overthrow the "Cuban dictatorship" is about destabilization "from below" and "from within." It is necessary to clarify here that the Cuban government is a revolutionary government and therefore a true grassroots movement, on behalf of the people, not the elite. Yes, there are problems in Cuba: fifty years of embargo and constant aggression by the US government have interfered in the normal functioning of the island, such as the maintenance of the revolutionary alert and therefore lack of elections. However, as demonstrated above, the existence of elections in polyarchies is a fictitious exercise because it turns the populous, as well as the executive power, into slaves of the elite.

It should also be considered that Obama follows the Brookings Institute project that calls for loosening the 1962 trade embargo in order to allow US offshore oil and gas companies, as well as renewable energy companies, access to Cuba.[5] The special concern is to offset Venezuela's oil investments in the Caribbean, as Obama asserts "some commentators fear that Chávez threatens oil markets and regional stability" (Obama 2008). Since Cuba formed part of the *Bolivarian Alliance for the Peoples of Our America* (ALBA) from its inception, this has become a struggle between two competing spaces, one hegemonic and the other counter-hegemonic. The contention between these two spaces became clear when Honduras joined ALBA on August 2008 and the battle between popular democracy and polyarchy emerged. Now that the discourse has been deconstructed the analysis can move to the actual practice in US–Cuban relations.

On April 13, 2009 Obama granted Cuban-Americans the right of unlimited travel to the island and the sending of unlimited remittances to their relatives – until then, laws only permitted one visit every three years and the sending of remittances was restricted to a maximum of US$300 per quarter (Hursthouse and Ayuso 2010: 5). Besides these two very important steps forward, the Department of the Treasury's Office of Foreign Assets Control also allowed US-based telecommunications businesses to operate in Cuba (Rodríguez 2010: 3–4). However, the lifting of the 1962 embargo and the closing of the US Guantánamo Bay Naval Base in Cuba are still pending. Paraphrasing Peter Smith, it may be said that these two contradictory issues represent the "talons of the eagle" because, on the one hand, Obama demands that in order to ease the embargo, Cuba call for free and fair elections, institute free press, the freedom of speech, the freedom of assembly and release of political prisoners (Rodríguez 2010: 2).

On the other hand, the inevitable question is: did Cubans' vote for Obama? What kind of freedom and democracy is Obama referring to when he does not allow Cuba to be free and interferes in the island's internal affairs? The fifty years of the embargo, according to Cuban Foreign Minister Felipe Pérez Roque, has cost Cuba about US$89 billion;[6] Cuba has already paid a very high price, and fifty years is enough. Therefore it is profoundly unethical and undemocratic to use the embargo as a coercive blackmailing tool to open the doors to corporate freedom and polyarchy – as the 1982 external debt was utilized towards the rest of Latin America, the Caribbean and beyond. The embargo should be lifted without asking for any concessions on the part of Cuba, and the US should respect the type of trade that Cuba may want to implement once the embargo is lifted. This is a debt that the United States has with Cuba and not the other way around.

The maintenance of US Guantánamo Bay Naval Base as a detention and torture center for prisoners suspicious of terrorism cancels the authority of President Obama to demand the release of political prisoners in Cuba. On January 22 2009, Obama signed an executive order declaring that Guantánamo should be shut down in less than a year from that date and prohibited the utilization of torture as an interrogation method – the document went beyond Guantánamo when demanding that the CIA close its entire network of secret prisons. Considering that the cost of maintaining a prison within the United States would save about US$180 million a year, it was proposed to move the Guantánamo prisoners to an empty maximum-security detention center in Thompson, Illinois (Gavin 2010: 4). The first steps would be to revise the status of the 245 detainees in order to determine if they should be transferred, released or prosecuted (Gavin 2010: 3–4).

Bearden, based on the analysis of new classified documents,[7] mentioned that an oversimplified "threat matrix" was designed to decide whether a prisoner should be held, transferred or released. In this matrix the prisoners were categorized according to a "risk level" that was very loosely defined and what were seen as potential signs of danger included "wearing a Casio F91W watch, traveling without documents, claiming to be a farmer, cook, or in the honey business, and being uncooperative" (Bearden 2011: 1–2). Moreover, the "risk levels" were based on the testimonies of other prisoners under the pressure of torture and were even based on those of mentally ill prisoners; as a result, many innocent men have been incarcerated while some high-risk prisoners have been released (Bearden 2011: 1–2). It is estimated that about half of the prisoners were innocent (Gavin 2010: 5); this demonstrates that Obama did not "set the example" that he had announced (see Obama 2008: 3). Thus, the embargo, the closing of the Guantánamo prison and the return of the territory of Guantánamo Bay – which is a colonial residue – are key issues at stake in order to produce "change" in US–Cuban relations; so far, an outdated Cold War diplomacy has prevailed.

The dichotomy between polyarchy and popular democracy reappeared in the Honduran crisis. The promotion of polyarchy in Honduras took place in the 1980s during the Reagan Administration, and the power of the elite was locked into the neo-liberal constitution designed at that time, as Edelberto Torres Rivas explained: "democratization did not imply a transition, it was instead the result of agreements amongst fractions of the military, business and political elite guided by 'the Embassy'" (Torres Rivas 2010: 57). The "constitutions from above" ensured that the wealth of the country remained in the hands of the fourteen richest families and, by doing so, intensified poverty and the abuse of human rights in the country (Torres Rivas 2010: 56). These families dominated in both political parties, the National Party (conservative) and the Liberal Party – President Zelaya belonged to the latter – and both parties opposed Zelaya due to his search for popular support and his policies were seen by the elite as a "betrayal to his own class" (Torres Rivas 2010: 61). Zelaya called for elections and, on June 28, 2009, a military coup d'état ousted and deported him to Costa Rica.

The main reason behind the military coup was the fact that in June 2007 Zelaya joined the Bolivarian Alliance for Our Americas (ALBA), led by Venezuelan President Hugo Chávez, signed a contract to buy cheaper oil from *Petrocaribe* and invited Presidents Chávez and Ortega to Honduras. However, more than that was at stake. Zelaya clashed with the legislative power; he wanted to appoint his own people in the new Supreme Court, especially because he wanted to call for a referendum to modify the Honduran Constitution to allow for the presidential re-election. If this had taken place, Zelaya would have been President until 2014. Thus, Zelaya's "problem" was to join the counter-hegemonic construction of space, to try to reduce the power of the Supreme Court – the heart of polyarchy and the reproduction of social injustice – and modify the constitution to strengthen the executive power. In other words, he was trying to undo polyarchical domination.

The international reaction against the coup was massive, especially on the part of the Latin American countries; however, the US took a contradictory standing. At first, Obama joined the other criticisms and condemned the coup as illegal but, because Zelaya was a Chávez ally, he also had to respond to the Republican opposition at home. When Brazil intervened to press the United States to help with Zelaya's return to Honduras, Obama opted for a diplomatic solution by sending assistant secretary of state Thomas Shannon to the region. The result was the signing of an accord in which both sides agreed that Zelaya could return to Honduras, that the elections in November would proceed and that the results would be respected by everyone. However, Latin Americans wanted the democratically elected Zelaya to continue in power independently of the results of the new elections. It happened that the fraudulent "elections" were won by the leader of the conservative National Party, Porfirio Lobos. With this result, the US retained Honduras, its Central American military bunker, under its polyarchical domination/conservative control, but relations with the rest of Latin America were profoundly damaged (see Hursthouse and Ayuso 2010: 2–3; Lowenthal 2010: 4; Shifter 2010: 68–70; Torres Rivas 2010: 61–6).

Promoting "security": police militarization, elite "justice" and genocide

The second of Obama's Freedoms, Freedom from Fear/Security, seeks to halt violence, gang activity and to tackle organized crime and drug trafficking. Mexico, Central America and Colombia are the main targets, and the policies suggested to combat insecurity include the support for the development of an independent police and juridical institutions through the US Department of Justice (DOJ) and Homeland Security (DHS), and to continue the support of the Mérida Initiative and the Andean Counterdrug Program initiated by his predecessors (Obama 2008: 5–7). Obama's objective was to extend hemispheric security by creating a "Regional Partnership on Crime and Security"; to this end, he stated that

Barack Obama believes that we need a new security initiative with our Latin American neighbours – an initiative that extends **beyond Central America**. This initiative will foster cooperation within the region to combat gangs, trafficking and violent criminal activity. And it will marshal the resources of the United States to **support the development of independent and competent police and judicial institutions in the Americas**.

(Obama 2008: 5)[8]

Comparing Obama's plans as presidential candidate and his actions towards the region once in power, it seems that hemispheric security reforms are replacing the FTAA as a regional hegemonic project. In fact, there is a notorious shift from the previous emphasis on trade to one on security and an interest in disembedding the police and the judicial institutions from the state, from the public to the private – as was previously the case with central banks and public enterprises. However, rather than promoting security, these measures can only intensify violence and corruption. Putting the police in the hands of the elite – what Obama calls "civil society" – is leading to the extermination of the poorest in society, and putting the judiciary at the service of the elite will justify and make legal that extermination. The impact of this interventionism into the internal affairs of other nations will be illustrated below with the cases of Mexico, Central America, Colombia, Peru, Ecuador, Argentina, Paraguay and Bolivia.

On April 16–17, 2009, Mexico was the first Latin American country to be visited by President Obama just before the Trinidad and Tobago Summit and, although the agenda included immigration policy, climate change and trade, the focal point was how to curb cross-border drug violence (Gay-Stolberg 2011) and the role of the Mérida Initiative. The Mérida Initiative is a security partnership between the United States and Mexico, Central America, Haiti, and the Dominican Republic which was signed on June 30, 2008 during the Bush Administration, and which was supposed to endure until September 30, 2010, yet its timeline has been extended. According to the U.S. Bureau of International Narcotics and Law Enforcement Affairs (BINLEA), the partnership represented a "shared responsibility" to "confront criminal organizations whose actions plague the region and spill over into the United States ... we confront this regional threat with a regional solution". The Initiative includes the funding for inspection equipment, communication technologies, technical advice and training to the institutions of justice, and the provision of helicopters and surveillance aircraft (BINLEA 2010). So far, about US$400 million a year has gone to Mexico and about US$100 million to the other countries in the program; a total of US$1.42 billion in the above-cited effects, not in cash, has been transferred to the signatory countries of the Mérida Initiative. Notwithstanding this effort, the so-called "war on drugs" has not stopped the cross-border flow of narcotics to the US nor the flow of American guns into Mexico, with which the violence has reached unprecedented levels.

In fact, during the six years of the Mérida Initiative, 60,000 Mexican lives have been lost and, according to Soltis, the trafficking of arms, particularly

AK-47 semi-automatic rifles – which can perforate bulletproof vests – from the United States increased from 2,000 in 2007 to 5,000 in 2009. In 2007, the Mexican police seized 9,562 arms and in 2009 this figure reached 32,332 (Soltis 2011). On March 3, 2010, the tension between the two countries escalated when the existence of the US "Operation Fast and Furious" was made public in CBS news (Carlsen 2011: 1). The aim of this operation, carried out by the Bureau of Alcohol, Tobacco, Firearms, and Explosives (ATF) office in Phoenix Arizona, was to allow more than 2,500 AK-47s and Barret.50 caliber rifles to be sold to suspicious traffickers in order to be smuggled into Mexico and guide the ATF towards high-ranking individuals in crime organizations. However, once the guns crossed the border, the ATF lost track of them (Carlsen 2011; Soltis 2011).

When it became known that one of these guns was being used by the drug cartels to kill agent Brian Terry, an American Border Patrol, Homeland Security Secretary Janet Napolitano and Attorney General Eric Holder were interrogated regarding the existence of the "Fast and Furious Operation" (Carlsen 2011: 2). President Obama defended Holder in both Univision and CNN and stated that neither him nor Holder knew about the operation, which led Carlsen to advance two conclusions: that either "Holder authorized an operation that likely violated U.S., Mexican, and international law and armed dangerous drug traffickers" or "the head of the Justice Department is presiding over rogue staff that decided not to tell their boss about an operation that poses major legal, ethical and diplomatic breaches" (Carlsen 2011: 2). One of the reasons advanced by Soltis regarding Obama's inability to curtail gun trafficking is due to the influence of the National Rifle Association (NRA) lobbyists, who argue that policies towards that end infringe upon their Second Amendment rights (Soltis 2011: 2–3). This insecurity at the heart of Obama's engine for a regional security partnership is very dangerous for both the US and the Americas as a whole, and indicates the fragility and inability of elected governments to produce "change" when they are under polyarchical domination. Under these circumstances, security agreements will inevitably be followed by trafficking in guns and the intensification of genocide.

On March 6, 2001 a massive "March for Peace" which took place in Mexico demanded that President Felipe Calderón put an end to the war on drugs, for justice – not elite justice – dignity, and called for the immediate demilitarization of the country. A protester mentioned that the war on drugs was "leaving out the most important part – eliminating political corruption and financial corruption, the foreign interests and businessmen that give them the money", while another claimed that "Under the pretext of the war on drug-trafficking, they're exterminating the lower levels of society.... We can't let the logic of war prevail. It's unacceptable that it's cheaper to kill the poor than to end poverty" (cited by Carlsen 2011b: 2).

Notwithstanding this panorama, on June 10, 2010 Secretary of State Hillary Clinton signed a security partnership with the Caribbean Community (CARICOM) known as the Caribbean Basin Security Initiative (CBSI), in which the US committed to US$45 million in 2010 and requested US$79 million for

2011,[9] an amount approved on June 22, 2011. The CBSI complements Reagan's Caribbean Basin Initiative, which led to the expansion of *maquiladoras* into the region, showing the continuation of the Republican and Democrat projects. Time will tell if this security armor will lead to the intensification of violence as happened in Mexico. The CARICOM includes among its members Saint Vincent and the Grenadines and Antigua and Barbados, the Caribbean islands that form part of Chávez-led ALBA. It will be interesting to research how being in two different economic blocs can affect the development of the islands. The US is recovering its spatial domination, first in Honduras and now locking in Saint Vincent and the Grenadines and Antigua and Barbados.

As Senator, Obama has opposed President Bush's Plan Colombia and the US–Colombia FTA due to the poor human rights records of the country and the assassination of union leaders. However, as President, Obama continued the policies of his predecessor and his policies also mirrored those of his northern conservative neighbor, Prime Minister Harper, who, despite the strong opposition of Canadians, signed an FTA with Colombia in 2010. There is a vicious circle that engulfs free trade agreements, the intensification of violence and corruption. On the one hand, an FTA with the United States, a country that strongly subsidizes its farmers, will jeopardize the possibility of Colombian farmers to compete with imported food, and therefore this will inevitably push more Colombian farmers towards the more profitable cultivation of coca, what neo-classical economists call the "supply side" of drug trafficking. On the other hand, the production of coca is driven by a high demand for drugs in its main market, the United States. When neo-classical economists talk about the "demand side," or consumption, they point to a social health issue. However, it is deeper than that; it is a structural issue. Neo-liberalism has increased inequalities by eliminating redistributive policies, pushing both, namely the marginalized who do not see any way out of poverty to consume drugs, and the coca farmers in the Andes to produce the only crop that pays enough for their survival. It is the middlemen who move between the illegal and legal world who profit from the marginalization of the addicts and peasants.

Thus, when policy makers emphasize either the "supply" or the "demand side" or try to "regulate" or "legalize" drugs, they do not attack the core of the problem, which is the structural matrix, the neo-liberal model, which forces farmers in the Andes to produce coca and the marginalized in the North, who do not find a way out of poverty, to consume it once it is processed into cocaine. This scapegoating works as a smokescreen that hides the real beneficiaries of drug trafficking. So far, the economic cost of the "supply–demand equation" has been US$7.3 billion dollars for the US and US$55 billion for Colombia (Suárez Montoya 2011); and as the social cost, 5.2 million forced displaced Afro-descendants and indigenous peoples (CODHES 2010) and thousands of deaths – including about 2,200 union leaders murdered since 1991(Witness for Peace 2011); while in the US the majority of the population in prison due to drugs offenses are African Americans, even when the main drug users are white (Reiss 2010: 30). This has led Suzanna Reiss to argue that it is necessary to move beyond supply and demand, that the question to be answered is "Who gets to supply what and who gets to demand?" She states,

> Focusing on the commodity overshadows the people and political struggles at the heart of the 'drug' conflict. It is not drugs per se, but rather competition to control their production, distribution, and consumption that has generated violence over the last half-century.... Despite the frequently staged spectacles of drug enforcement officers burning marijuana fields in California or airplanes fumigating coca fields in the Andes, it is necessary to restate the obvious: The United States has never waged a "war on drugs". Rather, it has waged various "wars" on specific groups of people ... the power hierarchies of who gets to supply and who gets to demand also ripple through racial, economic, and social disparities.
>
> (Reiss 2010: 30)

Since its inception in 1971, under the Nixon Administration, the war on drugs has cost more than US$1 trillion and hundreds of thousands of lives, yet the production of coca has not diminished (Curtin 2011: 1). Reiss recognizes that the unstated goal of the "war on drugs" is the global expansion of US military hegemony, that "the United States does not so much wage war on drugs as wage war with drugs" and that, since the 1961 Single Drug Convention, it sought to control the "legal" market, for which the main consumers of coca leaves were the pharmaceutical companies that were authorized by the US government to produce the flavoring extract for Coca-Cola, research and medicinal use. Reiss states that "while the United States spends billions of dollars attacking 'drugs', the legal drug industry is regularly among the top five most profitable industries in the country" (Reiss 2010: 28). This answers the question of who produces fear and insecurity, an insecurity that intensified when President Obama signed a ten-year defense cooperation with President Uribe to establish seven military bases in Colombia, five airbases and two naval installations, one on the Pacific and the other in the Caribbean. According to "Global En Route Strategy," a white paper produced by the U.S. Air Mobility Command, the Palanquero airbase – one of the five in question – could become a "cooperative security location" from which "mobility operations could be executed" as "nearly half the continent can be covered by a giant C-17 (military transport) aircraft without refuelling" (quoted in Matsunaga 2009; see also Lowenthal 2010: 4; Shifter 2010: 70).This incident produced a strong reaction from all the South American heads of state, who called for an urgent meeting of UNASUR in Bariloche, Argentina, in which Presidents Uribe and Obama were invited to explain the motives behind this militarization and to guarantee that the operation was restricted to Colombia. President Obama declined the invitation but Uribe participated in the meeting.

At the meeting, President Cristina Kirchner of Argentina mentioned that she "had never heard that loads of drugs would be bombarded, drugs were not combated with C-17 planes, even less with the placement or radars," that "the establishment of military bases looked more as a project for conventional wars rather than for combating drug trafficking" (LatinoAméricAhora 2009). For his part, President Fernando Lugo of Paraguay argued that "the security of our countries is at stake" (LatinoAméricAhora 2009), and the most vociferous of all the South American presidents were Rafael Correa of Ecuador, Hugo Chávez of Venezuela, Evo Morales of Bolivia and Lula da Silva of Brazil. Correa, who ended a ten-year agreement with the United States – an agreement that allowed the northern country to utilize Ecuador's Manta airbase as a regional hub for anti-drug surveillance operations – and, a year earlier, had broken relations with Colombia when Colombian troops bombarded a FARC rebel camp in Ecuadorian territory (Oualalou 2009; Piette 2009), argued that

> it was unnecessary to ask for military help from the United States to combat drug trafficking and terrorism ... that Plan Colombia had failed ... experience has shown that in those places in which the Drug Enforcement Agency (DEA) was expelled, the capture of drugs had improved.
>
> (LatinoAméricAhora 2009)

In the same vein, Evo Morales considered that Colombia wanted to "justify the unjustifiable," that with all the foreign military help Colombia had received, "drug-trafficking and terrorism should have been eradicated (from the country)," that "the *pueblos* will never again allow the interventionism of the United States" (LatinoAméricAhora 2009). For his part, Chávez referred to the Colombian agreement as a "declaration of war" and that it responded to "the United States global strategy of domination" (LatinoAméricAhora 2009).

Uribe's response to the criticism of the other South American heads of state was that he felt that Colombia was a "victim ... of a strong political interventionism," and he sustained that this conflict should be dealt with within the frame of the Organization of American States (OAS), not at its back. Lula strongly disagreed with Uribe and, according to him, the place where this conflict should be treated was the Defense Council of UNASUR, not the OAS. Lula added that the United States, as the world's principal consumer of illegal drugs, should combat drug trafficking within its borders rather than doing so in South American territory (LatinoAméricAhora 2009). Lula was especially uncomfortable with the fact that one of the Marines' bases was located on the doorstep of the Brazilian Amazon. Moreover, Lula mentioned that American floats where just below the oil reserves discovered in Brazil in 2007 (Oualalou 2009). The only South American country that sided with Colombia and the United States was Peru, whose President Alan García had signed, in December 2005, a Free Trade Area (FTA) with the United States, which entered into effect in February 1, 2009.

As it happened, in Mexico, when NAFTA entered into effect and the Zapatistas rebelled, the US–Peru FTA was followed by massive Amazonian indigenous peoples' protests. The implementation of the FTA meant that indigenous peoples would lose their common lands, and the doors of the Amazon would be opened to transnational corporations such as mining, timber, oil, gas and hydroelectric and biodiversity companies, for which laws were de-regulated to facilitate their entrance into the jungle. When land and nature were put up for sale, indigenous peoples initiated peaceful protests in all five departments of the jungle region, blocking highways and gas and oil pipelines. García sent the police and the military to attack the protesters, resulting in a massacre. Indigenous peoples reported fifty people dead and about 400 disappeared, and indigenous peoples mentioned that many of those disappeared were burned and thrown into the river to hide the massacre. Instead, the government reported that eleven indigenous peoples and twenty-three police officers had died. Alan García accused the indigenous peoples of being "terrorists," "savages," "assassins" and "extremists," and that they formed part of an "international conspiracy" led by Bolivia and Venezuela who feared that Peru's development would turn into a competition in the gas and oil sectors. García even dared to say that those who opposed intensive exploitation of the Amazon region were like "orchard dogs" who "don't eat or let anyone else eat" (Zibechi 2009). It seems that García wanted to have it all and, by doing so, become part of the transnational capitalist class. When seen from the viewpoint of the South, free trade agreements mean the implementation of an unethical and criminal legal system that generates population displacement, massacres and the looting of natural resources, and, by destroying the soil through intensive exploitation, deepening climate change, a reality that is very different from the one expressed in the North, where neo-liberal governments argue that trade is attached to human rights.

On September 30, 2010, a small group of Ecuadorian police officers led a mobilization that may be characterized as a mixture of strikes and an attempted coup d'état. The police action was triggered by a law passed by Congress that would put an end to the practice of giving medals and bonuses with each promotion. The fact is that the mobilization spiraled out of control, the Congress was occupied, airports and motorways were blocked, borders sealed, banks and supermarkets looted, and President Rafael Correa and the Minister of Interior were physically attacked, kidnapped and held hostage in a police hospital. The reaction against the attempted coup was not only internal but external; internally, the armed forces and a massive popular demonstration defended the democratic order, the police exercised repression and about seventy-four people were injured; meanwhile, the President was smuggled out of the hospital in a wheelchair. Externally, all the Latin American heads of state and the UN Secretary General Ban Ki-moon repudiated the coup, Colombia and Peru sealed their borders in solidarity, and OPEC nations pushed global oil prices to nearly US$80 a barrel (the *Guardian* newspaper). Although the OAS has pronounced against the police mobilization, it has never called it an attempted coup d'état, which shows the little respect for democracy of an organization that is supposed to represent all the nations in the continent.

At the beginning of February 2011, an US Air Force C-17 transport plane was seized by the Argentinian custom authorities at the Ezeiza International Airport in Buenos Aires because it brought camouflaged, undeclared sensitive material into the country. According to the Argentine Ministry of Foreign Affairs, the illegal cargo contained weapons, equipment for intercepting communications, various GPS, technological equipment with secret codes and a trunk full of different types of drugs, among them morphine. Argentine customs officials considered the cargo to be "war material" (Lantos). President Cristina Fernández de Kirchner sustained that the US Air Force had attempted "to violate Argentine laws by bringing in hidden material in an official shipment," and the Argentine Foreign Affairs Minister, Héctor Timmerman, added that "The United States must understand that they can't send war materials without informing the government," and he expressed outrage at the fact that the Assistant Secretary of State Arturo Valenzuela "refused to cooperate with the investigation" (AFP 2011). Moreover, Valenzuela expressed "concern on behalf of the US Defense Department over the seizure of items related to the security of the United States" (AFP 2011). The State Department spokesman Philip Crowley added that "we are puzzled and disturbed by the actions of Argentine officials," because they conducted "an unusual and unannounced search of the aircraft's cargo." He then added that "the material seized was routine for exercises in which US military experts train the Argentine federal police in advanced hostage rescue and crisis management techniques" (AFP 2011). The big question is: how can the United States decide to train the Argentine federal police without the Argentine government's knowledge? It is an undemocratic practice to interfere in other countries' internal affairs. Yet, interference had occurred again in Paraguay and Bolivia in the last week of June 2012.

On June 21, 2012 the Paraguayan Senate impeached the democratically elected President Lugo for a series of pre-fabricated charges. It should be noted that the Senate represents the opposition to Lugo's Patriotic Alliance for Change and it is the powerhouse of the country's large landowners. In Paraguay, about 2 percent of the people own 77 percent of the land – land concentration occurred during the thirty-five years of Alfredo Stroessner's dictatorship – thus the Senate, the heart of the Paraguayan polyarchy, speaks on behalf of that 2 percent. Among the impeachment charges were the fact that the Senate did not like the constant confrontation and struggle of social classes in the country; that President Lugo had allowed a conference of the "Latin American Youth for Change" to take place at a Paraguayan military base; that Lugo had signed a regional treaty affirming the respect for democratic principles without the approval of the Senate; and the principal charge, namely the President's "weak performance" when on June 15 landless peasants in Curuguaty occupied land owned by Blas Riquelme, an influencial member of the right-wing Colorado Party, leading to the eviction of about a hundred families. The result of the conflict was a massacre in which eleven peasants and six policemen were killed. Although Lugo sent forces, he was charged for failing to suppress the peasants. President Lugo was given only twenty-four hours to respond to the charges, after which time the Vice-president, Federico Franco, a member of the right-wing Colorado Party, assumed the presidency of Paraguay. Due to the short window given to President Lugo for his defense, what happened in Paraguay was labeled a "parliamentary coup d'état" with Franco as an illegitimate president. It should be noted that the coup happened just a few days before the presidency pro-tempore of UNASUR was due to be handed in to Paraguay. Thus, the coup was not just against Paraguay but against all South American nations.

The main issue at stake was land, particularly for soy production, which is dominated by Brazilian agribusiness, the so-called *brasiguayos*,[10] and Monsanto's name appeared in the news as one of those responsible for the coup. Domingo Laíno, a politician of the Authentic Liberal Radical Party (PLRA-*Partido Liberal Radical Auténtico*), the progressive line of the Liberal Party, mentioned that another contributor to the coup could have been the transnational aluminium smelter Rio Tinto Alcan, of Canadian, British and Australian capital, whose mega-project was going to need almost all the energy of the country to produce a massive amount of aluminium ingots. Besides, Laíno also mentioned that the de facto President Franco wanted to privatize the airports, which was why he sustained that the Senate's impeachment was ideological rather than political (López San Miguel 2012: 22). Moreover, Van Auken has mentioned that in the year previous to the coup, the Obama Administration more than doubled US aid to Paraguayan security forces, from US$3.9 million to US$8.2 million, and, did so under the banner of the "war on drugs." However, the Amambay Bank, the bank headed by one of the leading figures in the impeachment against Lugo, Hugo Cartes, was identified "in a confidential State Department cable published by WikiLeaks ... as being responsible for the 80 percent of money laundering in Paraguay on behalf of the drug traffickers" (Van Auken 2012). Thus, the "war on drugs" has been utilized once more by the United States as an excuse to interfere in Latin American politics.

While the gathering at a Paraguayan public TV station became the symbol of the peaceful protest against the parliamentary coup d'état and most Latin American countries withdrew their ambassadors from Paraguay to defend Lugo and the continuation of the democratic order, the de facto government was recognized by the Vatican, Spain, Germany and Canada. Two weeks later, MERCOSUR and UNASUR held meetings in Mendoza, Argentina. At the MERCOSUR meeting it was decided that Paraguay be suspended, which allowed for the entrance of Venezuela to the common market. This is because the Paraguayan Senate blocked President Lugo's interest to allow the entrance of Venezuela, an interest shared by the other MERCOSUR members, Argentina, Brazil and Uruguay. The day after, at the UNASUR meeting, it was decided that the presidency pro-tempore of the union should pass to Peru rather than to Paraguay. The new representatives of the Paraguayan government, who appeared in Mendoza, were not allowed to participate in the meetings and were asked to return to their country.

At almost the same time that the parliamentary coup d'état was taking place in Paraguay there was a police riot in Bolivia. About 300 young police officers in La Paz began a strike on June 12, 2012 to demand better pay. The young officers broke into the National Intelligence Directorate and the National Police headquarters, smashing windows and destroying documents. It seems that right-wing extremists were inciting riots at the moment when a legitimate march of the Tipnis, indigenous peoples from the jungle, were entering La Paz to demand that the plan for building a road through their territories be canceled. This attempted coup d'état against President Evo Morales was aborted by the government.

In sum, the meaning of Obama's Political Freedom/Democracy is to militarize and arm the Latin American police to produce a new type of coup d'état, to continue with FTAs that favor the entry of foreign companies that loot, displace and assassinate Afro-descendants, indigenous peoples, and all those living close to the natural resources desired by the transnational corporations. In other words, it is to strengthen the polyarchical structure that emerged in the 1980s, together with structural adjustment programs.

Promoting "freedom" from hunger, vultures and "humanitarian aid": the case of Haiti

The third of Obama's "freedoms," Freedom from Want/Opportunity, represents a reassertion and continuation of the Millennium Development Goals (MDGs) and the Heavily Indebted Poor Countries Initiative (HIPCs), which, as discussed above, represent an authoritarian social contract, a market approach to health, education and other social provisions. This time the target country was Haiti, the poorest country in the Western Hemisphere. Obama refers to Haiti as a "fragile country with a history of political instability," as a country that was hit by the world food crisis, in which the price of rice, the local staple, soared, producing hunger, which led to massive food riots. According to Obama, what restored the calm was the arrival of foreign aid and subsidies that lowered the price of rice. Obama announced his short-term and long-term policies towards Haiti, the short-term policy being to provide food assistance, and the long-term policy to provide technical assistance and job training. This would be done as always by supporting "freedom" and "democracy" (See Obama 2008: 8). The questions that arise from "Obama's New Partnership for the Americas" are: Who produced Haiti's history of political instability? What policies led Haiti, a country that until the 1980s was food self-sufficient, enter into a severe food crisis? What are the consequences of foreign "aid" and subsidies? For what purposes are technical assistance and job training given? For sweatshops?

Although Obama is not prone to look at the past, history matters, and it is precisely through a historical analysis that these questions can be answered. Haiti's political instability is a result of French colonialism, three American occupations, Canadian complicity, structural, superstructural changes and the commodification of livelihood through the so-called "poverty reduction strategies," which leaves the reduction of poverty in the hands of the private sector. When France recognized Haitian independence in 1825, thirty-four years after the slave revolution took place, France demanded that Haiti pay an indemnity of about 150 million French francs for the loss of its property, namely the slaves (Robinson 1996: 262). According to Ashley Smith, the equivalent today would be about US$21 billion (2010: 4). Haiti finalized paying this debt in 1947, which meant that Haiti did not have the means to develop economically, politically and socially. To this

should be added that the US occupation during 1915 to 1934 was used as justification for the existence of political instability in Haiti; however, the objective
was to allow the entrance of American corporations and the installation of the
Haitian National Army to secure American capital and repress the peasants who
opposed the corporations when being displaced from their lands. When the US
ended the occupation in 1934, it continued intervening in the politics and the
economy of Haiti – with a pause during the Carter Administration. Indeed, it supported the genocidal administrations of "Papa Doc" and "Baby Doc Duvalier"
(1957–1986), whose aim was to convert Haiti into an offshore assembly site for
US corporations, secured by the army and the Tonton Macoutes, the death
squads. This crystallized during the Reagan administration and the President's
Caribbean Basin Initiative (CBI), which not only opened up the area to maquiladora industries but also to agricultural corporations, with which local farmers
could not compete. This of course, was coupled with "democracy promotion"
measures that led to the creation of polyarchy and a transnational capitalist class.
Until that moment, Haiti was self-sufficient in rice production but the heavily
subsidized US rice and wheat pushed the Haitian producers out of business and
off their lands. The peasants migrated to the cities, where only a few of them
were hired in sweatshops, which, as many say, represent "modern-day slavery."
It is this scenario of exploitation that gave rise to the Fanmi Lavalas movement,
headed by the Liberation Theology Catholic priest Jean-Bertrand Aristide, abort-
ing the formation of a Haitian polyarchy. In the 1990s Aristide won the elections
and, a year later, President George Bush Sr. backed a military coup against Aristide, which was followed by three years of a brutal regime (Smith 2010: 8). In
1994 the US restored Aristide to power with the condition that he implement neo-
liberal policies; however, it was René Préval who two years later would put them
into practice. In 2000 Aristide won the elections again and took a mixed
approach; on the one hand he raised the minimum wage, built schools and
demanded that France refund the US$21billion colonial debt that Haiti was forced
to pay between 1824 and 1947. On the other hand, to maintain the calm of the
aggressors, Aristide allowed new sweatshops to be installed in Haiti. Nevertheless, due to his progressive actions, the US, Canada and France imposed economic sanctions and Aristide was forced to seek exile in South Africa. The US
delegated the occupation to the UN, to MINUSTAH, mostly formed by Brazilian
troops, which are still there today. In 2008 the food crisis spiraled out of control
with no locally produced food and the inability to pay the price of American-
produced rice, Haitians had to survive by eating mud cakes. Of course, rebellions
ensued, as did repressive measures. As a result, UN Secretary General Ban-Ki-
moon appointed Bill Clinton as Special Envoy to Haiti. Clinton was accompanied
by Paul Collier, a former World Bank research director, with the task of reacti-
vating Haiti's economy. The so-called Collier Plan was anchored in three main
measures: investment in the tourist industry, sweatshops for the cities and mango
plantations for the countryside (Smith 2010).

On January 12, 2010, an earthquake of 7.0 on the Richter Scale struck Haiti,
leaving about 230,000 people dead and three million affected – out of a total

population of 9.7 million (Gupta 2010: 1). Obama appointed Bush Jr. and Bill Clinton to collect donations through the Clinton-Bush Haiti Fund. Stories soon began to emerge regarding the militarization of what was called "humanitarian aid"; some mentioned that the US aid resembled a military occupation (Gupta 2010; Smith 2010; Waterfield 2010), that aid was slow to arrive, and that the relief efforts seemed to be a replay of Katrina (Gupta 2010). The American troups were obstructing the arrival of what Haitians needed most, namely doctors, medicine and food. It is unconceivable that in such a dramatic moment the trafficking of children was on the rise and that Monsanto donated hybrid seed maize to farmers. La Vía Campesina considered the donation to be a "deadly gift" that would eventually erode the farmers' food sovereignty, and is why 10,000 Haitian farmers marched in protest against Monsanto (La Vía Campesina 2010). Moreover, the lucrative business of reconstruction in the hands of foreign companies uncovered what type of "aid" and freedom from want may be expected from the United States.

In sum, it is the interventionism of foreign powers that did not allow Haiti to develop. If global justice would be implemented to restore to Haiti what belongs to Haiti, France should return the US$21 billion, and the US should indemnify Haiti for the ninety-seven years of criminal and corrupt interventionism. The same goes for Canada, since it became involved in this new colonial mission. Brazil should be held accountable for its role in MINUSTAH, and the UN Secretary General Ban-Ki-moon for the irresponsibility of giving the task for economic recovery to the same people who destroyed the economy of the country – and the entire world. Foreign corporations should leave the country and allow Haitians to generate their own businesses and grow crops for themselves; that is popular democracy; that is the real meaning of freedom.

Promoting freedom from energy dependency and the question of biofuels: the case of Brazil

Finally, "Working Towards Energy Security" is a call to invest in renewable energy with the objective of achieving independence from oil-producing countries – a contradiction of Obama's interests in Cuban and Venezuelan oil and Canadian tar sands – and to combat climate change. Obama sees Latin America as a magnificent source for renewable energy, and mentions that in 2007 the US entered into a biofuels partnership with Brazil, a country in which half of the cars are flex-fuel – they can run either on ethanol or gasoline (Obama 2008). Brazil is the target country for biofuels from sugar cane – note that Cuba has also shifted to sugar cane biofuels – but Obama's plan was more ambitious, namely to create an "Energy Partnership for the Americas"; in his terms, to

> help Latin American nations become more energy independent and promote sustainable growth for the region. The partnership also will create additional markets for American biofuels and American-made green energy

technology. Obama will enlist the World Bank, the Inter-American Development Bank and other international organizations to support these efforts.

(Obama 2008)

This strongly hegemonic discourse was also apparent a year earlier, when Obama sustained that

> We need a global response to climate change that includes binding and enforceable commitments to reducing emissions, especially for those that pollute the most: the United States, China, India, the European Union, and Russia. This challenge is massive, but rising to it will also bring benefits to America. By 2050, global demand for low-carbon energy could create an annual market worth $500 billion. Meeting that demand would open new frontiers for American entrepreneurs and workers.
>
> (Obama 2007: 7)

Thus, the objective of Obama, or a green capitalist approach to the environment, is to create new environmentally friendly industries, increase green employment and open up a new market niche for American-made clean energy technology. This could be a way out of the crisis for the United States, but it is not so for the majority of the countries that will have to open their doors to this new foreign technology, whether they want to or not, because they will be forced to do so through their link to free trade agreements. As Heather Rogers put it, "Green capitalism is an approach that says we can use the levers of the market to fix the broken environment" (2010: 1). It is this commodification of the environment that has led to the creation of a fictitious commodity such as the carbon market, and which results in what Bumpus and Liverman call "accumulation by de-carbonisation" (2008).

Biofuels can be produced from sugar cane, corn, wheat, sugarbeet, manioc, palm oil, soy beans, cellulosic – especially from eucalyptus – cassava, vegetables, sorghum, as well as jatropha, algae and waste. However, the two main products utilized for biofuels so far are corn and sugar cane; while the former reduces only 18 percent of greenhouse gas emissions, the latter reduces them by 91 percent, making sugar cane more "efficient" than corn, environmentally speaking. However, if the impact on society is brought into the picture, a very different result pops up. First, all of these products, besides algae and waste, need land, and therefore it becomes an engine for population displacement by the corporations that invest in this type of production. In the case of Brazil, sugar cane for ethanol is produced in the vicinity of Sao Paolo but, by doing so, it pushes cattle into the Amazon, intensifying deforestation, as pointed out by the Brazilian Landless Movement (MST). Second, it increases the value of both land and food, forcing the world into a food crisis. Other issues left out of the studies on biofuels is that the burning of sugar cane necessary to produce ethanol releases a huge amount of greenhouse gases into the atmosphere, as does the mechanized harvesting and transportation to the processing plants. To this should be added that the use of fertilizers and pesticides has a negative impact on the environment. In sum, this is a new field that requires an interdisciplinary study in order to evaluate the pros and cons of biofuels.

By the time the sixth Summit of the Americas took place, on April 14–16, 2012 in Cartagena, Colombia, inter-American relations were in a deep crisis. The OAS, which organized the summits, had lost the little credibility it had, and the anger of the Latin American heads of state towards the United States and Canada for their aggressive foreign policies in the region did not match the central theme of the Summit, namely "Connecting the Americas: Partners for Prosperity." Many Latin American heads of state did not participate in the Summit, and the requests put forward by the southern nations at the Summit were rejected by the northern nations. Latin American nations requested that Cuba be included in the OAS, that the OAS support Argentina's sovereignty over the Malvinas Islands, and that the international drugs trade be dealt with by alternative methods than the one utilized by the United States. The Summit ended with no agreement and no final declaration, and the anticipated unity of the Americas was broken. However, this failure strengthened the alternative organizations that had been created in Latin America and the Caribbean, such as the South American Common Market (MERCOSUR), the Bolivarian Alliance for the Peoples of Our America (ALBA), the Union of South American Nations (UNASUR) and the Community of Latin American and Caribbean States (CELAC). Henri Lefebvre was right: in order to survive, it is necessary to build a counter-hegemonic space. Individual nations would never have achieved what a united Latin America, by placing its people and dignity at the center, and embracing solidarity to fight for the independence and sovereignty of the region as a whole, has achieved.

To conclude, Part I has argued that the reconstruction of the New *Pax Americana* took place along four ten-year developmental planning stages that had the objective of weaving the Americas together. Each of these evolutionist stages deepened the crisis of social reproduction and inequality in the continent. Indeed, in the 1980s the disciplinary neo-liberal ideas, designed by the Council for Inter-American Security in the Santa Fe I document, were put into practice by President Reagan through the new global managerial infrastructure. Development was equated to "free markets" and democratization became the ideological tool to facilitate the acceptance of SAPs, which represented the new macro-economic mechanism to shift from a Keynesian to a neo-liberal World Order, as was demonstrated in the Southern Cone context. However, the implementation of SAPs gave rise to the competition state, and its attack on welfare led to the dialectical emergence of women's movements. Meanwhile, in security terms, the bipolar Westphalian system of states that endured all through the Cold War was also called into question, leading President Reagan to end the politics of the containment of communism. While the Central American region was the last context in which the "old civil wars" were taking place, the Caribbean Basin Initiative was ending the last vestiges of Keynesianism in the islands.

In the 1990s, the focus of the Santa Fe II document was on the struggle against Gramscian thought, particularly its cultural and juridical aspects. This coincided with the re-definition of development as "good governance" or the internationalization of the American Constitution. This new constitutionalism was implemented through multi-scalar agreements: at the global scale, the WTO joined the international financial institutions and Russia was incorporated into the G-7, becoming a "G-8 nexus"; at the regional scale, the old protectionist economic blocs lifted the barriers to trade and new ones were created; at the national scale, states were reshaped from within, giving rise to new managerialist states and a new public administration that intensified the modification of local constitutions and legal codes in favor of capital. The same modifications took place at the subnational and ethnic/community levels. This produced a shift in the gender and ethnic orders, and women's and indigenous peoples' social rights (welfare and land) were curtailed and commodified while political and civil rights were strengthened. Only a minority of these groups were beneficiaries of this new order. Women's movements were fragmented and indigenous peoples' struggles sprang up all over the continent.

In the new millennium, the Santa Fe IV document uncovered nine new threats and various privately led "poverty reduction" strategies were implemented, among them the Heavily Indebted Poor Countries Initiative, the Poverty Reduction Strategy Papers, the Impoverishment Risk and Livelihood Reconstruction model and the Millennium Development Goals. While it was expected that the FTAA was going to pass at the fourth Summit of the Americas in Mar del Plata, the "New Left" showed its strength by rejecting it and, since then, has started to build its own geo-economic and political space. By doing so, the 2008 economic crisis found Latin America in a stronger position than the European countries. Entering into the second decade of the new millennium it is argued that the Obama Administration represented a fourth moment of the New *Pax Americana*; in the name of "freedom" and "democracy" the US has been penetrating Latin America piece by piece, and now it is the turn of the independent police, the judiciary, oil and renewable energy with the objective of creating a new market niche for green raw materials and American clean products – biofuels, wind, and solar and nuclear energy.

In order to produce radical change, it is necessary to start by moving away from polyarchy towards popular democracy, to shift from corporate freedom towards peoples' freedom, to reform or create a new architecture of World Orders, perhaps in distinct locations – not all concentrated in the US. This new architecture should modify the current structure of the World Order, re-embed the social to the political sphere, and to change the superstructure to solidify a new morality that eliminates power disparities and includes all human beings on the planet. This is not to return to the Keynesian World Order; it would be impossible to do so because we are in a different historical conjuncture. This new architecture must respond to today's needs. The current moment is way more complicated than the end of World War II, when Keynesianism was implemented. Indeed, at that time, for example, tax havens, the main distorters of the world economy did not exist, the military-industrial complex did not have the power it has today, technology was not as developed as it is today – computers,

cell phones, etc. did not exist. It is necessary to create something new by analyzing former ways of organizing society, by evaluating their positive and negative
characteristics, and this has been the passion and commitment of Karl Polanyi.

Latin America is not anti-American, as Obama believes. Latin Americans
admire the tenacity, creativity and values of the American people. What Latin
Americans criticize are the policies implemented by the American elite – both
Republicans and Democrats – and their counterparts in their countries, which
has led to the impoverishment of the majority, to the elimination of the social
cushion and to genocide. Obama may represent the American dream, but he cer-
tainly does not represent Dr. Luther King's dream: that dream is yet to come.
Democracy, as Aristotle put it, "is when the indigent, and not the men of property, are the rulers," something that Abraham Lincoln was very clear about when
he said, "As I would not be a slave, so I would not be a master. This expresses
my idea of democracy." Let us hope that there is a tale of a second Obama, as
Latham proposed, and that this time he knows the distinction between polyarchy
and popular democracy, to start building a better America, to eliminate the wid-
ening inequalities in his own country and to generate new forms of peaceful relations with Latin America and the rest of the world. At the time when this
manuscript was being prepared for publication, Obama was starting his second
administration.

Part II

Transnational mining corporations

Searching for "El Dorado" at the turn of the millennium. The Bolivian case

5 The Amayapampa and Capasirca gold-mines
Double movement and state repression[1]

This case study is inscribed within the new post-Cold War struggles. It is one of the first resource conflicts that took place in the continent, following the 1995 outbreak of the *Zapatistas* in Mexico. The Amayapampa and Capasirca conflict emerged the same year in which Bolivia was included into the Heavily Indebted Countries Initiative, yet it preceded the introduction of the Poverty Reduction Strategy Paper (the HIPCs conditionalities) by about three years.

The Amayapampa and Llallagua massacres of December 1996 marked the sad end of an eight-month conflict between the miners and rural communities of Northern Potosí, Bolivia, and the transnational mining corporation (TMC) Da Capo Resources Limited, of Vancouver, Canada, one of the pioneer mining enterprises investing in Bolivia. Da Capo had bought the Amayapampa and Capasirca mines at the beginning of that fateful year. The Bolivian government justified the killings as a legitimate state response to a terrorist movement. However, it will be argued here that the miners and rural communities of Northern Potosí were by no means part of any terrorist movement against the state and the TMC. Rather, their reaction represented a form of self-defense against the social, cultural and economic dislocations produced by neo-liberal restructuring in the mining sector, and the government's response highlighted the authoritarian character of the "competition state" and its international alliances.

To put it another way, the tragic December 1996 events represented the culmination of a conflict between two different ways of organizing society. On the one hand, there was the emergence of a "competition state" (Cerny 1997: 251; Gill 1997: 14). Step by step, it had replaced the nationalist populist developmental state, particularly after 1985 when Bolivia adopted a strict neo-liberal program. This shift brought about a re-invention of the state's role by political and market actors – transnational corporations most importantly. The state reformed its regulatory and political guarantees by enacting a new mining code and reducing mining taxes to attract foreign direct investment (FDI). By doing so, the state effectively internationalized itself. At the same time, multilateral organizations and the G-7 development agencies were advising Bolivia on how to attract mining investment while also promoting the creation of an international framework that would guarantee investor rights.

On the opposing side were mine workers and *pueblos originarios*, indigenous peoples who relied partly on subsistence production and were allied against the competition state and its international cohort. They considered themselves and not the state as the original owners of the natural resources of their region, and they were the ones who were directly harmed by the environmental contamination and social dislocations produced by mining.

Because the miners had been indigenous peasants in the past, their ethnic identity was as strong as their class identity. Their reaction against the competition state took the form of a mixed class and ethnic movement that aimed for the protection of nature and peoples. These interactions between global and local forces – that is, the state, transnational mining corporations, multilateral organizations and their pro-business human rights apparatus "from above" on one side, and miners, *pueblos originarios* and community-oriented local and international human rights organizations "from below" on the other – form in essence what Karl Polanyi called "the double movement" of society against capitalism. They reflect, in other words, the ways in which initiatives from above to expand the realm of market power provoke a counteracting response from below.

This chapter is divided into four sections. The first section analyzes the shift from the "old" to the "new mining" in its global-local context, within which the interaction of international and national policies shaped the transition to a new mining production system. The second section examines the demands of the miners and *pueblos originarios* of the Amayapampa and Capasirca goldmines who were caught up in this "new mining" system. The third section explains how Da Capo Resources Limited/Vista Gold Corporation pressured the Bolivian state to comply with the interests of the international investors and the state's response to those interests. The final section explores the internationalization of the conflict and the situation as of mid-2003.[2] The goal is to present the conflicting interests of the different actors and explain their interactions.

From the old to the new mining: towards a transnational architecture of mining extraction

The passage from the "old" to the "new mining" in Bolivia may be analyzed in the context of changes in the structures of the World Order, specifically of the two phases of capitalist accumulation under US world leadership. In Bolivia, the shift from the Old *Pax Americana* (1947–1964) to the New *Pax Americana* (since 1982) – from the Keynesian to the neo-liberal World Orders – coincided with the transition from an "old" nationally oriented mining system based on tin, which did include some welfare concessions, to a "new" transnationally oriented mining extraction based on precious metals and stones (with an emphasis on gold) and the exclusion of societal interests.

The Old Pax Americana *and the old mining*

The first phase of *Pax Americana* emerged with the "modernization project" of the Bretton Woods institutions and financed national development programs of economic growth and social transformation with the aim not only of seeing Third World countries "catch up" with the industrialized West but also of ensuring their loyalty to it (McMichael 1996: 53, 79). This involved the creation of strong developmental states that could carry out economic policies of modernization and redistribution, including industrialization, agrarian reform and frontier colonization. The principal problem of the period thus derived from how the strength of these states was tied up to external financial resources and depended directly and indirectly upon the United States to help quell internal dissent and communism (McMichael 1996: 53, 79).

It was within this international context that a nationalist revolution took place in Bolivia in April 1952. The revolution was carried out by a coalition of workers, miners and peasants, led by Víctor Paz Estenssoro and his Nationalist Revolutionary Movement (MNR – *Movimiento Nacionalista Revolucionario*) – a group composed mainly of young army officers and petit-bourgeois intellectuals (Estellano 1994: 35). This amorphous coalition came together because its members shared a common goal: to remove from power the traditional bourgeoisie of landowners and mining magnates. The most important policies implemented towards that end were agrarian reform and the nationalization of the tin mines from the "tin Barons," the Patiño, Hochschield and Aramayo families. The expropriation of the tin mines was followed by the creation of the Bolivian Mining Corporation (*Corporación Minera de Bolivia*, COMIBOL), a state corporation that subsequently set up a social welfare infrastructure to benefit its workers. In fact, a system of housing, schools, health care and subsidized food through the *pulperías* or company stores was established in every single nationalized mine (Aillón Gómez 1999).

The populist model was feasible because the state monopolized tin production and appropriated the surplus generated by it. It did so through the implementation of two main mechanisms: the mining code of 1965 and the tax system. While the mining code excluded foreign mining companies from operating in Bolivia (Aillón Gómez 1999: 84), the tax system was designed to allow the state to capture all of the income and benefits generated by mining extraction. However, most of the state's income from the sector was not re-invested in mining in the Andean region. Instead, over the following decades (the period of transition between the Old and New *Pax Americanas*, the *Impasse*, 1964–1982) public support and foreign loans from the United States, the World Bank and the Inter-American Development Bank (IADB) were increasingly channeled towards the Amazon region to subsidize other sectors of the economy such as oil and agro-export sectors, dominated by local elites and eventually also by foreign capital. As this transfer of resources towards the east of the country increased, so too did the tension between the highly organized mine workers and the nationalist developmental state.

The mine workers from the Federation of Mine Workers of Bolivia (FSTMB – *Federación Sindical de Trabajadores de Bolivia*) criticized the reformist solutions as insufficient and considered nationalization a farce because political decisions taken in Bolivia could not affect the price of tin, which was dictated by the principal actors in the world market (Nash 1993: 263). Nevertheless, the workers accepted the 1952 revolution as a first step towards socialism.

The relationship between the miners and the state eventually broke down in 1960, when President Paz Estenssoro signed the Triangular Plan with the Inter-American Development Bank, West Germany and the United States. The Plan initiated a denationalization of the mining industry by allowing the penetration of foreign capital and the possibility of massive layoffs. In response, the miners orchestrated a general nationwide strike that threatened to explode into open rebellion, hence Paz Estenssoro's turn to the US for aid to stop the revolt. A year later General René Barrientos seized power, setting a pattern of military coups (backed by Washington) and the systematic repression of mine workers (Nash 1993: 270–272). The weakened foundations of the "old mining" system finally collapsed under the weight of two crises: the debt crisis of 1982 and, four years later, a crash in tin prices.

The New Pax Americana *and the new mining*

The transition towards the New *Pax Americana*, or "disciplinary neo-liberalism," was initiated in the 1970s with the expansion of offshore production and financial markets.[3] The globalization of production and money was facilitated by the Bretton Woods institutions through the creation of new legal frameworks in the global, regional, national and subnational arenas. This "new constitutionalism" refers to the norms and regulations that attempt to insulate "key aspects of the economy from the influence of politicians or the mass of citizens by imposing internally and externally, 'binding constraints' on the conduct of fiscal, monetary, and trade and investment policies" (Gill 2003: 132). In fact, as Gill argues, these macro-economic rules, by tying the hands of local governments, limit the possibility of local democratic control.

This supranational process of decision making led to a new model of development. Instead of being a nationally managed process, development was re-defined as "world participation by producers and states" (McMichael 1996: 111). Transnational corporations became the main recipients of financial assistance, thus supplanting the state as the guarantor of national and local development. The multilateral institutions themselves promoted the transition from the old to the new mining, from an inward- to an outward-oriented extraction system buttressed by two main policies based on neo-liberal structural adjustment programs (SAPs) and the World Bank's Poverty Reduction Strategy Papers (PRSPs). While the structural adjustment programs brought national control over minerals to an end, the World Bank's Poverty Reduction Strategy Paper proposed (among many other macro-economic rules) a new constitutionalist global mining extractive system, consisting of reformed mining codes and tax regimes and the creation of strong mining institutions. The Poverty Reduction Strategy Papers coincided with high global demand for gold, due to the increased consumption of gold in Asia, the use of gold in most high-tech products (to connect chips to circuit boards), and fears that the scarcity of oil could lead to the outbreak of an inflationary process, together with, according to the World Bank, the development of capital markets prepared to invest in mining, such as the Vancouver and Toronto stock exchanges (World Bank 1996).

In Bolivia, as in many other developing countries, the 1982 debt crisis provided the perfect opportunity for multilateral institutions to press the government to change its economic and legal structures to favor an open economy. In 1985, Paz Estenssoro once again assumed the presidency, this time with Harvard economist Jeffrey Sachs as his principal economic advisor (Klein 1992). Paz Estenssoro turned to the International Monetary Fund and the World Bank for loans, and the country has since been handcuffed by the package of conditionalities imposed by the Bretton Woods institutions. Indeed, the New Economic Plan (NEP) was little more than the local expression of structural adjustment programs, which included the privatization of national enterprises and the elimination of welfare programs. The main objective of the New Economic Plan was the closing of the Bolivian Mining Corporation's mines, leading to 30,000 layoffs between 1986 and 1992 and the weakening of the labor unions (L. Gill 1997: 293–294). The role of the Bolivian Mining Corporation also changed dramatically as it was transformed from a mechanism for state-led mining extraction to an administrative body for joint-venture contracts between transnational mining corporations and private Bolivian companies (Aillón Gómez 1999: 87).

Once the terms of the structural changes were finalized, the World Bank proposed the implementation of the Poverty Reduction Strategy Paper, designed for those countries that were completing the structural adjustment reforms. Bolivia was considered one of those "reforming countries" in Latin America, together with Argentina, Ecuador, Mexico and Peru.[4] The mining section of the Poverty Reduction Strategy Papers included the reform of the legal and investment regimes, the creation of public mining institutions (PMIs) that would enforce the new policies, such as the Ministry or Department of Mines, Mining Registry Office, Geological Survey and Mining Environment Office (World Bank 1996). Rather than having the state directly tackle social issues, the new rules and regulations facilitated the entrance of transnational mining corporations to the region. Poverty was to be addressed indirectly through the economic growth that was expected to flow from the reforms. To accommodate the "new constitutionalism," the Bolivian state converted itself from a nationalist and developmental state into a transnational "competition state," from a "civil association to an enterprise association" (Cerny 1997: 272).

The "competition state," in accordance with the misnamed poverty reduction strategies, introduced a new mining code and tax regime. In contrast to the mining code of 1965, which excluded foreign direct investment in the sector, the 1997 mining code opened the doors to transnational capital (Art.30). While the state remained the owner of all mineral resources in Bolivia (Art.1), it had the right to grant concessions to private investors. Furthermore, all those who attempted to prevent the transfer of mining properties to new concession holders would be held liable to pay compensation and be subject to possible criminal prosecution (Art.39). In a very threatening tone, Article 14 of the mining code gave the *Superintendente de Minas* the authority to use force, if necessary, to defend the "rights" of the new concession holders. Significantly, the mining code was drafted after the conflict in the Amayapampa and Capasirca mines had begun, and it was approved a few months after the "Christmas massacre,"[5] which undoubtedly contributed to the authoritarian character of the legislation.

The new law combined two types of taxes. One was based on profits while the other was based on the value of production, involving a floating rate tied to fluctuations in mineral prices in the international market (Medinacelli Monrroy 1999). This meant that every time mineral prices in the world market declined, Bolivia would receive less tax income. In effect, the reform was designed to shift the costs of an international market crisis in minerals onto the backs of Bolivians and other societies that depended on mining extraction. Another neo-classical insight, known as "Hottelings' Rule," complemented the mining tax. It held that if mineral prices decreased, the owner of a non-renewable resource should post-pone production until sometime in the future when prices rose again. The application of Hottelings' Rule would seriously affect mine workers, who would lose their jobs during periods of low international mineral prices, turning them into a flexible labor force that would bear the costs of the country's integration into the global political economy.

The new mining code and tax system were accompanied by a series of national and international laws that provided guarantees for foreign investors. Among the areas of national law affected were investment, sector regulation, stock markets, insurance, arbitration and conciliation, and property loans (see C-PROBOL 1998: 4–5). The institutions and international agreements signed by Bolivia that guaranteed investment include the International Center for Settlement Related to Investments Disputes (ICSID), the Multilateral Investment Guarantee Agency (MIGA), the Overseas Private Investment Corporation (OPIC), the World Intellectual Property Rights Organization, the Paris Convention and the Trade Related Aspects of Intellectual Property Rights (TRIPS) (C-PROBOL 1998: 7).

Another ominous aspect of the new investor rights regime, the 1996 secrecy law, represented an agreement between the state and the corporate sector. While transnational mining corporations have taken over mines formerly exploited by the Spanish conquerors in the Andes, in the western part of Bolivia a large number of foreign exploration companies also planned to move into the Amazon rainforest in the east, a region rich in gold. Yet once companies enter Bolivian territory they are protected by a secrecy law; the release of information regarding the mining companies is strictly forbidden. Another protective and public relations strategy adopted by transnational mining corporations is the utilization of Spanish or Pre-Columbian names which they change constantly to protect the identity of investors and prevent the rise of a nationalist sentiment against them.[6]

Other characteristics of the "new mining" model include the introduction of open pit mines, which are considered more efficient and competitive than underground tunnels; the introduction of new technologies, including the use of capital-intensive methods that reduce the number of workers and therefore social conflict; new levels of environmental contamination due to the use of toxic chemicals such as cyanide and arsenic; new forms of labor relations such as flexible or intermittent employment; and finally, an indifference to and disrespect for local culture.

In sum, the shift from the old to the new mining may best be understood in the context of the different phases of the *Pax Americana* or American-led hegemony. The old mining, based on tin extraction, coincided with the first phase. In the postwar settlement era, the new Bretton Woods agencies financed a modernization project based on national development programs of economic growth and moderate social concessions, a project deeply embedded in the politics of Cold War containment of communism. A nationalist and developmental state emerged through breaking the power of the traditional bourgeoisie of landlords and "tin barons," and later on modified the mining code and mining tax regime to develop an inward-oriented model of economic growth and social transformation. However, due to its dependency on external financial sources, the developmental state could not respond to the demands and organizational power of the mining labor movement, which led to socio-political conflict, military coups and a systematic repression of labor.

By the 1980s the inward-focused modernization project was being reversed. Development was given a pro-market meaning, thus giving rise to an outward-oriented model that, through neo-liberal structural adjustment programs, put an end to the old mining system and eliminated the social provisions attached to it. The poverty reduction policies coincided with the ascendancy of the competition state and the creation of the new mining economy, based on gold and capital-intensive production carried out by transnational mining corporations, whose entrance was facilitated by a new mining code and mining tax system. The Canadian company Da Capo Resources Ltd. was one of the first transnational mining corporations to install itself as a pioneer mining enterprise in Bolivia's newly reformed mining sector. The expansion of the transnational mining market contributed to a larger process of disembedding society. Not surprisingly, the people of the region of Northern Potosí reacted strongly to these developments, taking steps to defend themselves from cultural annihilation.

A progressive counter-movement: miners' and *pueblos originarios'* demands

The exclusion of miners and *pueblos originarios* by the New Economic Plan and its institutional expression, the internationalized competition state, led to the crystallization of an oppositional movement. In the Amayapampa and Capasirca mines, resistance to the new manifestations of capitalism unified the voices of miners and *pueblos originarios* in a counter-movement,[7] as they articulated joint historical, socio-economic and cultural demands in defense of their livelihoods and natural surroundings – demands that Da Capo Resources/Vista Gold Corporation did not understand.

Historical demands

The history of Northern Potosí – the poorest region in Bolivia and one of the poorest in Latin America – is defined by an enormous contrast between the wealth of its mineral deposits and the deep poverty of its inhabitants. It is a history that blends greed and exploitation with poverty and blood, and the people living in the district have paid with their lives in the millions (APDHB 1998: 1; Núñez and Jungwiry 1997: 5).

For about 300 years the Spanish exploited the silver mines of the Cerro Rico de Potosí and the gold-mines of Amayapampa and Capasirca. With all the silver that the Spanish took from the Cerro Rico, it is said, a "silver bridge stretching from Potosí to Madrid could have been built" (Absi 1997: 36). From the end of the nineteenth century until 1985 the Llallagua mine, located only a few kilometers north of Amayapampa and Capasirca, was known for having the largest tin deposits in the world, making Bolivia the top world producer of tin for more than a century. It would also become involved in the conflict with Da Capo Resources/Vista Gold. In the 1970s, the Garafulic family took control of the Amayapampa mine, and the Yaksic Ostoic family bought Capasirca.[8] According to Pedro Gómez Rocabado, a researcher for the Centro de Promoción Minera (CEPROMIN) in Bolivia, these Bolivian owners left the workers free to mine on their own, however they might decide to do the work, with no set hours of work.[9] In return the miners gave the owners half of what they extracted, and marketed the other half themselves. For almost three decades the mine workers used the same methods of extraction, and the owners made little if any investment in machinery or salaries. Still, by 1996, these local families owed many years of royalties to the miners. Raúl Garafulic himself extracted about ten to fifteen kilograms of gold per month, which permitted him to become the owner of a large national television network and a major shareholder in three local newspapers (Radio Pío XII 1997: 141–143).

Thus, over a period of 500 years, a small number of people had made a great deal of wealth from this land – in sharp contrast to the inhumane conditions of life experienced among those "poor who walked on gold," a common saying in the region. As a result, foreigners who arrive to Potosí in search of gold are not trusted; indeed, a history of distrust colors the social, economic and cultural demands of the region's people. In addition, as events would show, they had very good reason for that distrust.

In April 1996 one such foreigner, David O'Connor, an Australian geologist who was a shareholder of Da Capo Resources – he controlled 20 percent of Da Capo's shares, the rest comprising Canadian capital[10] – bought the mines of Amayapampa and Capasirca, the former for US$8 million and the latter for US$2 million (Núñez and Jungwiry 1997: 34). Amayapampa and Capasirca had estimated gold reserves of 50 tons, which represented about US$700 million (Radio Pío XII 1997: 146–147). That same year, Da Capo Resources merged with Granges Incorporated, based in the United States, to form Vista Gold Corporation, with O'Connor as general manager.

Socio-economic demands

Earlier, in 1983, during a time of drought, peasant unions had been formed for the first time. The miners, in negotiations with the corporation, would channel their demands through the Workers' Confederation of Bolivia (COB-*Confederación Obrera de Bolivia*) and the Federation of Mine Workers of Bolivia (FSTMB-*Federación Sindical de Trabajadores Mineros de Bolivia*). Meanwhile, the *pueblos originarios* would communicate their position through the *Consejo de Ayllus*, a pre-Columbian organization known for its "spatial, political and ethno-cultural connotations", as well as for its relative isolation: its "social and economic reproduction has been very weakly related to national society" (Núñez and Jungwiry 1997: 15). The *ayllus*[11] maintain a complementary economy across two ecological levels, the highlands and the valleys, bartering products between the two areas. The establishment of the peasants' unions did not undermine the existence of the *ayllus*; rather, the two managed to co-exist (Núñez and Jungwiry 1997: 15–17).

Not surprisingly, with the transfer of ownership to the new foreign owners, the miners were afraid of losing their jobs, and the local people in general felt a tremendous sense of insecurity. One of the testimonies recorded by the Bolivian Permanent Assembly for Human Rights stated, "We were sold like animals without any compensation ... they have treated us like dogs."[12] There was no consultation with the workers or the local communities. Still, the initial demands of the miners and *ayllus* presented to Vista Gold Corporation were little more than the demands that had been made previously, without success, to the Garafulic and Yaksic families. The demands, issued in Capasirca in 1996, included the right to retain their jobs, a recognition of seniority, social security and health services, and subsidized food through the *pulpería*. They asked for a salary increase of 50 percent (later raised to 65 percent), with payment in US dollars. Their demands also included a call for better equipment, machinery and tools to make the work less dangerous (e.g., the electrical system in the mines was deficient, and the mines needed stronger pumps to take the water out of the mines from a depth of forty-five meters). For its part, the company announced plans to institute regular hours of work, establish salary levels, and alter a whole range of practices that would make the mining conform with how transnationals generally operate (APDHB 1998: 14; Radio Pío 1997: 147; Núñez and Jungwiry 1997: 35).

Cultural demands

The true beginning of the conflict in Capasirca, though, came with the new ownership's attempt to eliminate the *pijcheo* – an ancestral cultural practice that consists of the workers chewing coca leaves before starting their day in the mine (Aillón Gómez 1999: 83). *Pijcheo* has a strong religious connotation – associated with the mythical figure of the *tío de la mina* or the uncle of the mine[13] – and it gives strength, fortifies resistance and eases hunger. From the workers' point of view, as June Nash (1993: 200) notes, the chewing of coca "makes the inhuman conditions of the mine tolerable," and attempts to eliminate coca breaks have historically led to rebellion. The new mine owners decided that it was inefficient for the workers to lose time chewing coca. Adding to the insult, when two leaders asked the company not to eliminate the time for *pijcheo*, they were detained for twenty-four hours (APDHB 1998: 38).

At the end of November 1996 the *Consejo de Ayllus* formed the Council for the Defense of the Dignity and Interests of the *Ayllus* of the Province of Bustillos (CODDIA-PB), through which they extended their demands into the national and international arenas, with a particular focus on indigenous peoples' organizations abroad.[14] Following the establishment of the Council, the *pueblos originarios* sent letters to different national authorities, informing them of its creation and their demands regarding mining in the territory of the *ayllus* of Northern Potosí. The letter concluded by stating "that in many cases large mass movements are uncontrollable."[15] This last sentence would later be used by the government as evidence of the emergence of a subversive movement in Northern Potosí.

During the eight months of negotiation with the Vista Gold Corporation in 1996, the demands of the miners from both Capasirca and Amayapampa and the *pueblos originarios* began to coalesce. The *Consejo de ayllus* or council of *pueblos originarios*, believing that they – and not the state – were the original owners of their region's natural resources,[16] went on to demand that 50 percent of the gold production stay in the country; that the company pay royalties to the region (Núñez and Jungwiry 1997: 36) and compensate them for the contamination of the environment; that Bolivia's new mining code be rejected, that rural communities had the right to consultation (a right established in Article 171 of the Bolivian Constitution and Convention 169 of the International Labor Organization, 1989); and human rights be respected.

Meanwhile, the workers continued to mine for gold as they had always done. In response the company accused them of theft and started to lay charges against them. According to Rocabado's account,

> When the company saw the workers meeting and discussing, it told them, "If you want to have meetings, you have to have them outside of working hours." And the workers said, "What working hours? We have always worked when we need to produce, or we haven't worked."

The development of events

Although various agreements were reached, the company never honored them. To make matters worse, by September 1996 the miners were still owed four months' pay, a debt incurred by the previous owners. As a consequence, on September 18, 1996, the miners of Capasirca took a Vista Gold engineer, Guillermo Cordero, hostage in order to get the company to respect their demands and pay their missing salaries. Cordero was quickly freed, but the incident provided fuel for the government's argument that a subversive movement was emerging in the Andes. Government officials also found the perfect body of evidence to support their claims of subversion in the *Tesis de la Chojlla*. According to the government, the thesis made reference to a plan – to be led by members of the FSTMB and the COB – to take over all the public and private mines in the region. Clearly, the government was convinced that a dangerous mass movement was unfolding that would damage government efforts to attract private investment for mining development in Bolivia.[17]

On November 14, the government sent 130 police officers into the area, guided by O'Connor, to detain Capasirca's union leaders. Backed by a judicial order, the police aggressively broke into the homes of the union leaders and laid legal charges against them. The population responded immediately and forced the police and the manager out of Capasirca. Members of the community took the police officers' guns, although they returned the weapons the next day to the *Prefectura de Potosí*, providing a clear indication that the miners of Capasirca were attempting to defend their rights peacefully (APDHB 1998: 15; Núñez and Jungwiry 1997: 36).

This incident became a turning point in the conflict, with the Amayapampa miners and the rural communities unified against Vista Gold on the one hand and the company and the state allied on the other. The conflict also quickly became regionalized against the enterprise–government alliance embedded in the competition state. The coalitions were clearly demarcated. Both the progressive and the repressive movements were gaining strength; and neither was prepared to give up its interests.

Nevertheless, one more effort was made to resolve the problem peacefully. On November 19, 1996, the different parties in the conflict signed an *Acta de Intenciones*, according to which further dialog would begin only after police forces were removed from the mines. Vista Gold Corporation was to drop its legal charges against the union leaders, and, finally, workers were to allow company representatives to enter the mine.[18] Initially, all three parties complied with the agreement, but after several days the union leaders realized that the legal document through which the corporation was supposed to lift the criminal charges against the union leaders was in fact falsified. Indeed, the legal official of Oruro, who purportedly signed the document on December 3, 1996, had actually left his position four days before he signed the document. Because the document was not legally valid,[19] the union leaders asked for a new one.[20] In addition, the unions demanded disclosure of the document used by the company to buy the concession. The unions knew that while the company claimed to have paid US$2 million for the Capasirca concession, the document of sale mentioned only US$400,000, which meant that the company would pay taxes on only that lower amount – instead of US$2 million.

At first the conflict had been entirely centered in Capasirca, but as the government, Vista Gold and the unions were meeting in November regarding Capasirca, the mine workers of Amayapampa, together with members of the surrounding *pueblos originarios*, took over the Amayapampa mine and assaulted three engineers employed by the enterprise, one of them a Canadian. At the same time they demanded that all people who worked for the company and the police leave Amayapampa.[21] In response, the government shifted its discourse. While it had previously argued that the conflict was being promoted by a subversive movement, it now accelerated the rhetoric: the coalition of miners and rural communities became a "terrorist movement." This shift in discourse was a prelude to what was to come.

The repression: Vista Gold Corporation and the competition state

The Vista Gold Corporation and regional government officials actively promoted the idea that the local opposition amounted to a terrorist movement against the state. The company demanded that both the regional and national governments ensure compliance with the mining code, which stated that nobody had the right to oppose mining concessions granted by the state and that any opposition could be subject to both compensatory claims and criminal charges.

The letters written to the government by David O'Connor always held to the same format.[22] O'Connor would begin by highlighting the economic and social benefits that Vista Gold Corporation would bring to the Northern Potosí region and the country, and then refer to how uneconomical and polluting the small-scale mining had been. He would conclude by warning that if the government did not intervene in the Amayapampa and Capasirca conflicts, the possibility of attracting future foreign direct investment would be ruined. It was a "good-vs.-evil" discourse. In a messianic tone, O'Connor presented Vista Gold Corporation as the generator of economic growth in the poorest region of the country. He pointed out that the company would invest US$65 million, with its operations contributing between US$720,000 and US$920,000 each year to the local economy; and about US$2.5 to US$3.5 million would be spent annually in both the local and regional economies. All this, according to O'Connor, would have a total impact in the Bolivian economy of somewhere between US$6.2 and US$7.4 million annually. The country would also receive US$3 million in taxes every year. O'Connor also emphasized the social benefits that Vista Gold would bring to the local population, such as the creation of 250 to 270 new jobs, improved health and education services, new roads, and organized sporting, cultural and other activities.

In addition to stressing his own "good intentions," O'Connor accused the mine workers of stealing some US$150,000-worth of gold per month from the mine by using the obsolete technology from the previous owners that was uneconomic, insecure and highly polluting. O'Connor considered the demands of the workers illegal and illegitimate. He seemed astonished that "a reduced group of people are trying to prevent the installation of the enterprise and the initiation of their productive and social projects," especially when the enterprise was in favor of economic and human development. In a letter dated November 19, 1996 to President Gonzalo Sánchez de Lozada, O'Connor asked the government to intervene, even suggesting the particular military force to be used: "Currently there is a force led by Colonel Eduardo Rivas of 150 armed men at Catavi awaiting instructions." According to O'Connor, the Amayapampa miners were demanding that the company withdraw all of its personnel and equipment from the mine within forty-eight hours. The letter's last paragraph referred to the costs to be paid if the government did not intervene:

> As you are aware, as a public company traded on both the American and Toronto stock exchange, such an impairment to our assets would require public and shareholder disclosure. If we are forced to withdraw on Thursday morning then disclosure would be required on Friday. In addition, we have already begun discussions with international banks (who today look favourably on Bolivia and our project) regarding financing for $65 million required. However, this goodwill would be lost if we cannot work or occupy our mines.[23]

The President, himself a mine owner and the architect of neo-liberal restructuring in Bolivia, clearly understood this strong message. Gonzalo Sánchez de Lozada was the major shareholder in *Compañía Minera del Sur* (COMSUR) (Sanabria 1999: 65), a company that had been active in setting up joint ventures with British, Canadian and US enterprises, including Río Tinto, Orvana Minerals Corporation and Apex Silver Mines, which had invested in various mines, such as Bolívar (lead, silver and zinc), Don Mario (gold, silver and copper), Colquiri (tin and silver), Porco (zinc) and Rincón del Tigre (Platinum-palladium).[24]

The President's reaction thus not surprisingly reflected his mixed public and private interests. There was too much at stake; those contributing to unrest had to be "disciplined" once and for all. If the workers would not agree with the new mining system, they would be forced to accept it. On December 19, 1996, some 800 to 900 members of the military and police forces – armed with machine guns, bazookas and gas launchers – arrived in Amayapampa by air and land. Members of the FSTMB and Bolivia's Permanent Assembly for Human Rights (APDHB) asked police comandant General Willy Arriaza for a one-hour truce: he agreed to give them only thirty minutes. Within fifteen minutes, however, General Arriaza gave the order to attack Amayapampa. The miners and rural communities resisted for about six hours, using their fists, sticks, stones, old rifles and dynamite. The conflict took seven lives, with about thirty people wounded by bullets (Radio Pío XII 1997: 144).

One of the eyewitness accounts pointed out that the community could not understand why this level of violence had been used against Amayapampa when the only conflict in this mine (as opposed to the events in Capasirca) had taken place after the union leaders were detained when they asked the company not to cut the time for the *pijcheo*. This insult to their customary practices led them to take over the mine two days before the assault.[25] Another human rights activist described how General Arriaza told her that he had "orders from above" to restore order and return the mine to its proprietors. According to her, General Arriaza declared, "I have orders from the Ministry of the Government and just in case you do not understand lady, I have orders from Mr. Goni Sánchez de Lozada to enter the mine and return it to its owner, because the mines do have owners, foreign businessmen." Arriaza said he had orders to return the mine to the company owners before 6 p.m., "even if I have to pass over all of them" – pointing, as he said this, in the direction of the peasants and miners on the mountain.[26]

Women were also very active during the conflict, some of them fighting alongside the men while others rushed off in search of food and medicines. They had never seen anything like what happened in Amayapampa: "it was the first time that we saw so many soldiers" and "bullets fell like hailstones," one of them said. The women were so afraid that they "could not sleep and had nightmares" and were convinced that the government was promoting a "psychological war" against the population.[27]

The day after the attack in Amayapampa, a military force in eight caiman tanks tried to pass by Llallagua on its way to Amayapampa and Capasirca. The entire population of Llallagua, however, had blocked the road. The military attacked the population of Llallagua to break the blockade – two people died and many were wounded. Ironically, this happened on "Miners' Day." In fact, December 21 was a date that commemorated the Miners' Massacre of 1942, when the Bolivian government defended the interests of Simón Patiño, one of Bolivia's former "tin barons" (Radio Pío XII 1997: 145).

Immediately after the December 21 attack a negotiation commission was formed by a large number of unions and human rights organizations, with the task of stopping the military entering Capasirca. Although the negotiation commission was successful, the police officers initiated a "psychological war" against its members. The military filmed and took pictures with the intention of intimidating commission members. The conflict ended on December 22 with the Pacification Agreement, which stipulated the removal of the combined military–police forces from the vicinity of the mines, recognition of the right of Northern Potosí to receive a portion of taxes and royalties for the exploitation of natural resources, compensation for the families of the people who died in the attack, and the return of the mines to Vista Gold Corporation (Radio Pío XII 1997: 146).

The internationalization of the conflict and other developments

During those three days that shocked Northern Potosí, two key actors entered the conflict: Radio Pío XII and the Bolivian Permanent Assembly for Human Rights (APDHB – *Asamblea Permanente por los Derechos Humanos de Bolivia*), and both would play a fundamental role in raising international awareness of the conflict. Radio Pío XII was the only media outlet to inform the region and other countries about the killing of miners and *pueblos originarios*. As a result, President Sánchez de Lozada received numerous letters from abroad calling for an end to the aggression and respect for freedom of the press. The government responded by accusing Father Roberto Durrete, Director of the radio, and other journalists who worked for Radio Pío XII of responsibility for the conflict and of forming part of the resistance against Vista Gold Corporation. The government initiated a campaign to discredit the radio station and its director (Radio Pío XII 1997: 149).

The Bolivian Permanent Assembly for Human Rights (APDHB) denounced the conflict and how the government had created an imaginary terrorist movement. At the end of January 1997 the President of the APDHB, Waldo Albarracín, was kidnapped by the police as he approached a taxi in front of his house. The police tried to make the abduction seem like the act of a terrorist group. It appears, moreover, that the police originally had "orders from above" to assassinate Albarracín, but those orders were changed and, after being tortured, the APDHB President was taken to a police clinic. By this time, however, many human rights organizations from around the world – including Amnesty International, the International Federation for Human Rights, the International Federation of Christians for the Abolition of Torture (FACAT), the Andean Commission of Lawyers, the Lawyer Committee for Human Rights and Washington Office on Latin America (WOLA) among others – had begun to place growing pressure on the government to stop the violation of human rights (APDHB 1998: 70–71).

President Sánchez de Lozada responded by dismissing General Willy Arriaza, but at the same time he guaranteed impunity to all those responsible for the incidents (APDHB 1998: 36). In a very clever move, the President invited the Inter-American Commission for Human Rights of the Organization of American States (from now on the OAS Commission) to investigate the conflict, including the government's claim that what it had been doing was attacking a terrorist group (APDHB 1998: 72). Between April 7 and 11, 1997, the OAS Commission sent a technical team of experts on criminal law to visit the mines and interview all the actors involved in the conflict. It issued its final report in August 1997.

A two-tiered human rights system

The Organization of American States Commission (OAS) report agreed with the Bolivian Permanent Assembly for Human Rights (APDHB) report with respect to the narration of the testimonies of the miners and rural communities. However, the analyses and conclusions of the two reports differed widely. The OAS Commission began by noting that it did not have the competence or authority to establish individual responsibilities. It also placed heavy emphasis on the illegal takeover of Amayapampa and Capasirca, but failed to analyze what had provoked the miners to occupy the mines. Although the OAS Commission met with the manager of Da Capo Resources/Vista Gold, there was no word in its sixty-six-page report about the illegal conduct and abuses of the company, the very activities that were at the core of the conflict and violence.

In the end, the OAS Commission report's conclusions whitewashed the government's role in the December killings. Although it did not support government claims about terrorism, it nevertheless rationalized most of the government's actions. Specifically, the report concluded that, from the point of view of international law, the use of public force by constitutional governments to maintain order is legitimate (APDHB 1998: 77; OAS Report 1997: 62–64). Moreover, it found that the high authorities of the Bolivian state were not involved in giving orders and could not be held responsible for the dead and wounded; after all, it argued, the government of Bolivia itself had invited the Commission to investigate the events that took place in Northern Potosí. Even more outrageously, the Commission indicated that during its stay in Bolivia its members found no evidence that the government had ordered the repression in Amayapampa, Capasirca and Llallagua. According to the report, the only responsibility of the state in the matter rested in investigating the conduct of the military and police officers actually involved in the operation; and the Commission recommended that the state compensate the victims' families, improve socio-economic development programs in the area, and increase the monitoring of work practices to ensure that labor legislation was respected. The report ended by reaffirming the democratic nature of the government and stating that no systematic violations of human rights had occurred in the country.

The Bolivian Permanent Assembly for Human Rights (APDHB) report countered with a stern rebuke of the OAS Commission. In contrast to the OAS document, the Permanent Assembly's own report, issued a year later, argued that it was necessary to track down and make accountable all those responsible for the massacre so that justice could be seen and done. Its report listed twelve people who should be investigated, starting with the President of the country, members of government ministries, and high-ranking military and police officers (APDHB 1998: 79). For the APDHB, the root of the conflict could be traced to the lack of consultation with the people of Amayapampa and Capasirca when the mines changed ownership. In fact, it may be argued that Da Capo Resources violated the ILO Convention 169 concerning indigenous peoples, which states (Article 7) that the communities:

> have the right to decide their own priorities for the process of development as it affects their lives, beliefs, institutions and spiritual well-being and the lands they occupy or otherwise use, and to exercise control, to the extent possible, over their own economic, social and cultural development. In addition, they shall participate in the formulation, implementation and evaluation of plans and programmes for national and regional development which may affect them directly.[28]

The Bolivian Permanent Assembly for Human Rights (APDHB) also highlighted the violation of human rights in the context of globalization and criticized the

OAS for giving the international community a false image of the Bolivian government, a regime that the Permanent Assembly considered "anti-democratic and anti-constitutional" (1998: 9). The conflict of Amayapampa and Capasirca thus brought to light the existence of a two-tiered human rights system: one tier responded to transnational corporations and the competition state in their joint bid to impose a neo-liberal economic model; the other to the rights and needs of Bolivia's people.

Situation in Amayapampa as of mid-2003

The members of the Amayapampa community remained in a difficult situation over the following years. The OAS Commission did not return to Northern Potosí to make sure that its recommendations were followed up by the government and the mining company. The enterprise did not compensate the families of the dead or those wounded in the "Christmas Massacre" of 1996. Instead, for each dead person the government paid US$13,000 to the families and US$6,500 for each of the wounded. In the interim, the company changed its name from Vista Gold Corporation to *Minera Nueva Vista S.A.* (MNV) and, as of mid-2003, put off any start-up production or investment in technical equipment. From April 1998 to April 1999, *Minera Nueva Vista S.A.* paid a subsistence bonus of US$26 per month to some of the unemployed workers and granted permission to the miners to earn additional income by collecting minerals in the mines. The company argued that it is not likely to start operations for another ten years owing to the low international price of gold.[29] After seven years without jobs, and with the prospect of having little or no income for many years to come, members of the local population began to try to negotiate other solutions with the company.

The terms of those negotiations differed according to the richness of the mineral deposits in each of the mines. Capasirca has less gold than Amayapampa; therefore it was easier for its miners to reach a favorable agreement. Capasirca miners organized themselves into a cooperative and proposed to buy the mine from *Minera Nueva Vista S.A.* and pay the company in gold; the company accepted that proposal. When the Amayapampa miners made the same proposal the company said that cooperatives were not effective and that it would be better if miners organized into a corporation that encompassed all inhabitants of the region, including the *ayllus* or rural communities. *Minera Nueva Vista S.A.* would retain ownership and then rent the mine to the people of Amayapampa. The company argued that this was a "fairer" arrangement than what they characterized as "the everyday illegal appropriation of gold by the miners."

On July 31, 2002, the population of Amayapampa formed the *Empresa Minera de Amayapampa S.A. (EMASA)* and proposed a ten-year rental agreement to *Minera Nueva Vista*, but the company would only agree to a five-year contract. EMASA, formed by 230 of the 250 miners in Amayapampa, would be responsible for improving conditions, equipping the mine and financing all the costs of production. In the first two years EMASA would pay the equivalent of

300 grams of gold per month in US dollars to the company, and in the last three years of the contract the payment would double. Meanwhile, the company would only contribute $1,000 – the contract did not clarify whether these were Bolivianos or US dollars – to cover the cost of medicines and the salaries of a nurse and teachers.[30]

The main problem the Amayapampa miners faced was that they owned an enterprise, EMASA, but lacked the start-up capital to make it work. They had a name but no funding, and feared they would not be able to meet the rental payments. In addition to financing, the miners needed new and modern equipment, and technical assistance. Moreover, while they intended to export the gold they produced, they did not know how to go about doing so. They also expressed concerns about the prospects for the community's widows and their children – people who have no jobs or protection. The communities needed a high school and scholarships for their teenagers to continue with technical or university studies. The miners also wrote of intimidation by the company personnel – in fact, of "terror" tactics – and of the need for guarantees for freedom of expression and the defense of human rights and natural resources.

The experience of these communities makes clear that development projects that depend on world market participation by producers and states essentially transfer the risks from the global economy to the workers and communities of the local economy. Transnational mining corporations can afford to sit on their investments, perhaps for ten years or more or until the prices of the minerals rise, stalling much-needed local investment and production. Meanwhile, "those poor who walk on gold" go unemployed, hungry, and suffer abuses of all kinds at the hands of the corporate managers and the state. In effect, local actors lack bargaining power and thus options. Indeed, the people whose lives were changed forever by the 1996 killings, including the many wounded, are still waiting for social justice and economic opportunity.

In conclusion, the implementation of the "new mining," as a poverty reduction strategy designed by the World Bank, has had the opposite effect, increasing the gap between the rich and the poor and leading to corruption and a systematic violation of human rights. The World Bank argued that corporate-led mining projects would benefit developing nations through an increase in tax income and the creation of jobs. However, the competition for foreign direct investment has forced governments to reduce taxes – even to go so far as to forge concession documents to declare an amount paid that was lower than the real cost of the mines, to help the company avoid higher taxes.

As for the creation of jobs for mine workers, the positions never amount to more than 200 or 400 intermittent jobs that depend on the price of gold in the international market. When the price of the mineral is low, workers are dismissed from their jobs; when it increases, workers are rehired. The year 1996 was a key time in which gold-producing transnational mining corporations began installing new operations in the Americas, with the number of active corporations increasing year after year. However, with the low price of gold since then, workers have been unemployed for years; meanwhile, the corporations have received financing from multilateral banks, they have been insured against risks and their managers have received their monthly salaries. If mine workers protest, they are considered subversives or terrorists and are intimidated and repressed. Indeed, the 1996 repression in Bolivia demonstrates very clearly how a combination of the competition state and international organizations turned democracy into a façade, empowering an autocratic alliance that undercut liberal democracy through a new constitutional and legal architecture. In this new architecture protesters are terrorists, state murder is justifiable self-defense and unethical activities are law.

The next chapter will discuss a case study also based in Northern Potosí but one that involved the displacement of an indigenous community by a transantional mining corporation.

6   Multilateralism, population displacement and resettlement in San Cristóbal silver mines

This chapter offers a detailed account of mining and displacement in Old San Cristóbal, Bolivia. It refers to the relationship between global multilateralism and global and local forces' induced displacement; and it is a story about the ethically questionable practices of compensatory displacement in the face of valued beliefs and traditions that are threatened once displacement commences. This story is historically located in the third neo-liberal period addressed in this book: the new millennium and the global experiments with "poverty reduction."

The Old San Cristóbal was a town located in the Bolivian Andes at 4,200 meters above sea level, in the Northern Potosí region and close to the Chilean border. It was built at the turn of the seventeenth century by the Spanish conquerors. In 1998, Apex Silver Mines, an American transnational mining corporation (TMC) with its headquarters in the Cayman Islands, discovered that the Old San Cristóbal had the largest open pit silver and zinc deposits in the world. Not surprisingly, Apex was keen to get the concession for the mine. The main obstacle to the project was that the Old Town sat atop the minerals and was between two silver mountains, the *Jayulla* and the *Tesorera*. As a solution, Apex Silver Mines, supported by multilateral financial institutions, initiated negotiations with the people of San Cristóbal in order to relocate the town and start with the exploration phase. After complicated negotiations, the company built a New San Cristóbal, where the people who were displaced from the Old Town were resettled in 1999. When research was conducted in the New San Cristóbal in the summer of 2000, much dissent was sensed among many of the population regarding the displacement resettlement project.

This chapter will argue that this new mining project is based on a socially unsustainable plan. This plan envisages the full proletarianization of indigenous communities, which, for many, will lead to their alienation from their deeply rooted and meaning-giving environment and from other peoples with whom they ecologically, socially and economically interact. This plan is likely to cause the breakdown of the complex reciprocal relationship within the circulation of labor and production which has been culturally cemented through kinship ties and within their cosmology, or religion. Meanwhile, the mega-projects replace the traditional livelihood of indigenous peoples by offering jobs in the mines until the minerals are extracted – generally mines have a life expectancy of about seventeen years. However, the jobs are dependent upon the price of the minerals in the international market. This means that in some cases miners did not have jobs, salaries or a social insurance structure for many years and, once the project comes to an end, they will be unemployed and without the previous kinship ties embedded in the "vertical control of multiple ecological zones", which permitted the social reproduction of the *ayllu* or kinship group. Such processes within this case study demand that we assess the normative aims driving the projects that cause development-induced displacement (DID) and the model put forward to ameliorate it, the World Bank's Impoverishment Risk and Livelihood Reconstruction (IRLR) model.

Research for this paper in Bolivia was conducted in the summer of 2000 and interviews were carried out with people in San Cristóbal from different gender and age groups as well as with members of the transnational mining corporations, non-governmental organizations (NGOs), academics and human rights activists. This information is complemented by documents related to the negotiation process between Apex Silver Mines and the community, newspaper articles and internet resources. Hence, this chapter starts by critically analyzing the Impoverishment Risk and Livelihood Reconstruction model, the interpenetration of global/local forces, how the community described their everyday life in the Old San Cristóbal, the negotiation process between the community and the transnational mining corporation, and finally addresses how the community was resettled in the New San Cristóbal.

The Impoverishment Risk and Livelihood Reconstruction (IRLR) model

The now standard model for development-induced displacement is the Impoverishment Risk and Livelihood Reconstruction model (IRLR), designed by Michael Cernea, the Senior Advisor for Sociology and Social Policy at the World Bank. This model acknowledges that it is necessary to solve the problems of population displacement and impoverishment inherent in development, and posits a "problem-solving" theory based on comparisons of the same variables across cultures, countries and temporality. Cernea's model highlights eight possible intertwined risks that lead to impoverishment and offers recommendations for their reversal. These risks include: landlessness, a loss of access to common property, homelessness, joblessness, food insecurity, marginalization, increased morbidity and social dis-articulation. According to the author, minimizing these risks requires setting up a more equitable resettlement plan that assures land property, shelter programs, employment, food production and "community reconstruction and host–resettler integrative strategies" (Cernea 1995a: 251–253; 1997: 1572–1575).

Hackenberg (1999: 440) claims that the Impoverishment Risk and Livelihood Reconstruction model's main objectives are to incorporate the "fallouts of globalization" into the global economy, while one of Cernea's clearly stated aims is to halt impoverishment in order to avoid conflict (Cernea 1995a). Even though

Cernea recognizes that between 1985 and 1995 around eighty and ninety million people were displaced by hydropower and irrigation dams and urban development (including transportation infrastructure) alone, every year a new cohort of about ten million people become displaced (Cernea 1995b: 92), and that the number of internally displaced people (IDPs) has already surpassed the number of refugees from wars and natural disasters (Cernea 1997: 1570), he still maintains that displacement-inducing development projects should continue because development is indispensable for national socio-economic development (Cernea 1995b). In fact, the Impoverishment Risk and Livelihood Reconstruction model features prominently in the World Bank's operational directive 4.12 on Involuntary Resettlement, which was recommended for approval by James Wolfensohn (President of the World Bank) on September 28, 2001, though he also considered that a review would be necessary after a period of two years from the implementation of the policy.

The Impoverishment Risk and Livelihood Reconstruction model is presented as a critique of previously dominant neo-classical perspectives on development-induced displacement and it is saturated in an ideological discourse or *trasformismo* aimed at legitimating its ends. It contains ubiquitous phrases like "development from below," "getting ahead collectively" and "putting people first," appearing as more rhetorical than substantial when the model is actually used. In practice, however, the Impoverishment Risk and Livelihood Reconstruction model raises few serious questions about the institutions that construct mega-development projects or about the projects that produce population displacement. In methodologically comparing the same variables across cultures, countries and time periods in a search for what is universal regardless of different historical and geographical contexts within which people are set, the effect of the model appears to erase difference or cultural identity on behalf of homogeneity. If one of its main objectives is to avoid conflict between the communities affected by development projects and transnational corporations (TNCs) by anticipating and averting risks, or by making slight reforms, it is a model inimical to the production of fundamental change that would acknowledge the demands coming from the displaced themselves.

Finally, despite the avoidance of the eight risks detected by the Impoverishment Risk and Livelihood Reconstruction model, this hardly constitutes equity, let alone equal exchange. Transnational corporations receive millions of dollars from the multilateral financial institutions that fund them, insure themselves against risks and directly benefit from the natural resources they extract. Yet, even in the best of scenarios, the displaced populations may only be compensated for their material losses, and what can really compensate them for the socio-cultural dislocation they have experienced? The Impoverishment Risk and Livelihood Reconstruction model, far from being a "development from below" model, appears to put the interests of transnational corporations first, and then reconciles these with those of those displaced afterwards, reworking the latest new progressive vocabulary into conventional modernization theory that adroitly seeks to co-opt and appease critics.

Within the context of this case study, the Impoverishment Risk and Livelihood Reconstruction model will be analyzed from an ethno-feminist international political economy (IPE) framework. This framework draws from
neo-Gramscian and feminist IPE perspectives and Andean anthropology, and
will subject the Impoverishment Risk and Livelihood Reconstruction model to
three levels of critical analysis: the social construction of neo-liberalism at the
level of the multilateral institutions, or the *meso-level*; the *macro-economic* policies recommended by neo-liberals to developing countries; and through their
implementation and impact at the *micro-level*, with specific focus on its differen-
tial impact upon gender and ethnic relations. Accordingly, the focus is on agency
from both above and below, using a method that combines the shifting demands
on structures of the world order introduced by multilateral organizations since
the 1980s with ethnographic research analyzing how the affected communities
perceived and responded to the imposed changes. This combined methodology
will allow us to move from the more abstract global perspective to a more
detailed one that, hopefully, reflects people's own voices.

Articulating spaces: Apex Silver Mines Limited

With a tax haven address in the Cayman Islands, Apex Silver Mines Ltd. from
Denver, Colorado controls one of the world's largest portfolios of silver properties,[1] located mainly in Mexico and South America. In 1996, after conducting
exploratory work around San Cristóbal, Mintec, a Bolivian exploration company
confirmed that San Cristóbal had silver both underneath it and in the two mountains on either side of the town, the Jayulla and the Tesorera.[2] Both mountains
are the product of a volcanic eruption eight million years ago, with the crater
holding the main deposits measuring over an area of about 7.5 kilometers. It was
further estimated that proven and probable reserves contained 470 million
ounces of silver, 8.8 billion pounds of zinc and 3.1 billion pounds of lead.[3] These
data make San Cristóbal one of the world's largest silver and zinc deposits, and
the largest of the open silver pits. However, according to the company, "nine
major areas located in the vicinity of the crater, which are not included in current
reserve and resource estimates, have the potential to more than double the ore
body size."[4] This led Mark Lettes, the TMC's Vice-president and Chief Financial Officer, to declare that "This development clearly reaffirms that our flagship
mine is one of the most attractive and exciting projects in the world today."[5]

Mintec's geological study was complemented with two others studies. The
first study focused on regional issues, and the second on the silver price on world
stock markets. For the first study, Apex contracted Knight Piesold, an environmental consultant company (whose major clients are mining and oil companies)
to conduct, together with Bolivian consultants, socio-economic and ethnological-
archeological studies, and a study on the region's water, flora and fauna
resources. The second study, concerning the stock market, indicated that in the
1980s there was no interest in silver and the world stock of silver fell. This
meant that the decrease of the silver stocks would eventually raise the price of

silver in the international market during the next twenty years as demand out-stripped supply. Because of this exceptional situation, Apex decided to buy the concession for the mine and opened a subsidiary in Bolivia, Andean Silver Corporation (ASC Bolivia LDC), which later on changed its name to *Minera San Cristóbal S.A.* The company planned to start with the exploitation of the mine in 2002, estimating that the mine would have between seventeen and twenty years of life.[6]

Estimating costs and searching for funding

After completing these studies, the company initiated a domestic and international campaign to obtain investment sources of funding, much of it from top shareholders who also sought to increase exports. In fact, two multilateral funding agencies, the International Finance Corporation (IFC) and the *Corporación Andina de Fomento* (Andean Corporation for Promotion-CAF),[7] would work together with Barclays Capital and Deutsche Bank Securities Inc. to develop multilateral financing for San Cristóbal.[8]

Apex's significance for the new regime of Bolivia's political economy and its centrality as an actor in displacement may be gleaned from its estimated direct investments as US$520 million, US$460 million in the construction of the mine and US$60 million for a road to the Pacific Ocean for the export of the minerals, and its indirect investments as US$190 million. San Cristóbal alone will consume 75 megawatts in electricity, 56,000 liters of diesel per day, 4,500 liters of gas per day and 38,500 tons of lime per year. The Apex calculated an investment of US$7 million for the construction of a New San Cristóbal, of which US$1.5 million alone was set aside for the cost of moving the Christian temple from the old to the new town.[9] In 1999 mining represented 45 percent of Bolivia's GDP, of which Potosí was the major contributor, and the estimates for the mining sector percentage for the 2002 start-up[10] for San Cristóbal would be enormous. The estimated total revenue from exports from San Cristóbal was to be US$200 million per year, adding up to a total of US$3.7 billion over a period of eighteen years. This represented 40 percent of the mining exports in 1999 and would increase the exports of silver by 500 percent, lead by 300 percent and zinc by 100 percent.[11] Zinc was the main mining product exported by Bolivia in 1999, and Apex Silver Mines together with the Bolivian *Compañía Minera del Sur* (COMSUR)[12] planned the construction of a zinc refinery in Potosí, which would permit the export of value-added zinc. Bethlehem Steel Corporation had already agreed to buy all zinc ingots from them.[13] Economically, this would seem to be the perfect business.

A "social" cost-benefit analysis

Besides the economic impact of San Cristóbal, Apex and the government promoted the social benefits that the project would represent for Potosí and for the nation as a whole, particularly with the income generated by taxes and the generation of jobs, which would make San Cristóbal a "sustainable" development project. The total revenue from taxes was estimated to be US$675 million for the nation and US$12 million per year – 216 million for eighteen years – for Potosí,[14] which, according to President Hugo Banzer (1997–2002), would be reinvested in social programs.[15] The President also mentioned that the project would generate 3,000 jobs during the investment phase and about 600 stable jobs during the operational phase,[16] representing salaries worth US$10 million per year.[17] Thus, the San Cristóbal project was presented by both the company and the "competition state" as the engine of reactivation for the mining industry and also the Bolivian economy as a whole. However, the rosy picture presented by the TMC–state association regarding the social effects requires closer attention.

In fact, coincident to this information being released to the press, the government launched three new decrees; two of them tax incentives for TMCs, and especially implemented to favor Apex Silver Mines Ltd. and its San Cristóbal project. The first tax incentive – Law 25493/99 – considered that all infrastructural investment carried out by the TMCs would be tax deductible.[18] This means that the US$60 million road to the Pacific planned to be built for the export of minerals will be paid for by all Bolivians. The second tax incentive referred to the exemption from taxes for imports of machinery related to the construction of roads.[19] The third decree was directed to the small mining and mining cooperatives and established that the state would sell them all the equipment and machinery of COMIBOL, which would represent an income of between US$5 and 10 million for the government.[20] This equipment, of course, was obsolete. Thus, it was clear that the government discriminated in favor of the transnational enterprises.

Regarding the creation of 3,000 jobs during the investment phase and 600 stable jobs during the operation phase, it should be noted that the stable jobs for people of San Cristóbal during both phases will not amount to more than 400 to 600 openings. The rest of the jobs will go to foreign employees such as engineers, geologists, technicians, truck drivers and cooks involved in either building the plant and its surroundings or providing other types of services required in the mine.[21] One of the main characteristics of the "new mining" is that it is capital intensive and therefore needs very few employees.

It should be added that Apex Silver Mines Ltd. has its address in the tax haven of the Cayman Islands and that about 60 percent of money laundering that is taking place in the world comes from taxes (Palan 1996; Strange 1998). Tax havens are therefore one of the main generators of inequality on a world scale. In addition, though the mine should have initiated its operation sometime in 2002, the operation has been postponed until the price of silver rises, and until shareholders receive higher dividends.[22] Evidently, the ones who pay the costs for this delay are the workers, since many had moved to the New San Cristóbal in 1999 and are still waiting to work in the mines.

In sum, the evidence suggests that the majority of the population does not benefit from the mega-development projects that Cernea considers "indispensable for socioeconomic development" (Cernea 1995 UNESCO), and many suffer from displacement as a result. Such projects are only indispensable for speculative transnational elites – local and global – whose power is anchored in the competition state and multilateral organizations, particularly the "twin sisters": the World Bank and International Monetary Fund.

The everyday life in the Old San Cristóbal

Before analyzing the impact of international laws and policies in San Cristóbal, it is necessary to pay attention to the everyday life of its inhabitants, how people organized their lives before the negotiations with Andean Silver Corporation (ASC Bolivia LDC, Apex Silver Mines' subsidiary). It is precisely in the "commonplace world of everyday experience … where conflicts of interests are actually experienced and where change is most widely felt" (Sinclair 1999: 10). It is at the level of ethnic identity that we can better perceive how, while the neo-liberal project incorporates new groups into the global political economy, it produces cultural and social disarticulation of these groups at the same time.

This section will be based on unstructured interviews that were conducted in San Cristóbal in the summer of 2000, a year after the population was displaced from the Old to the New Town and two years before the silver mine was expected to start operating. The research methodology utilized here gave people the possibility of freely expressing that sense of cultural anomie produced by a sudden change of structures and rules. One of my informants referred to be living "a moment in which contradictions were emerging, a tragic moment, a dead point between the old and the new." The focus of this section is therefore on the Old San Cristóbal's physical landscape and the link between the social, spatial, religious, cultural, economic and gendered understanding of life of the *Lípez* of Northern Potosí, which is embedded in an alternative local Andean worldview that differs from the rational and unlinear evaluative frameworks derived from western modernities.

The Old San Cristóbal was built in the seventeenth century by the Spanish. In those days, San Cristóbal was the obligatory path between Chile and the *Cerro Rico* of Potosí, the richest silver mine that the Spanish exploited during their colonization of South America. It was seen as the center point of those who "passed by" carrying the silver on mules from the Potosí mines towards Chile. This is why the town was called San Cristóbal. San Cristóbal was the saint who carried Jesus from one side of a Sicilian river to the other and, since then, has been known as the saint of travelers, and today of bus drivers. San Cristóbal is considered the founder of the town.

An infrastructure adapted to the Andean cultural landscape

The Old Town had about 150 families, totaling around 600 inhabitants. The population speaks *Quechua*, the language of the Incas, though most of them also speak Spanish. The town was strategically located between two mountains which protected it from the wind and cold weather. Due to the altitude, the Andes are characterized by an enormous fluctuation of temperature between day and night. During the day the temperatures range between 10 and 14 degrees Celsius, while at night they drop below 0, even down to –35 in winter, especially in the months of July and August. The houses of the Old Town had one or two rooms and the majority of them were built of stone and some on adobe. The roofs were made of straw and the windows were very small and facing east in order to let the sun heat the house and keep it warm during the night. Since there was no electricity, people used either candles or kerosene lamps for lighting. The streets were covered with cobbled paving, preventing dust from entering the houses, and fresh water was available from a central water fountain in the middle of the town. Thus, the infrastructure and location of the town reflected the needs of the population in the context of the harsh Andean climate. The Old Town also had a school with about 300 students and a "Center for Mothers" that had a kitchen, an office, a store-room and an almost completed daycare center. Women met there, especially on Saturdays, when they had adult literacy courses, or they prepared natural medicines, spun, knitted, sewed, embroidered and took care of the children. The New Town built by the TMC for the community of San Cristóbal did not consider the cultural meaning of the type of infrastructure to which the population was accustomed, nor the women's need for a Center for Mothers.

The religious and symbolic world

The Old Town was not only strategically located on climatic terms but also especially on symbolic terms. The symbolic values could be understood as a mix of pre-Columbian and Christian beliefs in which the former predominated. At the center of the town there was a seventeenth-century Christian temple, with stone walls and a straw roof, sustained by cactus wood columns. Inside the temple there were many statues representing Jesus, Mary, a diversity of saints and a huge San Cristóbal. The pulpit was made out of pure silver carved with images from three centuries ago. The paintings on the walls were also of the same period. Surrounding the church was a cemetery. Because, for Andean communities life continues after death, the community wanted both the temple and all the bones in the cemetery to be transported to the New San Cristóbal that was to be built by the TMC. Apex agreed to this.

The company, however, could not understand the community demands to transport certain stones that had an enormous symbolic and sacred value for them and that responded to their traditional religion. These were the *achupalla*, the three giants, the sentinel and the frog. The *achupalla* was a stone at the center of the town. On this stone the Spanish had hung many indigenous people and for three centuries it was where people from San Cristóbal made their *costumbres* or pleas and offerings to their gods. From their gods from above and below they prayed for good harvests, abundant cattle, a house or a truck, but the offerings were also directed towards avoiding the anger of the gods, who according to Harris, could provoke "accidents, illnesses and even death" (2000: 47). They sacrificed llamas, a white one for the gods from above and a black one for the gods from below, and offered them coca leaves and *chicha* – an alcoholic beverage made from fermented corn. In sum, the *achupalla* was much more than a simple stone; according to the informants it was "charged with energy" and, as all other stones, it was a *huaca*, the ancestors converted into stone.

The three giants and the sentinel were the guardians of the town and the silver, and the frog was meant to bring silver and money to the community. An informant from the community mentioned that a truck from the company collided with the sentinel and broke a piece off it. The truck caught fire and the community understood this as anger from the gods for betraying them by moving to another town, creating some panic among the residents. As part of the dualistic vision central to the Andean cosmology, mountains also represent gods, and it will not be easy for the community to see the Jayulla and the Tesorera blown away by the company in order to extract minerals. Mountain peaks are viewed as sacred and powerful places, and are considered the guardians of people's lives. According to Olivia Harris, mountains are simultaneously the symbolic representation of protection and malevolent things. On the one hand, the mountain spirits are "God's sphere" to which belong the sun and the moon and bring fertility; on the other hand, they have an "evil, devil sphere," which is the source of bad weather, disaster and illness (Harris 2000: 47–48).

The Pachakutik, the Ayllu, work and migration to Chile

This fear of the supranatural world is precisely what I could perceive through another informant from the community when he mentioned that their ancestors used to say that "the year 2000 would see the end of the world, that there was going to be a lot of *plata* (Spanish word that means both money and silver) but no food." The Andean notion of the end of the world, or the *Pachakutik*, refers to a cataclysm that reverses the notion of space and time, the transition from one era to another (Montes Ruiz 1999: 453). What the informant perceived was a shift from a subsistence economy which meant food security for the *ayllu* – group united through kinship ties – to a market economy, one in which food sovereignty and the social reproduction of the *ayllu* was at stake. However, this does not mean that the people of San Cristóbal were not previously linked to the market economy; it just means that their incorporation into it was not complete and that this mixed economic system, or what Harris calls the "ethnic economy," was crucial for the human security of the group.[23]

The subsistence economy of the Andean communities of Northern Potosí had their roots in the pre-Hispanic, territorially based large kinship grouping known as the *ayllu* (Albó *et al.* 1990: 43).[24] The *ayllu* was a territorial group that connected different ecological zones, tied together through endogamous marriages (Harris 2000: 19). In the case of San Cristóbal, it connected just two regions, the *puna* or highland – located at 4,200 meters above sea level – to the valley – located between 1,200 to 3,600 metres above sea level. This connection was conducted through migratory movements between the *puna* and the valleys in which products from each region were bartered, completing the diet of the *ayllu* and strengthening the social relations embedded in it.

In the Old San Cristóbal region, each family had about 15 to 20 hectares of land – located about an hour and a half from San Cristóbal – but cultivated only one hectare per year. Every year they rotated to a different hectare because the soil is very poor in the highlands and nothing would grow in the same plot for two consecutive years. Generally the utilized plots were left fallow for about eight years. They grew quinoa, potatoes, onions, carrots, lettuce, parsley, barley, wheat and broad beans. They herded llamas – each family had about 100 to 180 llamas – and also sheep and lambs. At the household level, both men and women took care of the crops and the cattle, and the children helped them when they were not at school.

However, the household also received help from other members of the *ayllu* in two forms of reciprocal relations. According to Harris, one was the *ayni* system which consisted of labor prestations, a system by which a person or family helped another family with their crops and, later on, the latter would return that favor by working on the land of the former. The other social relations were established through the *mink'a* or when labor was reciprocated with produce (Harris 2000: 130). Until some years ago, the elders of San Cristóbal would travel for three months with a caravan of about 180 to 300 llamas to Tarija in the valley. They carried salt, potatoes, meat, quinoa and llama wool, and exchanged them for corn, broad beans, wheat, vegetables and *oca*, a regional tuber. The value of what was exchanged was fixed by tradition and what was compared was the level of generosity rather than the value of the product being transferred (Albó *et al.* 1990: 36). Today, younger people travel by truck.

This subsistence economy was combined with sporadic work, generally three months a year, in the market economy for cash. Before the entrance of Apex Silver Mines Ltd., there were other mining companies in the region that the people of San Cristóbal used to work for. However, the majority of the younger population migrated in search of wage labor, especially to the Chilean border and also to Argentina. Men and women migrated together and took their children with them. In fact, some members of the community mentioned that in certain periods of the year there were only about twenty people left in San Cristóbal and that schools had few students. Those who migrated to Chile went to the mining centers of Calama, Santa Rosa, Antofagasta, Chuquicamata, Quilcha and San Pedro de Atacama. While men worked mainly at the sulphur and copper mines or as construction workers, women worked as domestics or vendors. Those who migrated to Argentina went to Jujuy, Salta, Mendoza and Buenos Aires, both men and women working in agriculture, some men also working in construction. People went to both destination countries with a thirty days' working visa, but they generally extended their stay to about three months. Some people, however, stayed for five to eight years and others even stayed abroad on a permanent basis. Of note was that men's wages in Chile and in Argentina doubled that of women, with men receiving a monthly wage of about 700 to 300 *Bolivianos* for women, about US\$95 to US\$40, respectively.

In sum, the search for distributional and gender equilibrium that existed in the subsistence economy was shaken when the *ayllu* entered into contact, on a temporary basis, with the market economy and the gendered dichotomies that characterize the latter. This illustrates the interdependence between the cash economy and wage labor in the social reproduction of the "ethnic economy."

Gendered hierarchical spaces, Andean dualism and the vertical archipelago

The Andean "ethnic economy" was embedded in a cosmological, dualistic and gendered notion of space. The Andean dualism responds to the "logic of opposed complementarity" or the union of contraries and the constant search for equilibrium and reciprocity (Albó *et al.* 1990: 127). Instead, the logic of capitalism is based on the excision of opposing forces or dichotomies. For example, in Northern Potosí the town was divided into two *moieties* or parts. The upper half, at the right-hand side, was considered hierarchically superior and associated with masculinity. The second or lower half was at the left-hand side and considered inferior and associated with femininity.[25] However, both sides of the town were linked through kinship ties and relations of reciprocity, in which the one considered superior should be more generous in order to reach equilibrium. This hierarchical and gendered concept of space at the community level was reproduced at the inter-community level.

In the case of the Old San Cristóbal, the *puna* or highland and Tarija in the valley were the two "vertical archipelagos" or physical landscapes united through kinship ties and a reciprocal circulation of labor and produce. Because the highlands were considered superior, people living there were expected be more generous than the ones in the valley in order to restore the equilibrium. This generates good social relations and provides a more complete diet through products of both the highlands and valleys. These practices have proved a millenarian strategy for survival in very harsh environments; they may be seen as illustrations of sustainable development created from below. Gender relations, although cosmologically unequal, were nevertheless complementary through kinship networks and the economic and public work done at the community and inter-community levels.

Politics at both community and inter-community levels consisted of a rotative structure by which the authority changed every single year and "true leadership was only granted to those who served their community and treated its people with care and respect" (Astvaldsson 2000: 164). In sum, when a transnational mining corporation displaces people to a new town and does not understand the culture of that community, negative consequences ensue. Just a simple example: by allocating a new house on the left side of the New Town to someone belonging to a higher hierarchy that had previously lived on the right side of the town will subvert ancestral power relations, producing fissures at all levels of the community. As has happened in other parts of the world where people withdrew to their own cultural identity to defend themselves against the homogenization of culture pushed forward by the transnational capitalist class and multilateral organizations, in San Cristóbal, the introduction of a new economy and new social relations of production can lead to a cultural resistance to modernity, to what Gilberto Pauwels called a "process of re-ethnification" (1996: 5).

The asymmetric negotiation process

The direct negotiation process by which the community of San Cristóbal agreed to be displaced to a New Town to permit the exploitation of the mine linked only two actors: Apex Silver Mines Ltd. and the community of San Cristóbal. Neither wanted the interference of NGOs or regional authorities. This section will focus on the collision between two different types of knowledge and values, the reasons why the community decided to negotiate, the generational conflict this decision produced in San Cristóbal, and finally the agreement that was reached on June 9, 1999.

The encounter between Western and Andean knowledge and values

In this encounter, two different kinds of knowledge and values entered into a very complex and asymmetric dialog. On the one hand, the company possessed a rational and objectified knowledge, where development meant progress and modernization. This was a progress that could only be achieved through an association with the state, transnational corporations and multilateral organizations, which provided the information, connections, investments, and economic and political insurance to the mega-projects. For the transnational mining corporation the silver mountains meant a fast and secure path to wealth, and reaching an agreement with the community of San Cristóbal meant a close and final contract that permitted the exploitation of the mines.

On the other hand, the community's knowledge was characterized by a "permanent subjective and personal relation with nature and a constant tendency to maintain the relationship of the parts with the whole ... the Andean knowledge is based on the valoration of nature and the role of men within the cosmic order" (Albó *et al.* 1990: 137–138). In fact, instead of being associated with the state and multilateral agencies, the community was connected to nature, other human beings and the cosmos. Moreover, mountain peaks such as El Jayulla – male – and La Tesorera – female – formed part of the lower cosmos and were considered the guardians of community life. These guardians represented fertility and – like all the other Andean gods – could be both protectors or, if betrayed, bring disgrace in the form of catastrophes (e.g., earthquakes, fire, thunder, etc.), illness, accidents or even death (Harris 2000: 47). If we add that these mountains contain silver and silver is associated with the moon, the wife to the sun, who belongs to the upper domain of the cosmos (Harris 2000: 193), we can therefore understand that chopping into silver mountains feels like an amputation from nature and the cosmological order, a breakup of the individual and collective identity.[26] For the community, reaching an agreement with the company was not a closed contract because for the community negotiations were considered an ongoing process of always trying to reach an equilibrium between two opposing forces.

Reasons why the community decided to negotiate and the enterprise's proposal

The community of San Cristóbal decided to enter into negotiation with the enterprise owing to a combination of external and internal factors. The external factor that was always present was the fear of conflict, especially since the "Christmas Massacre" in the Amayapampa and Capasirca mines (see Chapter 5). Since then, the government was so heavily criticized that it remained outside the negotiation process with the communities, and the enterprises that wanted to invest in Bolivia understood that they were supposed to somehow compensate the communities in order to avoid conflict and be able to continue with the exploitation of mineral resources. Both Apex Silver Mines, through its subsidiary Andean Silver Corporation (ASC Bolivia LDC), and the community of San Cristóbal were clear that they did not want another massacre to take place.

There were five principal internal factors that the community of San Cristóbal mentioned in agreeing to negotiate with the transnational mining corporation. First, the space where the town was located became too small for the community, and there was no possibility to expand owing to the limits imposed by the mountains that surrounded it; some mentioned that long before Apex came to the region (since 1993/1994) the community wanted to move somewhere else. Second was the lack of jobs in the region and because so many members of the community were tired of migrating to either Chile or Argentina, where, especially in the twentieth country, they were subject to racial harassment. Third was the sense that because they confronted a "huge power" that they could not challenge, it made greater sense for the community to negotiate and "take from the company as much as they could" rather than ending up like the miners in Amayapampa and Capasirca. Fourth, people did not possess property titles over the land, allowing the company to boast that although they were not obliged to compensate the community because nobody had property titles over the land, they would do so anyway as a demonstration of their goodwill. Finally, a Foundation was created to promote alternative sustainable developments to that of mining.

The Andean Silver Corporation proposed that the community move about 20 kilometers from the Old Town of San Cristóbal. They promised to build a new, improved and more modern town, give members of the community jobs in the construction of that town and later on in the mine. The enterprise created two divisions to deal with the community; one was a task force in charge of the social relations in the mines and the other was a Foundation that had the task of generating a long-term economic plan independent from the mines and based on renewable resources such as agriculture and livestock. Some people in the community mentioned that having a stable economy would save them from having to migrate to the neighboring countries and children would be able to have continuity in their education.

Thus, the main objective of the Foundation was to prevent the emergence of "ghost towns" – as was the case in traditional mining – once mining ended with the exploitation of the non-renewable resource. The Foundation was formed by five members, two representatives from the community and three from the TMC, and had about US$2 million to spend during the twenty years that the company would be in the region. However, the problem is that the managers of the corporation, prone to a worldview characterized by modern and Western values, understand sustainability as the commodification of agriculture and livestock through micro-enterprises that will incorporate the community into the national and international market. Yet, massive production is not possible in an area that has very specific notions of land tenure. In addition, this project will collide with the traditional relations that the community has with nature, with other human beings at different ecological levels – kinship ties and circulation of labor and produce – and with the cosmos. It is a very difficult task that will need intensive discussion.

A generational debate and the final agreement

Nevertheless, the community started debating the possibility of relocating. The most enthusiastic were the young people, who in their work-travel experience in either Chile or Argentina had contact with a more Western type of life. They liked the company's offer of having new and more modern houses. The elders were against moving elsewhere; they liked their Old Town and did not trust the enterprise. Finally, the community decided to move if it was not opposed by San Cristóbal, the statue in the temple after whom the town was named. They were afraid of San Cristóbal because on one occasion they took him out of the church and strong winds started to blow, which was construed as the saint being angry – the Christian symbol was given the connotations and powers of the traditional Andean religion.

The company asked how they could know if the saint would want to move, the response to which was to visit different cities, visit the virgins in their temples, and then ask the opinion of an indigenous priest, known as the *akia*. The company offered to pay for the tour, at the end of which the final decision depended on the *akia's* response, who read the coca leaves and announced that the saint would *not* be angry if they moved him to another town. The company moved swiftly in order to reach to a written agreement.

On June 9, 1998, the community of San Cristóbal and Andean Silver Corporation signed an agreement stipulating that:

1   Each member of the community that previously had a house in the Old Town would have a larger and more modern house including a dining-room, bathroom and kitchen. Those whose houses measured more than forty-five square meters would have three bedrooms and those whose houses measured

smaller than forty-five square meters would have two bedrooms. Each house would have a terrain of 450 square meters, and would have access to drinking water, connection to a sewer system and electricity. In total, the enterprise offered to build 140 houses. The enterprise would also give sixty plots of 450 square meters with access to drinking water, a sewer system and electricity to the community so that they could distribute them among those who did not have houses.

2   The New Town would have an elementary and secondary school, a government building, a health center, a market, a Catholic church, a hotel, a soccer field, a gymnasium and a cemetery.

3   A Foundation would promote the social, educational and cultural development of the community. The enterprise would donate US$2 million over a period of six years and would conduct fundraising outside the community in order to promote the generation of the following micro-enterprises: the building and administration of a hotel, growing vegetables in solar tents and greenhouses, the production and commercialization of llama meat, wool (of llama, alpaca and sheep), quinoa and garlic. It would also promote tourism and a craft industry, implement a transport system and build a gas station.

The New Town was finished almost a year after the agreement was signed, and witnessed the arrival of the community on June 9, 1999. The negotiation process between two very asymmetrical forces and cultures was possible because of a host of reasons, external and internal to the community, combined in the final decision. It was clear that the traditional "ethnic economy," which had been sustainable for centuries, and even millennia, was feeling vulnerable under market pressures. Many young people in the community wanted a change and an improvement of life, but appeared unaware of the kinds of change or of the impact that dealing with a TMC would have on their lives. They faced an uncertain future despite their reliance upon their religious beliefs for guidance.

Displacement and resettlement in New San Cristóbal: the impact on everyday life

The displacement of the population from the Old Town and resettlement in a New Town by the mega-mining project did not produce the social reintegration of those uprooted as would be expected by the Impoverishment Risk and Livelihood Reconstruction model of population displacement. Instead, the process estranged the population from nature and their sacred location, producing alienation and introducing asymmetries in gender relations. The meaning of alienation here refers to the neo-Gramscian notion that expands upon Marx's ideas. While Marx considered alienation primarily in the sphere of labor and production, Rupert (1993) also incorporated a superstructural dimension to it. In the case of San Cristóbal, displacement produced not only a change in the economic structure but also affected a wide array of ideas within their belief systems, religion, conception of space and time, internal power relations and value system of the population. This process has also dislocated the equilibrium between genders. While some men will become fully proletarianized when the mine starts operating, women will be left with nothing. Having lost their land and the Center for Mothers, they will be relegated to the social reproduction of labor.

Fears, the exodus and the infrastructure of the New Town

On July 9, 1999, the community walked the twenty kilometers from the Old to the New Town carrying the Christian statues of their temple on their shoulders and led by the priest. Community members reported that it felt like an exodus. While the adults walked, the children traveled in a bus; almost all the people were crying. Some members of the community said it was the saddest day of their lives and that they were scared. When they arrived in the new San Cristóbal they thought of it as a strange place. The infrastructure differed widely from the Old Town. Madrid Lara's book on San Cristóbal captures this change very nicely when he compares the two towns as "from the warmth of the *Mallkus* to the cold of the cement." In fact, the Old Town was located between two mountains to protect it from the cold and windy weather. The stone and adobe houses with their straw roofs, ground floors and small windows facing east permitted the sun to warm them and help them maintain their heat. By contrast, the New Town was located on a *pampa* or flat terrain, open to wind and cold. The houses were built on cement and had cement floors, *calamine*, and metal roofs and large glass windows, all materials that retained the cold like freezers, especially at night when the temperature went down to –25/–35 degrees Celsius. People demanded that the company install wood floors to help make the houses warmer. The TMC complied but installed parquet flooring that was too thin and broke easily if not waxed. Women complained that they did not have money to buy the wax. In addition, the new streets were not cobble paved as in the Old Town, and houses became very dusty.

The New Town could be considered an improved version of the Old if we note that it had a better school, a parabolic antenna, sewage system, piped water, electricity and a health center. But appearances can be deceiving. The water in the New Town was not as drinkable as the water they drew from the fountain in the middle of the Old Town. Some said it contained a toxic element called *copagira* while others just said it tasted mostly of salt. The electricity proved hardly beneficial as people did not have money to pay for it; in the end the power was turned on for only two hours a day, from 7 to 9 p.m. As for the health center, it was just an empty building with no equipment, medicines or doctors. Once in a while a nurse came to the town to vaccinate the children. The main conflicts regarding the New Town centered around the fact that the company did not build a new Center for Mothers, which had enormous value for the women and children, and the fact that the traditional division between the two *moieties* was not respected effectively subverted the power relations of the town. Overall, young men and some young women liked the New Town, but the children, the majority of the women and the elders did not. Some of the more disgruntled residents built their traditional adobe ovens outside the new houses and even whole new houses out of adobe. Nevertheless, the location and type of these houses was left to the few members of the community involved, not to the enterprise. They did not know why only a few people were consulted who took the decision to move on behalf of the whole community.

The impact of leaving behind the non-human community: the sacred stones

The displacement of the population from their sacred site is probably the most delicate aspect of the process. Vanden Berg (1999: 271) had already warned about the danger posed by the economic focus of the Impoverishment Risk and Livelihood Reconstruction model and those development projects that compensated religious institutions, such as churches, mosques and temples, but which ignored the importance of traditional religious systems such as sacred stones in a shrine. His case study of the village of Banjiram in northern Nigeria showed that after fourteen years the population continues to suffer for the loss of their patron spirit represented by the stones. As Shettima also shows, even in the best of scenarios, resettlement changed both the means and the relations of production, where leaving behind sacred spots demonstrated how it is impossible to replace those "non-human community aspects such as cultural attributes and belief systems," and whose absence was akin to being "culturally stripped naked" (Shettima 1997: 68). As we saw in the case of San Cristóbal, leaving the mountains and the sacred rocks, the *achupalla*, the three giants, the sentinel and the frog, introduced enormous uncertainty among the people that the gods would get angry and send disgrace to those who betrayed them. Since the displacement the elders of the community have returned to the Old Town on occasion, though it has already been demolished. In the Old Town they weep and mourn its disappearance as if they have lost their souls, the very thing that gave them identity. When this problem was mentioned to the Director of the Foundation and the question was asked why the company would not transport those sacred stones to the New Town, noting that they had an enormous cultural value for the people, he responded in the following technocratic modernist terms:

> What is the value of all that when people are dying of hunger?... Those are existential problems, their importance varies depending on the lenses that one uses to look at them. The question of moving or not moving the stones, although they may have sentimental value ... means investigating how economically feasible it would be. The young people do not care about the stones, the elders yes ... but if the young have already been in Argentina, in Chile, the stones do not have any significance. They want to have a better job, to buy their CD player, even learn to use computers – what all children want – And once they start with the internet, culture goes to hell! So we will have to study the cost of moving those rocks for just four old men that are going to die in two years? Where is the equilibrium?... it is not from one

day to the next that the mentality of an elder can be changed. I am not going to be able to change their way of thinking and, even worse, it is here where the political component enters the game ... because ... those from ... let's say ... people with a Marxist ideology, well, for them it's all about the justice of those that have less against those that have more. So all these issues come up and they come to these towns and continue pressuring. Therefore, they [the community] have to oppose just because of the fact that we [the enterprise] are foreigners and white. Because they are not like us, they have to oppose and put up obstacles. If they offer you 10 it is because it is worth 1,000. You have to ask 1,000 and then that is the difference ... and no, no, no, if they are offering you 10 is because the one advising is saying that you have to ask 1,000 ... but if the man did not have 2 and he is being offered 10, the same thing happens because there is someone pressuring him to say you have to make it 1,000. Thus, they brainwash them. These people are always going to be unsatisfied. It will always be "them against us" they are the enemies and we are the sufferers ... it does not matter how beautiful the school is, how clean the hospital is ... oh no, it is just that I need my little stone.[27]

From his technocratic perspective, the Director of the Foundation appears rational in focusing on the economic costs of moving the sacred stones and equating culture with "sentimental values." He felt himself to be the owner of the absolute "truth" having the right and even the mission to help his inferiors change their backward culture. He also accomplished an adept switch in putting himself in the role of victim, attacked by "Marxist brain washers" and indigenous populations. Typically, however, his professed empathy with those "people dying of hunger" clearly did not extend to re-evaluating the beneficiaries of the proceeds of the mine. The company did conduct some studies about the meaning of the sacred stones but their interpretation was flawed by a purely economic calculus of costs and benefits. Where the company did do a marvelous job was in the transportation and restoration of the eighteenth-century Christian temple that was in the middle of the Old Town – a Western symbol. The people mentioned that when they entered the temple they "felt as if they were in the Old Town" and as if the move to the New Town was "just a bad dream."

Negotiating the agricultural and grazing lands and the loss of food sovereignty

Once the population was displaced to the New Town a second round of negotiations were initiated, this time regarding agricultural and grazing lands located on the hillside of the mountains surrounding the Old Town. Since traditionally the community used to exchange a llama for one hectare of land, the company offered to pay the cost of a llama or 500 *Bolivianos* (US$68) by hectare. The community opposed this offer and demanded 1,200 *Bolivianos* (US$160) for non-irrigated land and 1,700 *Bolivianos* (US$230) for irrigated land. The elders and women, however, did not really want to sell the land because it was their main means of subsistence and independence. They saw land as a permanent and secure source of food, while money was seen as a temporary means of getting food because "it just would not last." As one of the elders mentioned:

> [W]e did not want to agree because up there [Old San Cristóbal] we have plots that although they are not large, every year that we sowed they gave us [food], I have been living and sowing there for eighteen, almost twenty years ... and if I continue planting I will continue having food, but if we compare that with being paid [money] it would not last even a week ... that is why we are demanding to be paid more ... that is how they cheated us ... money is something to look at for a little while.

The company pressured members of the community by saying that they should be aware that they did not have property titles to the land and that the company was being very generous in negotiating a price instead of simply imposing the law, which stipulated that each hectare cost between Bs15 and 20 cents – US$0.2 cents. They finally agreed to sell the land for 1,200–1,700 *Bolivianos* – US$160– US$230. Now the people have to buy food in the market of Uyuni – on a weekly or monthly basis – which is about five hours by bus from the New San Cristóbal. As for the cattle, the people did not lose their sheep, but the llamas cannot adapt to the New Town, in part because there is no grass there, but also because their sense of orientation is accustomed to the Old Town and they tend to go back there.

A utopia: the gendered transition from an ethnic to a neo-liberal economy

The loss of their main means of agricultural production also broke the reciprocal social relations based in the *ayni* and the *mink'a* systems, the equilibrium between genders, and the vertical economy based on inter-community and kinship relations. Young men were incorporated as proletarians in the construction of the New Town, receiving a daily wage of 35 *Bolivianos* – US$5 – and eventually they will work in the mine. To this end, young men were trained to use modern machinery and as mechanics. Many men who had migrated previously to Chile or even Cochabamba and La Paz began returning to San Cristóbal in search of jobs.

Meanwhile, men over the age of 40[28] and all women were excluded from working in the mine. The Foundation was created precisely to provide for these latter groups. Its role was to generate jobs for the elders and the women and to help prevent conflict by either sending in psychologists to detect possible disturbances or grant concessions. The Foundation represented the institutionalization or the mechanism of incorporation of the elders and women into the national capitalist economy on a "full-time basis."

However, the transition from an ethnic to a neo-liberal economy in the New San Cristóbal will be an extremely complex process. It was just starting when the research for this book was conducted. The first issue to consider is that the climate is very harsh, and the extremely saline soils of the *pampa* are unproductive. The geologist director of the Foundation interviewed above considered the attempt to generate sustainable development in the Andes utopian because it was "not profitable." He said, however, that he would work for it even if could only achieve 5 percent of his goals. To this end, the company, along with some members of the community, focused on the creation of micro-enterprises. An agro-industrial and transport enterprise and a gas station, primarily for quinoa and llama meat, were planned that would employ men, and a hotel, tourist enterprise and crafts would employ women.

Regarding the agro-industry, the Director of the Foundation considered that the massive production of quinoa would require tractors, but tractors would not be viable owing to the Andean traditional division of land into small plots and the fact that no one in the community would disturb a plot where the "owner" was absent or had migrated. The production and commercialization of llama meat also ran into difficulties. Although the meat is very lean and does not contain cholesterol there is no market for it, since, due to cultural reasons and prejudice, the middle classes would never eat the same food as the indigenous peasants. Only tourists eat quinoa and llama.

Another experiment has been to build a greenhouse for the elders, but the greenhouse will cost US$40,000 and measures only 90 × 10 meters. Upon completion it will accommodate only four workers, and if they are going to plant lettuce – according to the Director of the Foundation – it would not be "profitable." With regard to a transport enterprise, everybody in the Andes dreams about having a truck, but at this point, without land or food production of their own, what are the peasants going to transport? The gas station is designed to sell gas to the mine, and as such it cannot be considered a sustainable development project. More problematically, the gas station, just like the proposed hotel, would create only a few jobs.

Nor are plans to generate tourism or crafts – that would create jobs for women – really serious economic projects. A mining region is not the most attractive or healthy spot for holidays – especially when cyanide is being used in the extractive process. While crafts might work, there is still the question of who would commercialize it. The Director of the Foundation suggested contacting an NGO to see if they would be interested in promoting the crafts, but few NGOs want to go to such a cold place as San Cristóbal.

Thus, while the Foundation saw its role as utopian, the community of San Cristóbal was feeling that the enterprise was abandoning them. The community felt that they were being offered many things before that remained unfulfilled, and that the company had "convinced them to move," "manipulated them," "put pressure on them to take a fast decision" and even "bought them" by promising jobs, a better town and better living conditions. Moreover, the community felt that their decision involved an "exchange of the minerals for a better life." Thus, the state, the company and the community of San Cristóbal claimed "ownership" of the minerals.

To conclude, the focus of this chapter was on agency from both above and below. It attempted to uncover how the changes in the World Order pushed forward by the neo-liberal development project modified the relationship between elites at the global and local scales. While multilateral agencies provided the information, the funding and risk insurance to transnational mining corporations, they also pressured for structural and superstructural changes at the national level or the inauguration of a new constitutionalism for disciplinary neo-liberalism. Moreover, the state adapted to the demands of global capital and became the articulator of the global and local mining elites through Bolivia's Mining Corporation (COMIBOL), now an administrative body that promotes the formation of joint ventures. All these changes responded to a particular historical conjuncture, the 1986 fall of tin prices in the international market and a new interest in the search for precious metals that has emerged since 1987 and is related to a possible increase of inflation due to an expected oil crisis.

These changes in the structure and superstructure had a strong impact on the social fabric. The privatization of the mines led to the displacement of 30,000 tin miners, who formed the social base of the once strongest Bolivian labor union, the Federation of Mine Workers of Bolivia (FSTMB). It has been a systematic attack against organized labor. The new mining based on precious metals searched for new mines, new spaces and a new type of displacement. In fact, while the former displacement was related to the destruction of the nationalist-populist welfare model and its social base, the new displacement was related to the specific sites where the precious metals required by disciplinary neo-liberalism were located.

This time, transnational mining corporations were trying to incorporate those displaced as workers in the mines. However, only a few of those men – whose ethnic economy was based on subsistence and sporadic work in the mines – will be able to have a job in the mines, since the majority of the workers in the new mining enterprise will be expert technicians coming from abroad. Older men and women will instead be excluded from entering the labor market and will lose the land that provided them with a subsistence economy.

The Impoverishment Risk and Livelihood Reconstruction model claimed to compensate those displaced by development projects through the restoration and amelioration of land, common property, homes, jobs, food, health, social marginalization and social disarticulation that was lost. We have depicted a far more complex reality, one that demands recognition of a specific town's physical landscape, a notion of space, the relationship to the cosmos and nature, kinship ties and a secure system of food production, all of which was embedded in an Andean vision of the "logic of opposed complementarity."

From the exploration of these relationships emerges a simple and obvious point: a compensatory approach cannot solve the problems created by displacement. This approach can never restore culture and identity since these cannot be "priced" and are not interchangeable with money. What is required are critical analyses of the alliances between multilateral institutions, transnational corporations and states, of the relationships of power between global and local forces, and the changes and conflict they produce at the level of everyday life.

Obviously, those in alliance with each other to effect this "development" are hardly so interested. Calling something "development" and invoking its compensatory implications may assuage the guilt of those who promote ethically questionable mega-projects and those who push legal changes that effectively justify theft and atrocities in poor countries. Doing so, however, cannot restore the lives of those displaced. For those questioning the practices of displacement in the name of development, it is in the detail of everyday life where it is possible to detect the fissures in a society and the eventual possible emergence of counter-movements, such that what Polanyi called the "double movement of society" gets mirrored, just as development does at the local and global scales.

7 President Evo Morales Ayma's *Pachakutik*

Re-founding Bolivia as an indigenous nation

The neo-liberal project of the privatization of natural resources found fierce opposition among workers and indigenous peoples. The violent repression of miners and *pueblos originarios* in Amayapampa and Capasirca during the first government of President Sánchez de Lozada (1993–1997 and 2002–2003) was just the tip of the iceberg. Other resource wars have emerged since the Poverty Reduction Strategy Paper entered into effect in Bolivia, such as the Water Wars in Cochabamba and El Alto, and two Gas Wars, in 2003 and 2005 – Bolivia is the second largest gas producer in the Americas, after Venezuela. As mentioned above, the mobilization of October 2003, and the repression and killings of about eighty protesters by military and police forces, led to the fall of President Sánchez de Lozada, who since October 17 of that year was exiled in Miami.

On February 21, 2005, Sánchez de Lozada, his defense minister Carlos Sánchez Berzain and the interior minister Yerko Kukoc were formally charged with genocide by Prosecutor Pedro Gareca in the city of Sucre, while the other thirteen cabinet ministers were charged with "complicity."[1] This fact highlights the inaccurate analysis of the 1997 Organization of American States Commission Report regarding the actions of the ex-President in the Amayapampa and Capasirca conflicts back in 1996, and that many lives could have been saved if, at that time, the Organization of American States would have condemned the authors of the "Christmas Massacre," because it was those same actors that later on became involved in the first Gas War.

Vice-president Carlos Mesa Gisbert (2003–2005), who assumed the presidency following Sánchez de Lozada's exile, sought to solve the Gas War by proposing the Hydrocarbons Law. Yet, his plan did not include the 50 percent royalties for the country requested by indigenous peoples, peasants and miners who, headed by the Aymara *cocalero* leader Evo Morales, now demanded the nationalization of gas and oil.[2] After massive blockades of La Paz – which became known as the second Gas War – on June 6, 2005, the President resigned and the President of the Supreme Court of Justice, Eduardo Rodríguez Veltzé, became the transitional President of Bolivia. Elections were called on December 18 of the same year.[3] Evo Morales won 53.7 percent of the votes in an election in which 84.5 percent of the national electorate cast their votes; Morales was sworn in on January 22, 2006, becoming the second indigenous president in the

Americas.[4] It is argued that President Morales Ayma's re-founding of Bolivia as an indigenous nation may be seen as the beginning of the shift towards a more humane World Order. It aims to demonstrate how Morales has tried to untie the neo-liberal Gordian knot from the bottom up, first at the national scale, then at the regional scale and finally at the global scale.

At the national scale: nationalizing natural resources and redesigning the national constitution

Nationalizing the hydrocarbons

On May 1, 2006, Worker's Day, Morales launched the Presidential Supreme Decree 28701 "Heroes of Chaco"[5] by which, faithful to his platform – which included the nationalization of natural resources and an end to the neo-liberal model – he nationalized Bolivia's hydrocarbons: oil and gas. In his speech "Upside Down World" at the oilfield of San Alberto, in the province of the Bolivian Chaco, Department of Tarija, under the control of Petrobras,[6] the President said:

> The pillage of our natural resources is over [and added that this was] just the beginning, because tomorrow it will be the mines, the forest resources and the land.[7]
>
> We wish to say that our coming to government – as president, ministers and members of parliament that effectively come from the original indigenous peoples – was not because we have come here with vengeance, rather we have come here with the hope of the Bolivian people and the property of the hydrocarbons – the natural gas that passes to the hands of the Bolivian state from this point onward. These resources being under control of the Bolivian people is the solution to our country's economic and social problems. Once we have recovered this natural resource it will generate employment.... I want to tell the Bolivian people that we came to the Palace on the 22nd of January with a fragmented and privatized State, and that with the new Law of the Regulation of the Executive Power (Ley de Ordenamiento del Poder Ejecutivo) we began to nationalize the State and now with this Supreme Decree we are nationalizing the hydrocarbons.[8]

Morales then referred to the Bolivian Army's new role:

> We are also grateful to the Military High Command for sharing and taking upon itself this process of change. If indeed previous governments have used the Armed Forces for the benefit of transnational corporations, the Armed Forces have now united for their country.... Similarly, the National Police force is with us here, with the High Command of this institution participating in, and providing protection for this process of nationalization.[9]

The nationalization of gas and oil affects about twenty transnational corporations, among them Spanish Repsol, British Petroleum (BP), British Gas (BG), the American Exxon Mobil Corporation, French Total and, especially, Brazilian Petrobras,[10] all of which now operate under the control of *Yacimientos Petrolíferos Fiscales Bolivianos* (YPFB – Bolivia's National Oil Company).[11]

Yet, the countries most affected would have been Brazil and Argentina, the main importers of Bolivian gas. Brazil imports twenty-seven million cubic meters of gas – 85 percent of the total gas that the country imports – and Argentina seven million.[12] This is why, three days after the Bolivian nationalization, on May 4, Presidents Morales, Lula from Brazil, Kirchner from Argentina and Chávez from Venezuela met in Puerto Iguazú, Argentina to discuss the question of energy security in South America.[13] Besides the Bolivan nationalization, they also discussed how this could affect the planned mega-gas pipeline that would bridge Venezuela, Brazil and Argentina. This so-called "Southern Gasoduct" would cover 10,000 kilometers and is expected to cost around US$23 billion.[14] In the meeting, Morales made it clear that the neighboring countries will continue to receive Bolivian gas, but at a higher price.[15]

According to Walter Mignolo,[16] this process of nationalization differs from the 1970s nationalist populism in the region, which he considered extremely pernicious; instead he sees in Evo Morales and Hugo Chávez the emergence of a new way of doing politics and economics, which consists of decolonizing the state and the economy as a response to the danger posed by transnational corporations.[17] Although agreeing with Mignolo that this is a distinct way of doing politics and not having doubts about the honesty of President Morales, there are three points worth noting: the distinct meanings of nationalization; the involvement of the Supreme Court of Justice and the Army; and the power of the mechanisms of hegemony at the global scale.

First, in the history of Latin America, nationalization has had two very different meanings whether it involves "compensation" or "expropriation". In the former case, it would mean "reformism," a problem-solving "band-aid" approach that involved payment to the capitalist for what has been appropriated by the state. This means that the state "bought" a company's assets, and by doing so, it maintained the status quo – the capitalist system. Instead, "expropriation" meant the non-payment, the non-recognition of private property and, therefore, the total breakup with the capitalist system – in the Americas this has only taken place in Cuba, in Chile under Allende, and in some specific cases in Central America during the civil wars.

What Evo Morales has proposed is a third meaning of nationalization; in fact, he made it clear that he would not expropriate the companies but would assume "control" over the companies, and that a large percentage of the income formerly appropriated by the transnational corporations would now be transferred to the state, to the people of Bolivia.[18] An analyst, W.T. Whitney Jr., explained this very clearly:

> Foreign companies will transfer 82 percent of their revenues from large fields to Bolivia's state oil companies Yacimientos Petrolíferos Fiscales

Bolivianos (YPFB). They now pay 50 percent, and revenues are expected to increase from $460 million in 2005 to $780 million in 2007. Owners of recently privatized companies will transfer 51 percent ownership to YPFB. If compensation packages and contracts for foreign companies to become service providers do not emerge from upcoming negotiations, the companies will leave Bolivia.[19]

In sum, the state would regulate the distribution of benefits in a more equitable manner. Juan Careaga, ex-minister of finances during the government of Víctor Paz Estenssoro, was also very clear when he said:

> This is not an improvised text [the Supreme Decree], it is very well thought because it does not confiscate anything but the state takes control over all the chain of hydrocarbons ... it allows the enterprises to operate and gives them the option to accept or reject the new rules of the game with a margin of negotiations that would take place during the next 180 days.[20]

This raises the question as to whether this is a new type of Latin American-designed state or a foreign-designed "new managerialist" one, a state that regulates the private sector instead of providing and managing these public goods as the previous corporatist or developmental state used to do.

The second concern is the involvement of the Supreme Court of Justice, the Army and the Police in the process of nationalization – institutions that the Santa Fe II document referred to as elements of what they considered to be "permanent governments" as opposed to the elected "temporary government." The judicial system, the Army and the Police have been modified in many countries in the South since the 1990s, but there are few studies in Bolivia or in Latin America regarding this shift. Yet there is plenty of daily information in the newspapers regarding the pro-market stance of the Courts and it is arguably hard to believe that the Bolivian Army and police forces – as well as that in any country of the region – which since General Barrientos' coup d'état back in 1964 had brutally and systematically repressed workers and miners will all of a sudden be transformed into the people's defenders.

The third concern is the global context, with the current reconstruction of American hegemony and the power exerted through the mechanisms of hegemony, especially the World Bank and IMF and, as demonstrated, the role of *trasformismo* in absorbing the discourse of women and now indigenous peoples – among many other cases – with the objective to neutralize them. How will the United States react to this cautious nationalization without expropriation? Let us remember that expropriations of American enterprises in Latin America and even reformist policies that included the compensation of American property; for example, the 1952 Guatemalan agrarian reform ended with American interventionism.

In Bolivia the nationalization of hydrocarbons affects the US Exxon Mobile Corporation and also Petrobas, which, as mentioned above, is 60 percent

American owned. If this type of nationalization expands to mining, land, forestry and even, as one journalist[21] mentioned, to those partially *capitalizadas* – privatized – enterprises such as energy, water, communications, trains and planes, would Bolivia be able to circumvent the new constitutionalist order at the local, regional and global scales? It seems that, although with many contradictions, Evo Morales found the way to do so.

Changing the neo-liberal constitution and creating a plurinational decolonized state

The constitution of Bolivia was drafted by a Constituent Assembly, an elected body that met for various months in 2007 in the cities of Sucre and Oruro. However, the constitution was the product of many years of difficult dialog among all sectors of society and it was finally approved by 62 percent of the votes in a referendum that took place on January 25, 2009. Two weeks later, President Evo Morales Ayma promulgated the constitution in the city of *El Alto*, stating that with the new constitution Bolivia was "re-founded as a unitary plurinational state" with the aim to institutionalize "communitarian socialism," a system based on the well-being of society as a whole by making wealth a communal affair (Morales, February 7, 2009).

In fact, the Constitution guaranteed the unity, equality and dignity of all women and men, of people who lived in rural and urban areas, of indigenous and Afro-Bolivian populations, and aimed at integrating the *Media Luna* – half moon, the name of the rich secessionist region in the east of the country – into the Bolivian *Luna Llena* – full moon. The constitution, Morales argued, was the result of the consciousness and struggle of social movements, peasants, indigenous peoples, workers, miners, intellectuals, university professors and coca producers, and its ultimate aim was to decolonize Bolivia and to fight against neo-liberalism and imperialism. This was, according to Morales, a "popular, cultural and democratic revolution" in which the Bolivian people have demonstrated its strength, patience and tolerance to peacefully construct a new society (Morales, February 7, 2009). Thus, the constitution represented a pluralist politico-juridical, economic and socio-cultural architecture to build a Bolivia in which many cultures could fit. In this design the Andean "logic of complementary opposition" of the integration of opposing forces – as distinct from Western epistemology based on dichotomies – is constantly present in the constitutional text. The cautious search for consensus with the elite is present in the political, economic and socio-cultural pluralist aspects of the constitution.

Political pluralism was embedded in the administrative, legislative, judicial and electoral machinery of the state. The creation of new ministries such as the Ministry of Autonomy, Cultures and Transparency against Corruption and the establishment of four administrative levels of government, namely departmental, regional (provincial), municipal and originary indigenous and peasant territories, shows some resemblance to liberal constitutions (e.g., multiculturalism and multi-level governance). However, the notion of autonomy (article 4) responds to a long-standing and worldwide indigenous demand. As Van Schaick has advanced, autonomy is the main success of indigenous peoples because it gives them the right of self-determination and self-government, rights incorporated into the 2007 *U.N. Declaration on the Rights of Indigenous Peoples* (Van Schaick 2008: 2–3). It should be added that it allows indigenous peoples to maintain individual and collective rights to the land, manage their renewable resources and maintain their customary practices.

In the legislative arena the objective of Morales was to eliminate the Senate in favor of a unicameral system, but because this would have benefited the MAS, the opposition rejected the proposal and the legislative branch remained intact (Van Schaick 2008: 3). However, a quota increasing the number of indigenous legislators, albeit the opposition, could now be passed. In the electoral turf, the presidential and legislative terms remained over five years but this time a one-term re-election was allowed – previously there was no re-election – and the "segunda vuelta" was installed where no candidate obtained the majority of the votes.[22] According to Van Schaick, Morales sought to obtain two more terms but, in order to achieve the consensus of the opposition, he agreed to just one more term (Van Schaick 2008: 3). Article 258 established popular referendum mechanisms in sensitive issues in international agreements, such as those that dealt with border issues, monetary integration, economic integration or the transfer of institutional rights to supranational institutions. This latter article represented a defense against the many transnational agreements that could lock in adverse laws to Bolivia.

The judicial system included the indigenous community justice at the same level as ordinary justice and a Plurinational Constitutional Tribunal with representatives of both systems. Morales highlighted that with this dual judicial system "something ethical was recuperated, the law left by our ancestors … the *ama sua, ama llulla* and *ama k'ella*" (Morales 2009). With regard to security issues, Bolivia defined itself as a peaceful country that would never declare war on a neighboring country unless it would be in legitimate defense. Only in the latter case would the joined forces of the army and police, "armed by the people and for the people," act to defend the country (Morales 2009). Article 268 reinforces that Bolivia will continue to search for a peaceful solution to regain its coastal territory in the Pacific – territory appropriated by Chile following the War of the Pacific between 1879 and 1884, and which turned Bolivia into a landlocked country. Finally, Morales added that the constitution

> will never allow the installation of foreign military bases, therefore there will be no ambassadors, as in the past, that appointed ministers and threw out ministers; ambassadors of the United States that authorized the entry of planes to the Chimoré airport. This has ended due to the rise of consciousness of the Bolivian people.
>
> (Morales 2009)

Economic pluralism was embedded in the "socio-economic and communitarian model" which included private, public and collective property; all of them guaranteed by the state (Morales 2009). Instead, basic services such as water, sewer systems, electricity, natural gas for domestic consumption, postal services and communication services became the responsibility of the state, as Morales asserted "they are a human right, therefore they will not be a private but a public service" (Morales 2009). According to the results of the referendum, the size of large estates would be restricted to 5,000 hectares starting from the moment the constitution was approved (article 398) – those which were larger than that size before the constitution was promulgated would remain untouched; they would not be expropriated. According to Borón, about half a million hectares of land were transferred to the hands of farmers (Borón 2009: 2).

Renewable and non-renewable natural resources were declared strategic assets and, while forests were considered the exclusive property of indigenous communities, all other natural resources belonged to the Bolivian people on behalf of their collective interest (article 349). Hydrocarbons were a special case and they would remain in the hands of the state, which would be in sole charge of its commercialization (article 359). Finally, coca, the sacred leaf, was considered the cultural patrimony of Bolivia and an important factor of social cohesion (article 384).

Socio-cultural pluralism was embedded all along the constitutional text. This section will address the two main points: religion and languages. Catholicism would cease to be the official religion of Bolivia; the constitution declared the right to religious freedom and all religions and cosmovisions were considered equal (article 4). Spanish and each of the thirty-six indigenous languages of Bolivia were recognized as official languages (article 5). Moreover, as Morales stated in his promulgation discourse, Bolivians "are obliged to slowly learn to speak an *originario* language and Spanish, but also a foreign language … to be able to communicate with the rest of the world" (Morales 2009). Those indigenous languages cited on the constitutional text were *aymara, araona, baure, bésiro, canichana, cayubaba, chacobo, chimán, ese ejja, guaraní, guarasu'we, guarayu, itonama, leco, machajuyai-kallawaya, machineri, maropa, mojeño-trinitario, mojeño-ignaciano, more, mosetén, movima, pacawara, puquina, quechua, sirionó, tacana, tapiete, toromona, uru-chipaya, weenhayek, yaminawa, yuki, yuracaré* y *zamuco* (article 5). Many Bolivians heard the name of these languages for the first time: how could all these indigenous groups be citizens of a country that was run by an elite that did not even know these groups existed?

In sum, the 2009 constitution of Bolivia meant the re-foundation of the country along a plurinational line, giving, for the first time, the chance to indigenous peoples and workers, women and men, the possibility to participate in its design and to be recognized as citizens of their country in their own right. Concessions to the opposition were given in order to placate them and avoid a civil war, and the secession of the *Media Luna*, but this should not overshadow the huge accomplishment of a president committed to construct a communitarian socialist path for a country where indigenous peoples represent the majority of the population. Maintaining an equilibrium between opposing forces, rather than the establishment of dichotomies, is central to Andean indigenous epistemology. Morales knew very well that changes at the national scale could not be sustained without weaving links to broader scales.

At the regional scale: between solidarity, autonomous integration and indigenous continentalism

Morales formed three very distinct regional alliances, first in 2006 with *Alternativa Bolivariana* (ALBA-Bolivarian Alternative) with Venezuela and Cuba, which was based on ties of solidarity among its members. Two years later he joined the *Unión de Naciones Sudamericanas* (UNASUR-Union of South American Nations), a hybrid union that encompasses all South American countries – with the exclusion of French Guiana – and that aims to achieve an autonomous integration – without the USA – into the global political economy. Finally, Morales remained an activist in the indigenous summits of *Abya Yala* – Runa indigenous name for the continent, it means continent of life – with whom he shared the ideal of communitarian socialism. Thus, Morales was at the crossroads of twenty-first-century socialism, autonomous liberalism and communitarian socialism; however, it is the latter that he embraced for Bolivia.

ALBA: solidarity, cooperation and complementary advantages

The Bolivarian Alternative's objective was to counteract the FTAA and, as such, it was an alliance aiming to foster social justice in the Americas. President Morales has called this Alliance the "Axis of Good."[23] Following ALBA's goals, Morales proposed the creation of a "People's Trade Treaty."[24] This agreement, signed in Havana, had the objective to promote "a market for small producers, artisans, micro-business owners, cooperatives, and community-run businesses."[25] In June 2009, ALBA's membership, initially formed by Venezuela, Cuba and Bolivia, expanded to include Ecuador, Nicaragua, Honduras, Antigua and Barbuda, Dominica, Saint Vincent and the Grenadines. Although it maintained its acronym, it changed its name to the Bolivarian Alliance for the Peoples of Our America, presenting itself as Pan-Latin/Hispano-Americanism. More recently, in 2012, Suriname and Saint Lucia joined the Bolivarian Alliance. This counter-hegemonic construction of space aimed at displacing from the region the hegemonic Monrovian Project of Pan-Americanism present in the FTAA (see Marchand 2005).

While the FTAA was an open "strategic regionalist project" comprising a state–TNCs alliance that aimed at locking Latin America into neo-liberal development and trade liberalization (Briceño-Ruiz 2007), ALBA was based on solidarity, cooperation and complementary advantages aiming at a Pan-Latin integration of energy resources (e.g., *Gasoducto del Sur*, *PetroCaribe* and *PetroAmérica*); finances through the creation of *Banco del Sur*, and communications through *Telesur*, which would be sustained by people's diplomacy (Serbin 2010: 11–12). However, the aim of this anti-capitalist regional formation was to generate strategic multipolar alliances for a global struggle against imperialism (Briceño-Ruiz 2010: 49). According to Borón, the international solidarity with Cuba and Venezuela allowed Evo Morales to build various hospitals and medical centers, be successful in the recovery of oil and gas from Brazil, and to carry out many infrastructural projects at the municipal scale (Borón 2009: 2). Morales' alliance with the Union of South American Nations (UNASUR) was very different from the one with ALBA.

UNASUR: redistribution, autonomy, diversification and security

The Union of South American Nations (UNASUR) was born on May 23, 2008; yet the union did not come into effect until 2011. UNASUR encompasses all South American countries with the exception of French Guiana. In this subregional formation of $17,694,335\,km^2$, a population of 382 million and rich in natural resources such as food, water reserves and hydrocarbons, Brazil became the leading power and Venezuela its main rival. The Secretariat is located in Quito, Ecuador and the South American Parliament in Cochabamba, Bolivia. According to Briceño-Ruiz, UNASUR is more of a political and social rather than an economic initiative and it may be seen as a revisionist "hybrid model" and not as an open regionalist one, as some authors perceive it. Briceño-Ruiz bases his argument on the fact that UNASUR never included an agenda of deep integration as the one proposed by WTO plus (Briceño-Ruiz 2010: 44–49).

The main characteristics of UNASUR have been the typical redistributive policies of the *Estado de Bienestar* or welfare model, such as education, health care, housing, public services, social justice and market regulation (Briceño-Ruiz 2010: 46–49). Keeping its distance from the United States and the diversification of international links were crucial in its search for an autonomous integration into the global political economy (Serbin 2010: 7–12). Infrastructure, energy, finances, the environment and defense were other important areas of action. The effectiveness of UNASUR was put into practice in August 2008 when, due to the constitutional conflict between Morales and the opposition and the massacre of Pando – where sixteen supporters of Morales' MAS were killed – UNASUR intervened in order to stop a coup d'état against the President.[26]

Indigenous continentalism: plurinationalism, reciprocity and self-determination

President Morales has followed up and even participated in some of the indigenous summits that have been organized since 1990 to counteract the "celebration" of the 500 years of the Spanish conquest. The objective of these summits was to initiate discussion and dialog between the Confederation of the Eagle – Abya Yala North – and the Confederation of the Cóndor – Abya Yala South – for their common struggle. This struggle involved the fight against oppression, for the achievement of self-determination, and the construction of a "new society, pluralistic, democratic and humane, in which peace [was] guaranteed."[27]

It should be noted that today, indigenous continentalism represents the broadest regional opposition – much larger in scope than ALBA and UNASUR – to the Pan-American strategic regionalist project (Roncallo 2010a).

> The sites of the gatherings were carefully and symbolically selected, they were all ceremonial centers or sacred sites of the largest indigenous civilizations of the continent, *Teotihuacán* in Mexico; *Quito* in Ecuador; *Iximché* in Guatemala and *Puno* in Peru – in a gathering in Cauca, Colombia, in 2010 it was determined that the next summit will take place in 2013 in Mexico. In each of these Summits the Indigenous peoples prepared a declaration with the main issues discussed in their meetings.
>
> (Roncallo 2010a)

Among the demands was the modification of the constitution in each country of the continent to include their own judicial, political, economic, cultural and social worldviews in co-existence with the Western ones, the rights of autonomy and self-determination of indigenous peoples, the collective rights to their lands, the defense of Mother Earth, "living well," balance with nature, climate justice, the millennial principles of complementarity, reciprocity, duality, gender equilibrium, traditional health and educational systems, spirituality, maintenance of their languages, food sovereignty, a dialog on plurinationalism and so on, in order to create a "Cosmetric Cultural Transformation of Humanity" (Roncallo 2010a). All of these items were carefully integrated into the Bolivian constitution. It should be noted that in the 2007 Summit in Iximché, Guatemala, entitled "From Resistance to Power," there was a dramatic shift of indigenous peoples' understanding of power. Previously, they rejected power because it was seen as inherent to the capitalist system and therefore a co-optation of indigenous peoples into it. The shift was due to the extraordinary advances carried out by Evo Morales in his first year in power (Roncallo 2010a).

Thus, at the regional scale, by joining ALBA, UNASUR and the indigenous summits, Morales moved between three very different worlds: one that aimed at creating a space based on solidarity, cooperation and complementary advantages (ALBA) to counteract capitalism; another that wanted to remain in the capitalist system but to be autonomus from the United States, for which it was necessary to diversify its alliances (UNASUR) and strengthen its defense mechanism; and finally, one that called for plurinationalism, reciprocity and self-determination, yet which co-existed with the Western world.

At the global scale: the tale of two climate change accords: the Copenhagen Accord and the Cochabamba Peoples' Accord[28]

Morales went beyond the regional boundaries when, in the face of the climate change crisis and in response to the failure of the Copenhagen Conference on

Climate Change, he called for a "World Peoples' Conference on Climate Change and the Rights of Mother Earth," which took place in Cochabamba, Bolivia, on April 19–22, 2010. This conference was attended by 35,000 people from 140 countries. In this conference, he argued that the heart of the climate change problematique was the capitalist system and its inherent separation and constant commodification of nature, of "Mother Earth." The conference was organized into seventeen workshops in order to produce the Cochabamba Accord, and the six main topics addressed were: (1) *Technology transfer*: it was considered that scientific knowledge should not be subjected to intellectual property rights because in the face of the emergency that the global climate crisis represented it was necessary to share knowledge between "Western science" and the "traditional knowledge of the people"; in other words, to intensify an "inter-scientific dialog" and to incorporate this dual knowledge into educational curriculums.[29] (2) *Mitigation*: it was stipulated that GHGs emissions should be reduced to 50 percent in the period 2013 to 2017 in order to be significant. This raised the concept of "climate debt" that Northern countries have with the South, yet financial compensation was not considered sufficient for "restorative justice"; what was needed was to restore "the balance, integrity and harmony of the Earth and its climate system."[30] (3) *Adaptation*: the Peoples' Accord rejected the idea of adaptation because it considered that adaptation meant a "resignation to impacts provoked by the historical emissions of developed countries." Instead, what was needed was to learn how to "live well" rather than "living better," to live in harmony with Mother Nature. For this, what was needed was a shift in agricultural practices, to prohibit the genetically modified seeds promoted by agribusiness which was responsible for the peoples' loss of food sovereignty, and to return to the agricultural system utilized by indigenous communities since millennia.[31] (4) *Financing*: developed countries needed to increase to about 6 percent of the developed countries' GDP to developing countries and that this should not include any kinds of "strings attached" (such as the implementation of more neo-liberal policies).[32] (5) *The REDD mechanism* was strongly criticized because it was considered that tree plantations under the Clean Development Mechanism (CDM), which would be used for agro-fuels, would threaten native forests and jungles, and as such was considered a false solution to climate change.[33] (6) *Carbon markets* were seen as another false solution to climate change because carbon credits just transferred the responsibilities of the reduction of GHGs emissions from the North to developing countries.[34] Moreover, it became an extremely profitable business for people in the North; as Clemençon had estimated, in 2006 the carbon credit market was worth US$30 billion and it had the potential to increase to several US$100 billion (Clémençon 2008: 73). In sum, the tension between the Copenhagen Accord and the Cochabamba Peoples' Accord represented two different worldviews and ways of life, a capitalist system that commodified everything along the way and a "living well" approach embedded in "communitarian socialism," which did not need the market to survive. The latter accord ended by suggesting a global referendum on climate change, to create a Global People's Movement for Mother Earth, an International

Climate Justice Tribunal, and to change the current capitalist system. At the Cancun meeting on climate change, President Morales said that he preferred "to be on the side of the peoples of the world that defend life in the face of aggression toward the environment and the planet."[35]

To conclude, Part II has dealt with the internationalization of mining extraction in Latin America, initiated by the mid-1990s and its impact on Bolivia, one of the four countries in Latin America considered under the International Financial Institutions' Heavily Indebted Poor Countries Initiative. This coincided with the United Nations First Decade of the World's Indigenous Peoples (later on extended for another decade, until 2015) and the emergence of indigenous peoples' movements and resource wars in the continent. The conflict in the Amayapampa and Capasirca gold-mines in 1996 was one of the first encounters between miners, indigenous peoples and a transnational mining corporation in the hemisphere, as well as one of the first cases in which workers and indigenous peoples were accused by the agents "from above" of being terrorists. Chapter 5 demonstated that the action taken by miners and indigenous peoples was in self-defense against the social, cultural and economic dislocations produced by neo-liberal restructuring in the mining sector.

The expansion of foreign direct investments in mining was dramatically intensified in the new millennium, when a new conditionality, the Poverty Reduction Strategy Papers, was added to the Heavily Indebted Poor Countries Initiative. The Poverty Reduction Strategy Papers included mining as a multilateral strategy, through the collection of mining taxes and their investment in social issues and the creation of jobs, would indirectly be expected to reduce poverty. The international financial institutions also created the Impoverishment Risk and Livelihood Reconstruction model as a social cushion for population displacement. The case study on the San Cristóbal silver mine (Chapter 6) demonstrated that although this was a peaceful interaction between a transnational mining corporation and indigenous peoples, the deterritorialization of the San Cristóbal population from the Old to the New Town led to the breakdown of kinship ties and the ethnic economy which allowed the social reproduction of the *ayllu*. Hence, transnationalized mining corporations' involvement in the social reproduction of the ethnic mining economy does not reduce poverty but rather increases it.

President Morales' re-founding of Bolivia as an indigenous nation may be seen as the beginning of a shift towards a more humane World Order. At the national scale, the President's creation of a plurinational state that incorporated the long-standing demands of indigenous peoples in their continental summits democratized the state apparatus. By joining ALBA, UNASUR and participating in the indigenous continental encounters, Morales moved between President Chávez' twenty-first-century socialism which rejected capitalism, the Union of South American nations which followed a hybrid model, and the indigenous ideal or "communitarian socialism." At the global scale, his call for reliable solutions to save "Mother Earth" rather than adopting a "fictitious" economic and technical approach to climate change has demonstrated the need to move the current World Order towards a more humane and pluralistic one.

Conclusion

Rethinking hegemony-development in the light of continentalism

Since the end of World War II, the United States has become the leader of the world and has started to construct a *Pax Americana*, an imaginary community that combines mythical and rational elements. Indeed, the myth of the Manifest Destiny represented the ideal of superiority, the strong belief of being the nation selected to carry the weight of guiding the whole world towards "freedom." This religious fundamentalism, drawn from the Protestant ethic, is embedded in the notion of progress and territorial expansionism. The myth was rationalized through the creation of universal rules and the invention of development geared towards the constant capture of new enclosures and the primitive accumulation of capital. This, then, is the element of continuity that underpins hegemonic thought on development.

Yet, that element of continuity was also countered and challenged with resistance from below, reflecting what Karl Polanyi called the "double movement." This dialectical confrontation of ideas has led to struggles within the hegemon regarding what would be the correct mechanisms of hegemony to implement in the changing historical situation. The result was a constant metamorphosis of the economic, political, social and environmental spheres carried out by positivist "problem-solving theory" with the aim of maintaining and fixing the status quo, the established conservative order.

The Coxian method of historical structures aims to capture the moments of rupture and transition between what was termed, following Gramsci's insight, the Old and the New *Pax Americanas*. Added to this was how gender and ethnic relations were reshaped, as seen through the lenses situated in the Southern Cone of the Americas, my region of origin – note that both the periodization and explanation will always differ from where and from whom – life experiences – the analysis comes from. This conclusion will look back at the Old *Pax Americana* to rethink how the New *Pax Americana*, the focus of this book, came about.

The Old *Pax Americana* (1947–1964) was built during the postwar "Golden Era" around the politics of containment against the external threat represented by the Soviet Union. At the forefront of the strong belief that Latin America and the Caribbean were on the brink of massive revolutionary movements, a set of "problem-solving" ideas emerged in the economic field, crystallizing into disciplinary modernization theory and the praxis of development. The aim was to achieve stability by "helping" traditional societies to modernize through industrialization, thereby creating urban middle classes, who in turn would be expected to fund Center-Left reformist political parties that would control social change and economic growth from above. By doing so, communism would be aborted and capitalism secured. Hence, economic growth was intrinsically linked to the construction of liberal democracy.

The United Nations declared the 1960s and 1970s as "Development Decades" and launched an "assault on poverty and underdevelopment" – the ideological component – which reshaped existing international organizations and created new ones. President Kennedy's Alliance for Progress, designed according to liberal modernization ideals, favored the articulation of the regional order with the underlying intention to avoid the formation of another Cuba in the Americas. This was accompanied by the creation of the "Green Berets," a temporary anti-guerrilla unit aimed at suppressing social movements until the "take-off" stage was reached. The Alliance for Progress was embraced by local petit-bourgeois reformists because its values were very similar – albeit it came from the outside – to those of the reformist Latin American students' movements and parties. This gradual, more permanent and peaceful approach of American hegemony led to the formation of developmental states based on corporatism and an import-substitution industrialization economic model, aimed at preventing the emergence of social struggles, and included a social contract as a tool for consensus building.

The result was the formation of a gender order linked to the nuclear family and the incorporation of indigenous peoples into the state through the creation of peasant federations controlled from above while also allowing both of them to maintain an autonomous space, informal and subsistence economic systems that gave security to the reproduction of each group. This reformist project was opposed by revolutionary movements inspired by the Cuban example of "actually existing socialism," in which workers and peasants became the owners of the means of production and political power. In fact, in Cuba, land was expropriated and redistributed to form a mixed economy based on agricultural co-ops, state farms and small private property, and political decisions were taken at people's assemblies. The state's role was to plan what was democratically decided at those meetings. Hence, this alternative model considered that when the means of production were in the hands of transnational corporations, growth would only be absorbed by them, and when political decisions were taken at the international scale, they could never be democratic.

The Impasse (1964–1982) was a period of crisis and transition between the old and the new. During that time, conservatives believed that economic modernization rather than containing communism was the cause. This led to a shift in the social construction of threats: the external threat posed by the Soviet Union was replaced by a belief that the threat was now *within* Latin America and the Caribbean; it was the result of internal subversion, and this time Brazil became the main concern of the United States. This paranoia accelerated with the end of the "Golden Era," the collapse of the Bretton Woods system and the 1970s world economic crisis. In this context, there was a retreat to disciplinary conservative ideals. The realist "hardliners" argued that the solution to the problem was political and not economic, and proposed to restore order through the strengthening of constitutions and military institutions rather than through development and foreign aid. For them, the source of stability was the country-side, not the cities, which implied an alliance with the Latin American traditional rural elites and the military instead of the "poor" and middle classes – contrary to what modernization theorists had proposed.

Institutions such as the U.S. Army School of the Americas – located at that time in the Panama Canal – and the University of Chicago had a central role during the Impasse. The former trained Latin American military officials in methods of terror and counter-insurgency techniques and the latter trained economists in the gospel of Friedmanite monetarism or supply-side economics. The "Mann Doctrine" represented a radical shift of the Alliance for Progress and inter-American relations. It put emphasis on the promotion of economic development and the protection of American private investments abroad, the maintenance of an anti-communist position, and disregard for both social reform and representative democracy. Hence, the re-articulation of the regional order was conducted through the 1964 "Military Assistance Agreement" signed by many Latin American states, which stipulated the need to combat internal subversion, and the implementation of what is called here an "authoritarian transitional development model." This included the internationalization of production, particularly of capital-intensive industries, export-oriented industrialization (EOI), and the internationalization of finances or the internationalization of American inflation through the implementation of a debt-intensive strategy. This led to the 1982 economic crisis and the incorporation of Latin America into the global political economy.

The new wave of dictatorial governments was the corollary of the economic warfare launched by the United States, giving rise to bureaucratic-authoritarian states. These bureaucratic-authoritarian states were dominated by a highly oligopolized and transnational upper bourgoisie, comprising the armed forces, large enterprises and some representatives of the state's civil bureaucracy. Their objective was to "restore order" and "normalize the economy"; the means utilized were the suppression of the channels of popular representation, of political parties and Congress. By doing so, citizenship was suppressed, and the "dirty wars" endured for almost twenty years of the Impasse. The result was the disappearance and assassination of thousands of workers, peasants, students, women, young people and children; the national security doctrines labeled them as the "new enemies of the nation."

Authoritarian governments enshrined masculinist and Catholic values, and did not agree with a gender order based on the nuclear family. Instead, they considered the extended family as the ideal because it could perform social welfare, political, economic and religious functions. In opposition to this repression, women's and human rights movements sprang up all over the continent. There was also a shift in the types of guerrilla wars that emerged in this interregnum. In fact, the "second-wave guerrilla wars" that emerged, especially following Ernesto "Che" Guevara's assassination in 1967, distanced themselves from Cuba, which was now seen as revisionist and pro-Soviet. Instead, they could be characterized as Maoist, nationalist and populist, and they endured until the end of the 1980s.

The New *Pax Americana* (1982–present) refers to the ongoing reconstruction of the American-led hegemony based on the last four ten-year developmental planning "stages" of the new global political economy. The external debt became the Gordian knot that tied up the Americas and allowed for the reconstruction of the Leviathan through the imposition of coercive conditionalities to build a kleptocratic structure favorable to capital (e.g., through the nationalization of the external debt, debt servicing, the privatization of public assets, shifts in the juridical system, the tax havens and especially capital flight towards them, the disembedding of the police forces and so on), which in turn intensified the crisis of social reproduction for the majority of the inhabitants of the region. In the 1980s, a New Right "historic bloc" emerged at the core, initiating its counter-revolution by re-defining development as "free markets." Established in the Santa Fe I document, *Inter-American Relations, Shield of the New Order and Sword of the U.S. Ascent to World Power*, also termed "The Reagan Doctrine," their building blocs included policies to end the "static containment" of the Westphalian bipolar order anchored in what the document called the "Soviet–Cuban Axis"or the "Evil Empire." The document also entailed a shift in discourse: previously, the oppositional social forces were called "subversives"; now they were labeled "terrorists."

In this geo-political context, the Bretton Woods institutions were given the role of managers of the private lenders and, by doing so, a global managerial infrastructure was created to implement rules-based procedures to deal with the Southern private forces' external debt – an external debt that was the result of the internationalization of inflation produced in the North, which in turn benefited Southern elites, the recipients of *plata dulce* or hot money. From then on, the international financial institutions used the package of conditionalities, attached to new soft loans given to Southern countries to service their debts, while at the same time introducing market reforms, giving rise to a "competition state," which acted as a "quasi-market actor." "Democratization" was the ideological tool that accompanied the introduction of structural adjustment programs, which included the free movement of capital, the gradual elimination of the social contract – public health, education, subsidies, etc. – and the privatization of public service enterprises – gas, electricity, water, communications and transport.

The free movement of capital allowed for capital flight to tax havens – a tool constantly utilized in the South to discipline progressive governments – and generally produced and ended with what has been termed in this book "economic coup d'états." For example, President Siles Suazo (1982–1985) of Bolivia had to resign after a capital flight produced a hyperinflation of an annual 2,177 percent in 1984, and 8,170 percent by mid-1985 (Klein 1992: 272). Another case is President Raúl Alfonsín in Argentina who had to resign in 1989 due to the unstoppable inflation produced after capital flight took place. The elimination of the social contract affected those who needed it the most, namely women, children, the youth and the elderly.

The privatization of strategic public service enterprises meant the appropriation of goods that belonged to the whole nation by transnational corporations – formed by both foreign and local capital. This does not mean that public enterprises worked wonderfully well, but because they were local they were more accountable to people's demands, they provided jobs and justice was monitored by unions. Meanwhile, transnational capital is geared only towards profits and it is careless of people's needs and concerns. The privatization of public enterprises created a new bourgeoisie by incorporating the previous nationalist populist leaders of the former developmental states onto corporate boards of directors and as private owners of the newly privatized enterprises. The objective behind this was to demolish the unions of the corporatist alliance; in other words, it was an attack on labor and the Keynesian model. Paradoxically, when everything was being privatized, the private external debt was nationalized. This meant that every single citizen in the South had to pay a debt that was contracted by the military and the elite, not the majority. As such, the debt is illegal because it was forced upon the majority by the kleptocrat bearers of power.

In this context, the Southern Cone's transition from authoritarianism to "democracy" should be understood as a shift towards a dictatorship of the market – similar to all the countries that have been subjected to SAPs. Hence, capitalist accumulation in the 1980s has taken place through debt servicing and the privatization of public service enterprises, which since then imposed tariffs according to the price of those goods in the international market, an excessively high price for the South, a price that did not match local wages. This happened at the same moment in which agricultural exports from Southern countries plummeted. As McMichael (1996) has acknowledged, by 1984 the flows of capital had reversed: the outflow from the South was larger than the inflow, reaching US$400 billion for the whole Third World, and in the 1990s the debtor countries owed 61 percent more debt than in 1982. This situation led to the 1980s being labeled the "lost decade." Yet, a lot more than a decade had been lost with the structural changes produced back then. Meanwhile, Central America followed the revolutionary path at a moment in which the American New Right was determined to end the Cold War, being the region with the last experience with the old revolutionary wars. In sum, the 1980s meant the demolition of both the residues of the old Keynesian demand-side economic model, and the Westphalian system of states with a balance of power.

In the 1990s, with the end of the Cold War, and following the Washington Consensus, development was re-defined as "good governance," also known as second-generation reforms – which, according to the literature on democratization, was expected to consolidate democracy. In contrast, it has been argued in this book that what good governance consolidated was hegemony. Indeed, the structural changes introduced in the 1980s became solidified through the social construction of transnational legal regimes, a fusion that Stephen Gill (2003) has defined as "new constitutionalism for disciplinary neo-liberalism." This juridical superstructure meant the internationalization of the American Constitution, and its aim was to strengthen institutions to facilitate trade and foreign direct investment, particularly the independence of the judicial powers and the armed forces.

A corollary was the reshaping of the US Armed Forces to deal with the post-Cold War "low-intensity conflicts" (LICs) which included terrorism, narco-trafficking, migration and natural resources. The "fight against corruption" and "peacebuilding" became the ideological tools to mask how a legal infrastructure was built to secure market or pro-free enterprise reforms, and thus, generating the globalization of corruption and violence rather than being an antidote to them. In this post-Cold War context, President George Bush Sr. announced the creation of a New World Order and at the center of this plan was the formation of a Free Trade Area of the Americas (FTAA), also giving rise to other new constitutionalist agreements at a range of spatial scales towards that end. At the regional level, under GATT and the WTO, the old protectionist economic blocs moved towards trade liberalization and lowered their tariffs to all countries based on the principle of non-discrimination, and created a new series of free trade areas and bilateral investment treaties. At the local level, all national constitutions were harmonized according to the "new rules of the game": equal treatment between local and foreign investors; most favored nation status, protection from expropriation and nationalization; and mechanisms for dispute settlement, such as international trade tribunals and domestic courts.

A masculinist new managerialist organizational strategy, with its roots in militarism, reshaped the states. The "managerialist states" were decentered, ejecting and privatizing two main aspects: the welfare structure which, since the implementation of structural adjustment programs in the 1980s, was emptied of its content; and land and natural resources. Hence the state, instead of providing and securing important issues for the reproduction of society, was transformed into a mere regulator of the private sector. Paradoxically, the re-privatization of welfare, which primarily affected women, children and the elderly, was carried out at the same moment in which women were incorporated into politics through the implementation of electoral quotas, and also into the labor market to offset the former autonomous space they had in the informal market. Yet, the women incorporated into the new political economy were a selected group of elite women who conformed to traditional masculinist values, and they were used to implement policies that were detrimental to the majority of women – an illustration of the role of *trasformismo*.

At the community level, the privatization of communal lands and natural resources affected indigenous peoples and other ethnic groups. The communal lands allowed them to maintain an autonomous space where their traditional authorities and subsistence economy could be maintained. Not surprisingly, the curtailment of this space was confronted with massive movements from Chiapas to the Southern Cone. Parallel to this, the United Nations declared 1995 to 2004 the Decade of the World's Indigenous Peoples – which was then renewed for a further ten years. As in the case of women – and the nationalist populist leaders in the 1980s – a group of indigenous peoples were incorporated into the political arena and also into the market through the system of micro-enterprises. This produced the division of the women's and indigenous peoples' movements and was seen as a co-optation to undermine and depoliticize these groups.

A particular role in the decentralization of politics has been played by NGOs and universities. The new NGOs maintained a distance from the old activist ones and became more technocratic, geared towards the formulation of policies, project execution and social services delivery, based on efficiency criteria – a shift produced through selective donor financing. Universities were also becoming "NGO-ized" and were shifting towards the training of public bureaucrats. It is noteworthy that the American New Right Santa Fe II document, *A Strategy for Latin America for the 1990s*, aimed at reverting what they considered the biggest threat of the post-Cold War era: "Gramscian Marxism." They made a distinction between "temporal governments," the elected officials, and, most importantly, "permanent governments" – the ones they wanted to reinforce to combat the Gramscian threat: the armed forces, judicial power, civil bureaucracy, democratic organizations – unions, business groups, commercial associations and educational organizations. Thus, in the 1990s, a new privatized organizational infrastructure for capitalist accumulation emerged but it was not yet strong enough.

In the new millennium, development was re-defined once more, this time as "poverty reduction," which echoed the origins of development back in the 1960s – the heydays of the modernization theorists and the launching of the UN development decades as the "war on poverty and underdevelopment." However, these were two different hegemonic models for "poverty reduction." The former was launched during the Cold War and was based on the Keynesian social contract, state-led approaches, and aimed at containing class struggle. The latter was launched in the post-Cold War, especially after September 11, 2001, and was designed abroad as an antidote to terrorism. It is an authoritarian social contract because the "aid" to reduce poverty falls into privatized health, security provision and educational systems – services that were ejected from the managerialist state in the 1990s – and it also fomented the privatization of strategic natural resources such as water, energy and mining.

These pre-emptive extractive mega-development projects financed by the international financial institutions are displacing ethnic groups, indigenous peoples and Afro-descendants from rural areas and create a constant state of violence with the objective of increasing profits through the selling of small arms, land-mines, sex trade and criminal acts and violence that spills over the cities. Consequently, policies, such as the Heavily Indebted Poor Countries (HIPC) Initiative, the Poverty Reduction Strategy Papers – the HIPC's conditionalities – the Impoverishment Risk and Livelihood Reconstruction model (IRLR) – which use a problem-solving approach to population displacement – and the Millennium Development Goals (MDGs) need to be analyzed more critically. As argued in this volume, "poverty reduction" is an ideological tool which masks the fact that the private sector is accelerating the infrastructure of globalization and the primitive accumulation of capital through the appropriation of welfare, land and natural resources. It is the South that, since the 1980s, has been developing the North, not the other way around. If the 1960s "war on poverty" failed and led to massive revolutionary movements, the new millennium "poverty reduction strategy" will also fail albeit for other reasons that have been detailed here.

Particularly alarming was the intensification of mergers of regional new constitutionalism, such as "NAFTA Plus" or "deep integration" of Canada, the United States and Mexico in the North, the Canada–Central America Four Free Trade Agreement (CA4FTA) and other free trade agreements in the region. Smaller bilateral investment treaties (BITs) and free trade agreements were being utilized to produce one big fusion, the FTAA; this treaty was expected to enter into operation in October 2005 at the fourth Summit of Americas in Mar del Plata, Argentina. Due to the opposition of five South American presidents and the strong critique of indigenous peoples at their second Indigenous Peoples Summit – held one week before the President's Summit – continentalism has been delayed.

The following years saw the strengthening of the Latin American New Left governments and their construction of counter-hegemonic spaces, such as the Bolivarian Alliance for the Peoples of Our America (ALBA), the Union of South American Nations (UNASUR) and the Community of Latin American and Caribbean States (CELAC) which deepened and strengthened Latin American integration and South–South cooperation, particularly with China, African countries, Russia, India and, in some cases, even Iran. These shifts in power relations loosened the previous dependency from the United States; thus, when the 2008 global economic meltdown took place, Latin America was in a strong position to radicalize its policies. Indeed, at the national scale, the state took control of the economy, and started implementing counter-cyclical policies, a better redistribution of the national income and the development of the internal market; favoring an industrialization process that could add value to local raw materials, the objective was to generate employment, reduce poverty and produce social inclusion. At the regional scale, ALBA, MERCOSUR and UNASUR continued on the path of integrating the region, lowering tariffs within it while increasing tariffs towards the outside; in other words, a regional protectionism. At the global scale, relations with China strengthened.

At the same time, in the United States Barack Obama won the elections and became the first African-American President in the history of that country. The voters responded to his promise for "change" and Latin Americans to his promise for "freedom," which included "political freedom," "freedom from want," "freedom from fear" and "freedom from energy dependency." However, after a year in power, the moment of "Obama-mania" started to wane, and it became clear that Obama's first administration was a continuation as usual, a fourth moment of the New *Pax Americana*, a "cosmetic hemispheric change," from Bush's controversial FTAA towards a "Regional Partnership on Crime and Security," from an economic to a security-based partnership. The latter involved the project of disembedding the police and juridical institutions from the state, which increased violence and corruption in those countries that signed a security agreement with the United States. The shadow of Obama's first administration includes the maintenance of the US Guantánamo Bay naval base and the embargo in Cuba, the coup d'état in Honduras and Paraguay, the "Operation Fast and Furious" in Mexico, Plan Colombia and the installation of seven military bases in that country, the militarization of "humanitarian aid" when Haiti was struck by an earthquake, not putting limits to Monsanto's GM seeds, favoring the formation of the carbon market which is leading to the appropriation of land by foreign companies, and the displacement of Afro-descendants and indigenous peoples. Notwithstanding these serious actions, Obama owes his re-election to the Latino population in the United States. Hopefully, for his second administration Obama will understand what a mistaken view he had of Latin America and that he needs to change those advisors who misled him.

The case studies on Bolivia (Chapters 5 and 6, this volume) are inscribed in the third moment of the American-led hegemony of the continent. The questions which emerged from interviews and documents in the two Bolivian communities showed the extent of the massive penetration of transnational mining corporations into the region. Bolivia, a small and impoverished nation, was a useful entry point for understanding a broad range of processes relevant to the region as a whole. For example, Bolivia provided a window on global finance, including the stock markets of specific wealthy countries and cities, and the tax havens where transnational mining corporations have their addresses. Although the Amayapampa and Capasirca mines were bought by a transnational mining company a few years before the new millennium, it was a pilot project that pre-announced the intensification of mining extraction in Bolivia (and the continent) as well as the discourse on terrorism that accompanied the emergent resource conflicts.

In fact, the Amayapampa and Capasirca miners and indigenous peoples were accused by the transnational mining corporation and the state of being part of a terrorist movement. On the contrary, they did not form part of a terrorist movement but rather their reaction was a form of self-defense against their annihilation by global and local capitalist forces – what Karl Polanyi called the "double movement" of society. The resistance in these mines and the internationalization of the conflict through the pro-people human rights organizations led to the dialectical reformulation of the relations between, on the one side the international financial institutions and the foreign investors, and on the other the miners and indigenous peoples.

In fact, this shift was most clearly reflected in Chapter 6, in the case study conducted in the San Cristóbal mines. The displacement of the population that lived on top of a silver mine took place at the time when the World Bank's Impoverishment Risk and Livelihood Reconstruction model was taking shape. Although the social cushion that this particular problem-solving model proposed, and the creation of the Foundation *Llama de Plata* reflected, may have reduced the emergence of resource conflicts, it was demonstrated that it is still an unsustainable plan for the displaced peoples because it separates indigenous peoples from nature by introducing capitalist relations. Moreover, it destroys the Andean notion of equilibrium based in indigenous peoples' cosmologies, their "ethnic economy" and kinship ties which are all intertwined. Finally, it modifies gender relations by subordinating women to patriarchal relations inherent in the capitalist system.

The election of Evo Morales to the Presidency of Bolivia in 2006, just as two years later with Obama's election, marked an ethnic shift in the leadership of the Americas. This shift was accompanied by the election of women to the presidency in the region: Michelle Bachelet in Chile, Cristina Fernández de Kirchner in Argentina and Dilma Rousseff in Brazil. Evo Morales re-founded Bolivia as a plurinational nation by incorporating the ethnic diversity of the country into the new national constitution. He nationalized the natural resources, joined ALBA, UNASUR and the indigenous continentalist movement at the regional scale and initiated a global contestation to the green capitalist approach to the environment. Hence, Evo Morales represented the antithesis to Obama's hegemonic position on the environment.

In retrospect, when analyzing development/hegemony, there are five warning signs that analysts generally gloss over. First, the social construction of threats that precede a shift from one evolutionary moment to another. Second, the creation of ideological baits, such as "democratization" in the 1980s, "fight against corruption" and "post-conflict reconstruction and peacebuilding" in the 1990s, "poverty reduction" in the new millennium and a "green economy" more recently, were all created to produce exactly the opposite, namely market and juridical reforms to secure the capitalist system and increase the primitive accumulation of capital.

Third, *trasformismo* or the absorption of the discourse of the opposition in order to neutralize it, the nationalist-populist discourse was designed as an antidote to Marxism; the legal and cultural reforms of the 1990s as immunization against Gramscian thought; women's movements and indigenous peoples' discourses were brought into the liberal pluralist paradigm to co-opt their elites, while applying detrimental policies towards the majority of women, Afrodescendants and indigenous peoples – the elimination of welfare and massive population displacements and murders to appropriate natural resources on Afrodescendants' and indigenous peoples' lands. The creation of the Heavily Indebted Poor Countries Initiative was also a means to neutralize the Jubilee 2000's – now Jubilee Research – objective to cancel the external debt of southern countries.

Fourth, the shift in the alliance of classes along the history of development/ hegemony: traditional liberals preferred an alliance with the "poor" and the middle classes; the realists preferred a link with the military and rural elites; and the liberal pluralists preferred links with the ex-nationalist populist leaders and an elite among women and indigenous peoples, in order to introduce policies detrimental to workers and the majority of women and indigenous peoples. Fifth, it is imperative to start analyzing and quantifying the massive transfer of resources from South to North to demand that the North pays what it has taken away from the South.

In sum, this book has aimed to demonstrate that development in its liberal and neo-liberal formats is a synonym of hegemony, while during the Impasse it was non-hegemonic because there was no consensus. Hence, hegemony under the New *Pax Americana* was defined as a masculinist and ethnocentric social construction of threats, markets, transnational juridical norms, the universalization of culture, and the conquest of land and the appropriation of natural resources. Threats and ideological baits precede the moment in which a dominant mode of production penetrates other subordinate modes of production, a juridical structure secures the terrain for the expansion of capital and the "globalization of the mind" aims at promoting the individual acceptance of the new rules of the game in the long run. By penetrating new territories, it modifies and recreates dependency on multi-scalar arrangements reflecting the regional, national, subnational and ethnic/community levels, the household and the body. It also subverts the former social fabric along class, gender and ethnic lines. The ultimate objective of penetrating new enclosures through the internationalization of welfare, land and natural resources is to accelerate the primitive accumulation of capital.

The contribution of this book is that it starts exploring the ways and the interdisciplinary literature that can explain how the changes introduced by the process of globalization are reconstituting the geo-economic and political unit of analysis from "Latin America and the Caribbean" to "the Americas" – including the United States and Canada – in both theory and praxis. The aim is to start building a new framework that covers the whole hemisphere, based on readings from all over the continent but analyzing it from the viewpoint of the South that could, in the future, fill the vacuum left by dependency theory.

With this objective in mind, this book expands on the Coxian method of historical structures to include gender and ethnicity, and adds the period that may be called the New *Pax Americana*, a period that Cox did not write about. In this later period, it was necessary to re-scale Cox's triad: world order, states and social forces to make sense of the changes produced by the neo-liberal multi-level governance approach. This book has critically analyzed the impact at the global, regional, national, subnational – provincial and municipal – and ethnic/community, household and body scales that neo-liberalism has produced.

This multi-scalar framework required the incorporation of a variety of disciplines, including history, geography, critical IPE, feminist IPE and anthropology. In addition, other disciplines and literatures were introduced when necessary, namely sociology, psychology, communications, education, culture, security, social movements. Since knowledge is not automatically transferable from one culture to another, documentary sources need to be critically interrogated from the reality of the South, while other locally construed concepts need to be brought to the fore to explain the specificity of the culture under scrutiny. Critical gender and ethnic epistemologies and ontologies were utilized here to maintain a distance from the liberal pluralist paradigm because the aim was to respect difference and not to include it as a smokescreen for the commodification of livelihood – welfare, land and natural resources.

The periodization is one of the most important contributions for a number of reasons. First, studies emerging in the northern context generally focus on the shift from the Keynesian (1945–1970) to the neo-liberal model (since the 1970s). From the vantage point of the South, it is crucial to pay attention to the period of transition or Impasse, which is a moment of military dictatorships, and when the seeds to change the structures of the World Order were planted (internationalization of production and finances). The objective here was to highlight that intermediate period of non-hegemonic conditions by introducing three periods: Old *Pax Americana* (1947–1964), Impasse (1964–1982) and, especially, New *Pax Americana* (since 1982).

Second, studies of neo-liberalism do not make the distinction between how neo-liberalism changed in the 1980s (structural-economic), in the 1990s (superstructural-juridical), in the new millennium (poverty reduction) and currently (green economy). Drawing on Stephen Gill's distinction of the shift between the 1980s and 1990s, this dissertation has extended it to the new millennium. Stephen Gill's is a very strong contribution because not understanding new constitutionalism and what Desai and Imrie (1998) called the fragmentation of the managerialist state into myriad service providers/NGOs in the 1990s leads to confusion regarding the real meaning of "poverty reduction" in the new millennium, which is the deepening of poverty, not its reduction. In fact, the Heavily Indebted Poor Countries Initiative, the Millennium Development Goals, the Poverty Reduction Strategy Papers and even the Impoverishment Risk and Livelihood Reconstruction model are intended to strengthen the privatized social sector, not the ones in need.

Perhaps the most important contribution comes from field research in Bolivia, such as linking the natural resource wars to the Poverty Reduction Strategy Papers. Generally the sparse literature on the Poverty Reduction Strategy Papers focuses on the analysis of welfare and macro-economic issues included in that policy framework but not on natural resources. On the other hand, the emerging literature on resource conflicts that comes from the political ecology approach does not link it to the Poverty Reduction Strategy Papers. Yet, some progressive NGOs are starting to make the link between the Poverty Reduction Strategy Papers and resource conflicts. This book is also one of the first works on the "new mining" and also on development-induced displacement in Bolivia; it brings up the origins of the discourse on terrorism in the 1980s (well before the attack on the World Trade Center), which points to the social construction of threats, and it pays attention to the shift from the old to the new pro-corporate human rights in Bolivia (see Chapter 5 on Amayapampa and Capasirca).

The case of Bolivia helps expand the understanding of the New *Pax Americana* by relating mining extraction – particularly gold and silver – to the stock markets of the world's largest cities. Central are the cities of Toronto and Vancouver that, as mentioned before, pressed the World Bank to include mining in the Poverty Reduction Strategy Papers frameworks; the tax havens and the international financial institutions. This global system is designed to favor a transnational capitalist class – global and local – who has appropriated the discourse on human rights, now understood as corporate human rights. It also serves to silence the oppositional forces and through the "good and evil" discourse legitimize its actions by addressing the "other" as a "terrorist" – as was demonstrated through the case study of Amayapampa and Capasirca.

The case studies also showed that the new hegemony tackles specific sites: those rich in mineral resources at the subnational scale. Yet, the crucial contribution is the detailed description of the encounter of Western and local knowledges and values, the friction between cultures when one wants to dominate the other through economic, political and social means, and the resistance to it. In the case of Bolivia, resistance has already led to the ousting of two presidents, showing the fragility of hegemony when "life" is at stake.

This leads to the final contribution, namely to show that the main issue animating the current social movements was a struggle between a new constitutionalism of global scope – which favors transnational corporations – and a local constitutionalism directed at mitigating the negative effects of transnational corporations; particularly on the areas of land, natural resources and directed at the erosion of the social contract as reflected in public spending on education, health and pensions. This is a struggle for life and a class struggle as well as for culture and identity. The mechanisms of control during the Old *Pax Americana* and the Impasse were based on the control of labor from above, through the anticommunist labor organizations: AFL-CIO, the Inter-American Regional Organization of Workers (ORIT – *Organización Inter-Americana del Trabajo*), and the unions and confederations created by the corporatist states. During the New *Pax Americana*, the objective is to control life from above through the commodification of water, food, health, education, energy, the environment, communications and culture. To reiterate, this book has sought to be a first articulation of new topics that make sense of today's reality and aims to spur future research projects in these areas.

Notes

Introduction

1 Note that the concept "dialogue" is drawn here from the indigenous movements, the World Social Forum and the Brazilian educator, Paulo Freire, who, in *Pedagogy of the Oppressed*, blended Marxism and Liberation Theology with the aim of creating an emancipatory approach towards education.

2 "Pluriversal" is a concept borrowed from Walter Mignolo and it refers, following the Zapatistas, to a world in which many worlds can co-exist (Mignolo and Tlostanova 2006: 216). This concept is central to Mignolo's "border thinking" and the "de-colonial project."

3 *Ayllus* are a pre-Hispanic, territorially based large kinship groupings that connect different ecological zones, and are tied together through endogamous marriages (Harris 2000:19).

4 When gathering the documentation for the Amayapampa and Capasirca case, it recalled for me the work of the Italian medievalist Carlo Ginzburg (1992, 2002) regarding the importance of trials in understanding the worldview of common people such as millers and "witches" in the sixteenth century – something that the studies of the transition from a medieval to a capitalist mode of production could not capture. To do so, Ginzburg searched the documents covering the trials conducted by the Inquisition to understand the beliefs of people that were considered "heretics" and who were sentenced to death by that Catholic institution. Inspired by Ginzburg, I thought that "good governance," the rights-based approach to development in the 1990s, which included the independence of the Judicial Courts – what the Santa Fe II document referred to as "permanent governments" – bore an uncanny resemblance to the medieval ages. In fact, the pro-market Judicial Courts act in similar ways to the Inquisition, especially when defending transnational corporations and labeling the oppositional forces to the neo-liberal model "terrorist," a label that within the Americas is especially used for indigenous peoples, the modern "heretics," whose cosmologies/worldviews differed from those drawn from Western knowledge.

5 Lucien Febvre, "Leçon d'ouverture au College de France, 13 décembre 1933" in *Combats pour l'histoire*, Paris 1992: 8 (quoted in Carlo Ginzburg, *The Judge and the Historian* (2002: 35–36)).

6 The unstructured methodology avoids the universalizing pitfall of those pre-set questionnaires of large samples that are later on turned into quantitative information to test the validity of the hypotheses. This universalizing result is because the focus is on the creator of the questionnaire and not on the different culture under study; therefore it tends to reflect the culture to which the researcher belongs – this methodology only works well when the researcher forms part of the same culture that she/he is studying.

7 The sacrifice of llamas is carried out during the month of August as offerings to *Pachamama* – earth deity. The belief is that Mother Earth is hungry and can take the life of

someone in the community in order to appease her hunger; therefore people offer her the sacrifice of llamas to appease her appetite and prevent somebody's death. As in the case of the cult of the Uncle of the Mine, those who do not participate in the sacrifice are held responsible if accidents or droughts occur (this explanation was given to me in San Cristóbal).

8 The *San Juan* bonfire takes place on June 23, the coldest day of the year. According to an old belief *Inti*, the god sun, was waning, and therefore, in order to prevent this from happening, precisely in the season when the land was to be left fallow, everybody in the community lit fires to give strength to the sun. The sun was the crucial ingredient for crops to grow (this explanation was given to me in San Cristóbal).

9 As Bieler and Morton have assessed, for Cox,

> Other forms of collective identity and agency are included within the rubric of social forces – ethnic, gender, green, national, religious, sexual – ... like class, they derive from a common basis of exploitation and marginalization ... it is through processes of hegemonic struggle that such contending social forces may arise.
>
> (Bieler and Morton 2001: 23)

10 Abya Yala is the name the Kuna people from Panama and Colombia used to denominate the continent and, since 1990, it has been adopted by all indigenous peoples in their documents and declarations. The objective was to reject the term "Americas" used by the conquerors.

11 The concept "global managerial infrastructure" was borrowed from McMichael (1996).

12 The concept "old wars" was borrowed from Kaldor (1999).

1 The 1980s: development as "free markets," the demolition of the old and the rise of the new

1 The authors of Santa Fe I were: L. Francis Bouchey, Roger W. Fontaine, David C. Jordan, Gordon Sumner and Lewis Tambs, and the introduction was written by Ronald F. Docksai, the founder of CIS. Patrick Buchanan, a member of CIS, became President Reagan's communications director; Fontaine was appointed Latin American specialist at the National Security Council (NSC); Sumner was the special consultant to the State Department's Bureau of Inter-American Affairs, and Tambs was assigned to the NSC and later as ambassador to Colombia and Costa Rica. By 1986 CIS had 70,000 members and, five years later, its membership increased to 200,000 – an increment that demonstrates the popularity of the Council. Source: www.disinfopedia.org/wiki.phtml?title=Committee_of_Santa_Fe (accessed May 24, 2004).

2 www.disinfopedia.org/wiki.phtml?title=Committee_of_Santa_Fe (accessed May 24, 2004).

3 I am drawing on a Spanish version of Santa Fe I (accessed September 18, 2004).

4 Note that during the Reagan years Reagan's ambassador to the United Nations, Jeane J. Kirkpatrick's distinction between "authoritarian" and "totalitarian" governments was taken as a pertinent one. For Kirkpatrick, "authoritarian governments" were "good" governments because they tried to preserve traditional values within a capitalist society (e.g., Latin American dictatorships). Meanwhile, "totalitarian governments were bad governments in the sense that they intervened and controlled both social and economic affairs – e.g., Stalin and Hitler" (La Feber 1993: 276). The "Good and Evil" discourse was also strongly evident in Kirkpatrick's definition.

5 This term was borrowed from Philip McMichael (1996).

6 It should be noted that John Hopton's study is on managerialism in the context of the United Kingdom. I am expanding his analysis on local managerialism to global managerialism. The United Kingdom, Australia and New Zealand were the first countries

where managerialism was implemented and where it started to unravel in the 1980s. In the case of the United Kingdom, it coincided with the "New Right"'s success in eliminating the social contract. New managerialism, together with new constitutionalism or transnational legal regimes, expanded to most countries in the world in the 1990s.

7 McMichael (1996: 128).
8 Public health, education and food subsidies.
9 Gas, electricity, water, communications and transport.
10 Instead, a neo-Gramscian perspective, by introducing the concepts of hegemony and passive revolution, aims to integrate both the external and internal dimension of democratization (see Abrahamsen 1997).
11 This was specifically the objective of the edited volume by Sonia E. Álvarez, Evelina Dagnino and Arturo Escobar: *Cultures of Politics, Politics of Cultures. Revisioning Latin American Social Movements* (1998).
12 See Abrahamsen (1997).
13 Cerny, op. cit. 1997: 267.
14 Op. cit. 1997: 269.
15 Op. cit. 1997: 269.
16 This was mentioned by Estellano (1994) for Bolivia, yet it is also the case for most countries in the region. More studies are needed regarding the formation of a new bourgeosie in Latin America since the 1980s.
17 Term borrowed from Van Der Pijl (1998).
18 Waylen's analysis refers to her empirical study in Argentina, Brazil, Chile and Peru.
19 For the Central American Civil Wars see: J. Dunkerley (1985, 1994); J. Dunkerley and R. Seider (1996); H.E. Vanden and G. Prevost (1993, 1999); K.M. Coleman and G.C. Herring (1991); T. Walker (1991); T. Wickham-Crowley (1989, 1998).
20 See Santa Fe I document; also Smith (1996: 184).
21 Ramsaran notes that the "Caribbean Basin" was an arbitrary term utilized by the Reagan Administration to refer to twelve countries in the northern tip of South America, Central America and the Caribbean, which, up until that point, were considered part of the Latin American bloc (Ramsaran 1982: 431).
22 Watson argues that the history of the colonial-imperialist project in the English-speaking Caribbean carried a deep and abiding racialization of class and other areas of social relations. Indeed, in 1845, South Asians were introduced in the region as indentured laborers and, eleven years after the abolition they formed an intermediate ethnic group between creole – white capitalists – and black laborers. The fact that the South Asian ethnics generated business forces from within and mostly in alliance with the white creoles disadvantaged the blacks, for whom it became almost impossible to penetrate the upper echelons of the capitalist strata. This racialization of class relations did not change with independence and it became a huge problem in Jamaica in 1968 and in Tobago in 1970. The CBI deepened these existing class relations between white power and black poverty (I wish to thank Hilbourne Watson for this personal clarification).
23 I wish to thank Hilbourne Watson for this personal explanation.
24 According to Hilbourne Watson, family and household units in the English-speaking Caribbean did not necessarily coincide with the cases studied by Helen Safa, the Dominican Republic and Puerto Rico. Jamaica, Barbados and other former British West Indian colonies have been heavily dominated by female-headed households, so there has been greater insecurity and vulnerability to the neo-liberal economy and financial shocks there than in the Spanish-speaking Caribbean (I wish to thank Hilbourne Watson for this personal explanation).

168 *Notes*

2 The 1990s: development as "good governance" and the consolidation of hegemony

1 According to Santa Fe I.
2 The authors of Santa Fe II were: L. Francis Bouchey, Roger W. Fontaine, David C. Jordan and Gordon Sumner. I am using a Spanish translation of the original document.
3 World Bank, http://web.worldbank.org/WBSITE/EXTERNAL/TOPICS/EXT-POVERTY/EXTPRS/0,,P... (accessed May 9, 2005).
4 See Williamson (2002).
5 For NAFTA's impact in Canada see Schneiderman (1996).
6 The Central American Common Market was integrated by Guatemala, El Salvador, Honduras and Nicaragua; the Caribbean Free Trade Association by Antigua and Barbuda, Bahamas, Barbados, Belize, Dominica, Grenada, Guyana, Haiti, Jamaica, Monserrat, Saint Kitts and Nevis, Saint Lucia, Saint Vincent and the Grenadines, Suriname, and Trinidad and Tobago. Meanwhile Anguilla, Bermuda, the British Virgin Islands, the Cayman Islands, and the Turks and Caicos Islands are associate members. The Andean Pact included Bolivia, Colombia, Ecuador, Peru and Venezuela. Chile was part of it but withdrew in 1976. The MERCOSUR members are Argentina, Brazil, Paraguay and Uruguay; however, in 2012 Paraguay was suspended following the parliamentary coup and Venezuela joined the common market. For the shift produced in MERCOSUR after the 1990s see Phillips (2001, 2004b); Estevadeordal, Goto *et al.* (2001).
7 A very important literature on new regionalisms has emerged in the past few years. See Devlin and Ffrench Davis (1999); Fix-Fierro and López-Ayllo (1997); Phillips (2003a, 2003b, 2004a, 2005); Philips, Breslin *et al.* (2002); Devlin and Estevadeordal (2001); Burfisher, Robinson *et al.* (2003).
8 For this shift produced in the public administration in the Canadian context see Arthurs (2001).
9 Note that Desai's and Imrie's piece cited here is a comparative study on new managerialism in the UK and India. There are no studies on new managerialism in Latin America and I think this is a crucial aspect to examine, in particular the role of foreign-funded NGOs in the replacement and privatization of welfare during the 1990s.
10 For new gender orders see Bakker (1999, 2003); Bayes *et al.* (2001);Bayes and Kelly (2001); Connell (2001); Donaldson (1993); Gherardi and Poggio (2001); Meyer and Prugl (1999); Young (2001).
11 For gender quota laws in Latin America see Baldéz (2006); Blondet (2002); Craske and Molyneux (2002); Htun (2003, 2004, 2006); Htun and Jones (2002); Jones (2004, 2005); Krook (2004, 2006); Molyneux and Craske (2002).
12 Note that parts of this section have been used in a presentation I gave at the International Studies Association (ISA). My paper was entitled "The PRSPs and New Constitutionalism: Deepening the Fissure Between the Americas. The Case of Non-renewable Natural Resources Regimes" and was presented at the International Studies Association (ISA) Annual Convention, *The North–South Divide and International Studies*, March 22–25, 2006 in San Diego, USA (isa06_proceeding_98500.doc).
13 For tax havens see Palan (1996, 1998, 2002, 2003, 2006).
14 See Chapters 6 and 7.
15 Le Billon (2001) has addressed this very well in the African context.
16 There is a very rich literature emerging on resource wars in other regions that can be a basis for understanding the current situation in Latin America. See Berdal and Keen (1997); Boge (1998); Duffield (1998); Fairhead (2000); Kaldor (1999); Karl (1997); Keen (1998); Leite and Weidmann (1999); Renner (1996); Reno (2000); Robin (2000).

17 The concept "complex political emergency" refers to countries that in the post-Cold War era go through a multidimensional crisis that involves a political uprising yet also natural disasters, produces enormous human suffering and the state is strongly contested or even collapses (Pearce 1999: 51).
18 Mexico Solidarity Network: http://mexicosolidarity.org (accessed February 2, 2006).
19 Mexico Solidarity Network, http://mexicosolidarity.org (accessed February 2, 2006). See also Harvey (1998).

3 The new millennium: development as "poverty reduction" and the commodification of livelihood

1 Parts of this section have been used in a paper I gave at the International Studies Association. My paper was entitled "The PRSPs and New Constitutionalism: Deepening the Fissure Between the Americas. The Case of Non-renewable Natural Resources Regimes" and was presented at the International Studies Association (ISA) Annual Convention, *The North–South Divide and International Studies*, March 22–25, 2006 in San Diego, USA (isa06_proceeding_98500.doc).
2 The literature on PRSPs refers to them as second-generation reforms – because it is law-bound – but also as third-generation reforms. I prefer to use the term "third-generation reforms" because they represent a third planning stage and contain structural, superstructural and social dimensions. I consider as third-generation reforms the Heavily Indebted Poor Countries (HIPCs) Initiative, the Poverty Reduction Strategy Papers (PRSPs), the Millennium Development Goals (MDGs) and the Impoverishment, Risk and Livelihood Reconstruction (IRLR) model – all policies that aimed to "solve" the poverty problematique. The reason I am focusing especially on the PRSPs is because these are the ones that deal with natural resources, and therefore they are an introduction to the second part of this volume: mining in Bolivia. Chapter 6 on Bolivia also deals with the IRLR model.
3 I am using a Spanish translation of Santa Fe IV. The editors of Santa Fe IV were Gordon Sumner Jr. and Lewis Tambs – the latter is a diplomatic, a historian and a professor at Arizona State University. The introduction was written by James P. Lucier, Staff Director of the Committee for Foreign Relations of the United States Senate. According to the Spanish preface written by Fernando Bossi of *Proyecto Emancipación – Comité Permanente Congreso Anfitriónico Bolivariano*, other participants in Santa Fe IV were: Roger W. Fontaine, David C. Jordan, Francis Bouchez, General John K. Singlaub and Jeanne Kirkpatrick (Santa Fe IV 2001).
4 The italics have been added to the original text and, as mentioned above, I have done the translation from Spanish to English, so there may be some differences with the original English version of the Santa Fe documents.
5 The difference between Bolivarianism and the Monroe Doctrine requires further clarification. Both had originated in the nineteenth century and were related to the expulsion of foreign powers from the Americas. However, Simón Bolívar's objective during the revolutionary wars for independence was to unify Spanish-speaking America against Spain and, when President Chávez today appeals to Bolivarianism, he does so in defense against American "imperialism." This has nothing to do with a Latin American "imperialism" as the Santa Fe IV document pretends to imply. Instead, the Monroe Doctrine always had a hegemonic connotation by which no extra-continental power was allowed to enter the Americas, a terrain that Americans believe they own. This is clear when the Santa Fe documents and many other US documents refer to South American natural resources as "our natural resources."
6 As mentioned before, the literature on PRSPs refers to them as second-generation reforms and also as third-generation reforms – both are rule-based. Here it was

preferred to use the term "third-generation reforms" to distinguish it from the 1990s rights-based development policies because they also include the new social policy, based on the privatization of livelihood.

7 For a mainstream perspective on the post-Washington Consensus policies and HIPCs see Birdsall and Williamson (2002); Kuczynski and Williamson (2003). For a critical perspective see Arthurs (2002); Dunkerley and Bulmer-Thomas (1999); Patel and McMichael (2004); Soederberg (2004).

8 World Bank Group, WWW.WORLDBANK.ORG/HIPC/ABOUT/HIPCBR/HIPCBR. HTM (accessed May 2005).

9 Yet this logic was not always followed. For example, Haiti, the poorest country in the Americas, was not considered a heavily indebted country.

10 For a critical analysis on PRSPs see Weber (2004, 2006).

11 See Kalima (2001); the Jubilee South Pan-African Declaration on PRSPs – May (2001); Bond (2004); Bullard (2003); Chávez-Malaluan and Guttal (2003); Demba Moussa Dembele (2004); Guttal (2002, 2003); Jones and Hardstaff (2005); Stewart and Wang (n.d.).

12 See World Bank Group: Poverty Reduction Sourcebook: http://web.worldbank. org/WBSITE/EXTERNAL/TOPICS/EXTPOVERTY/EXTPRS/O,,c.. (accessed May 2005).

13 World Bank Group, op. cit.

14 See Poverty Reduction Sourcebook, op. cit.

15 The Impoverishment Risk and Livelihood Reconstruction model is a problem-solving approach to development-induced displacement (DID). It recognizes eight intertwined risks that lead to impoverishment through development-induced displacement: loss of land, common property, homes, jobs and food security, increasing marginalization, morbidity and social disarticulation, and recommends policies to reverse these problems. However, it does not address the Poverty Reduction Strategy Papers, which are the source of the problem. As such, it is just another "band-aid" policy of the problem-solving approach of the international financial institutions.

16 Poverty Reduction Sourcebook, op. cit.

17 Francisca Relea: "Una lucha entre quienes quieren vender gas y quienes no. Cómo es Tarija, la Kuwait Boliviana." Página 12, Buenos Aires, Argentina, November 6, 2003 (www.página12web.com.ar/diario/elmundo/4–27759.html).

18 One of the main points of disagreement was the fact that Chile would make profits out of Bolivian gas. This is because the coastal territory where that pipeline would be built belonged to Bolivia until the Chileans seized it during the "Pacific War" (1879–1883). Since then, Bolivia became a land-locked country and the relations between both countries have been, and remain, bitter.

19 Konstantin Kilibarda, "Disappearing Bolivia: The Globe and Mail's Coverage of the Gas War. An En Camino Alert," November 1, 2003 (www.en-camino.org/ nov012003kilibarda.htm).

20 Raquel Gutiérrez Aguilar, "Bolivia: Recuperating Natural Resources, Rebuilding a Nation." Americas Program, Interhemispheric Resource Center (IRC), November 1, 2003 (www.americaspolicy.org). See also Konstantin Kilibarda, op. cit.

21 Raquel Gutiérrez Aguilar, op. cit.

22 Raquel Gutiérrez Aguilar, op. cit.

23 Poverty Reduction Sourcebook, op.cit.

24 ESAF refers to Enhanced Structural Adjustment Facility and PRGF to Poverty Reduction Growth Facility. In reality, ESAF was renamed PRGF when the PRSPs were launched. This shows that the latter are a continuation of structural adjustment programs yet under a different name. World Development Movement (www.wdm.org. uk/democracy/parliament/index.htm).

25 World Development Movement, op. cit.

26 Tabra Guerrero, Mario: Salvemos el Agua, Salvemos la Verdad. El Agua de los

Guayacundos. Factortierra, www.geocities.com/factortierra/chira/20050522/#subtitle 1 (accessed June 2, 2005).

27 Guido, Emiliano: El Acuífero Guaraní en Pantalla Grande, La Tierra Sin Mal, September 4, 2005 (http://eco21.com.ar).

28 Herraiz, Iñigo: Maniobras de la empresa española que se adjudicó la privatización ahora derogada. November 14, 2004. La Democracia del Agua (www.rebelion.org/noticia.php?id=7612).

29 Poverty Reduction Sourcebook, op. cit.

30 Personal Interview with Pedro Gómez Rocabado, researcher at the Centre for Mining Promotion (*Centro de Promoción Minera*, CEPROMIN, La Paz, Bolivia).

31 See: Smith (2002); Winn (2006).

32 Until 2005 there have been four Summits of the Americas: Miami (December 1994), Santiago de Chile (April 1998), Québec (April 2001) and Mar del Plata (November 4–5, 2005), and two special Summits: Summit on Sustainable Development (Santa Cruz de la Sierra, December 1996) and the Extraordinary Summit of the Americas (Monterrey, January 2004).

33 For NAFTA Plus see Ayres (2004); Campbell (2005).

34 For security in the post-9/11 World in the Americas see Nef (2005, 2006).

35 According to the Canadian government, there are "various outstanding issues in the agreement that could not be solved. For example, work remains in the areas of market access for textiles and apparel, as well as market access for agricultural products." See: www.dfait-maeci.gc.ca/tna-nac/ca4-en.asp (accessed August 5, 2006).

36 See "The Investment Chapter in the Canada–Central America Free Trade Agreement: Threats to Community Rights. A Briefing Note from the Americas Policy Group, A Working Group of the Canadian Council for International Co-operation," June 2, 2005.

37 See Cuzco Declaration document (www.comunidadandina.org/exterior/sudamerica. htm).

38 Inter Press Service News Agency, December 7, 2004 (www.ipsnews.net/interna. asp?idnews=26583).

39 See www.comunidadandina.org/exterior/sudamerica.htm.

40 See Interview with Isaac Bigio, Correo, Ayacucho, Peru, December 9 2004: Adónde va la CSN que hoy nace en Ayacucho? (www.americas.org/item_17139).

41 See ALAI Latin America in Movement, October 11, 2005 (http://alainet.org/active/9435&lang=en and www.spanish.xinhuanet.com/spanish/2005–10/02/content_167452.htm#).

42 See ALAI Latin America in Movement, October 11, 2005 (http://alainet.org/active/9435&lang=en).

43 These include the Mapuche Confederation of Neuquén (*Confederación Mapuche de Neuquén*), the Indigenous Commission of the Lawyers Association of Argentina (CJIRA – *Comisión Indígena de la Asociación de Abogados de Argentina*), Confederation of Indigenous Nationalities of Ecuador (CONAIE – *Confederación de Naciones Indígenas de Ecuador*), the National Indigenous Organization of Colombia (ONIC – *Organización Nacional Indígena de Colombia*), the Kuna Congress of Panama (CKP – *Congreso Kuna de Panamá*) and, over twenty other indigenous organizations from the Americas, including those from the United States and Canada (Porqué los pueblos se oponen, Mar del Plata, October 23, 2005 (http:www.prensadefrente.org/anticumbre/index.php/2005/10/23/setenta_organizaciones_indigenas_del_con_1)).

44 Porqué los pueblos se oponen, Mar del Plata, October 23, 2005 (http:www.prensadefrente. org/anticumbre/index.php/2005/10/23/setenta_organizaciones_indigenas_del_con_1).

45 The author of the document is Nilo Cayuqueo. The original version appeared in *Azkintuwe Noticias*, a Mapuche newspaper. A Spanish version may be found at Porqué los pueblos se oponen, Mar del Plata, October 23, 2005 (http:www.prensadefrente.org/

anticumbre/index.php/2005/10/23/setenta_organizaciones_indigenas_del_con_1).   An
English translation may be found at www.globalexchange.org/countries/americas/argen-
tina/3388.html.

46 Palabras del presidente de la República Argentina, Dr. Néstor Kirchner durante la
inauguración de la IV Cumbre de las Américas, en Mar del Plata, Friday, November
4, 2005 (www.ivcumbreamericas.gov.ar/DetalleDiscurso_53_ing_esp.html).

47 The acronym ALBA also means "sunset" in Spanish, a connotation for a new
beginning.

48 Costa Rica, Malasia, the Philippines and Uruguay (*Página 12*, 2009a).

49 Andorra, Anguilla, Antigua and Barbuda, Aruba, Bahamas, Bahrain, Belize, Bermuda,
British Virgin Islands, Cayman Islands, Cook Islands, Domininca, Gibraltar, Grenada,
Liberia, Liechtenstein, Marshall Islands, Monaco, Montserrat, Nauru, the Dutch Anti-
lles, Saint Vincent and the Grenadines, Samoa, San Marino, Turk Islands and Caicos
and Vanuatu (*Página 12*, 2009a).

50 Austria, Belgium, Brunei, Chile, Guatemala, Luxembourg, Singapore and Switzerland
(*Página 12*, 2009a).

4 Obama, "change" and the disembedding of security in Latin America: the tension between polyarchy and democracy

1 This chapter was presented at the Karl Polanyi International Seminar, "The World
Between Crisis and Change (Panel: Embeddedness & Disembeddedness)," jointly
organized by the Karl Polanyi Institute of Political Economy and the EMES European
Research Network on February 15–16, 2012 in Paris, France. It was chosen as an
EMES Conferences Selected Papers Series (ECSPs): Liege, Belgium (www.emes.net/
index.php?id=458).

2 http://nobelprize.org/nobel_prizes/peace/laureates/2009.

3 See Latham n.d.

4 Gavin has demonstrated that the US Guantánamo Bay Naval Base is a colonial
residue that dates from the end of the nineteenth century, when the Spanish were
defeated. The Spanish signed the Treaty of Paris, through which Cuba would remain
under the *temporary* protectorate of the United States. However, later on, the Platt
Amendment strengthened the Cuban dependence on the United States through two
key articles; article III stated that the United States had "the right to intervene for the
preservation of Cuban independence," and article VII that, in order for the US to
maintain Cuban independence, "the government of Cuba will sell or lease to the
United States land necessary for coaling or naval stations." In 1903, the Cuban–American Treaty was signed with the objective to take into effect article VII of the Platt
Amendment and, in 1934, a new treaty ratified that Guantánamo would be leased per-
manently to the US for $4,085 a year. Because Fidel Castro, due to the confusion of
the first years after the revolution, cashed one of those cheques, it was considered that
he legitimized the 1934 treaty (Gavin 2010: 2).

5 See Brookings Institute (www.brookings.edu/topics/cuba.aspx) and *Oil & Gas
Journal* 2009.

6 Cited in Rodríguez (2010: 2).

7 These classified documents were released to the *New York Times* and National Public
Radio and also through WikiLeaks on April 24, 2011 (Bearden 2011: 1).

8 The bold highlighting was added by the author.

9 See www.state.gov/r/pa/prs/ps/2010/06/142950.htm.

10 *Brasiguayos* stands for Brazilian Paraguayans.

5 The Amayapampa and Capasirca gold-mines: double movement and state repression

1 This chapter has been published in Liisa North, Timothy Clark and Viviana Patroni (eds), *Community Rights and Corporate Responsibility*, Toronto: Between the Lines (2006). Some changes have been introduced into that version. It was also presented at two conferences. First, at the *Conference on Canadian Mining Companies in Latin America: Community Rights and Corporate Responsibility* organized by the Centre for Research on Latin America and the Caribbean (CERLAC) at York University and Mining Watch Canada, May 9–11, 2002, Toronto, Ontario, Canada; and; then at the *Conference Latin America: Between Representations and Realities* organized by the Canadian Association for Latin American and Caribbean Studies (CALACS), October 24–26, 2002, Université du Québec a Montréal (UQAM), Montréal, Québec, Canada.

2 This was the final stage of my research for this chapter.

3 Stephen Gill defines disciplinary neo-liberalism as the structural or socio-economic form of capitalism that emerged in the 1970s, which

> relies upon the market, especially the capital market, to discipline economic agents. And it is premised on the fact that investors constitute a privileged stratum in capitalist societies....This is a form of the structural power of capital. Indeed, since discipline in the workplace is viewed by investors as crucial for confidence, it indicates that the indirect power of market forces is not enough to ensure the reproduction of capital. Direct power is also needed in the form of state action to ensure social control, and in the provision of laws and coercive potential to ensure that the owners of capital determine how production takes place.
>
> (Gill 2000: 4)

4 The World Bank also proposed that Chile and Brazil should shift to gold-mining production. However, neither of them are considered "reforming countries." Chile enters the World Bank category of the "reformed country" and Brazil is "still to be reformed" – together with Colombia, Venezuela, Guyana, Jamaica and Surinam (World Bank 1996).

5 Refers to the December attack in Amayapampa.

6 The information related to the characteristics of "new mining" comes from interviews conducted by the author in Bolivia with mining and other NGOs and human rights activists in the summer of 2000.

7 Karl Polanyi writes of the "double movement" – from above and below – as follows:

> the market expanded continuously but this movement was met by a counter-movement checking the expansion in definite directions.... This was more than the usual defensive behavior of society faced with change; it was the reaction against a dislocation which attacked the fabric of society, and which could have destroyed the very organization of production that the market had called into being.
>
> (Polanyi 1944: 130)

8 The Garafulics' dubious ownership of Amayapampa became the subject of a lawsuit that was still unsettled as of mid-2003. The Radic family claims ownership of the mine. See "Historia de un estelionato" in the newspaper *La Estrella*, Santa Cruz, December 21, 1998.

9 The quotation in this chapter from Pedro Gómez Rocabado is taken from his testimonial presented at the York University conference in spring 2002. His testimonial was published in North *et al.* (2006).

10 Report about the Participation of the Mining National Secretary in the conflict between the enterprise Da Capo Resources and the Amayapampa and Capasirca Workers' Union. Sent by Dr. Teddy Cuentas Bascope, Mining National Secretary, to

Dr. Jaime Villalobos, Minister of Economic Development. January 10, 1997. Database: Centro de Promoción Minera, CEPROMIN, La Paz.

11 Olivia Harris defines the *ayllu* as a

> [c]orporate descent group with collective ownership of resources, including lands and theoretical endogamy (marrying within the *ayllu*). Its members enjoy a relationship of mutual aid or reciprocity and, although they may be dispersed, retain their social linkage and rights to communal resources.

(2000: vi)

12 Testimony of Segundina Vargas, Community: Chuquiuta, Capasirca Mine. In APDHB 1998: 53.

13 In the Andes, every single mine has a statue of the Uncle of the Mine. The Uncle represents to the miners what *Pachamama* – earth deity – represents to the agriculturalists. The myth of the Uncle of the Mine dates from the Spanish conquest of America: when Inca Atahuallpa was about to be executed, he held up an orange (the symbol of gold, the sun and masculinity) and said, "this gold that for us it was easy to obtain, enters deep into the earth and, those who want to possess it should suffer and sweat to obtain it"; then the Inca held up an egg (the symbol of silver, the moon and femininity) and repeated the same words. The world then turned upside-down and some versions of the myth sustain that the Uncle of the Mine is the Inca who, as a result of the world turning upside-down, was now inside the earth, the *Manqhapacha* or the Kingdom of the subsoil. Other stories say that the Uncle is the son of the sun, dressed as a devil, enemy of the conquerors, and that he represents the resistance against them. Hence, the cult of the Uncle is profoundly religious; he has the power of the Inca and is the one whom the miners consult in their search for rich veins and also for moral and material strength. He is a giver and reaffirms the common identity of the miners which is one of cultural resistance to domination. Those who do not participate in the *pijcheo* and the *convite* or plea are seen as responsible for all the bad things that can occur such as an accident in the mines, loss of jobs or the disappearance of the veins. In the mines there is not only a *Tío* but also a *Tía*, an aunt, who is very jealous, and therefore women are not allowed to enter the mines because the aunt can make the veins of mineral disappear. This is a very strong belief in the Andes and has led to a gendered division of labor in the mines. In fact, women miners as the *palliri* can only work outside the mines (Aguilar 1996: 8–29; see also Poppe 1977; Gusmán Rada Cusicanqui 1999).

14 Resolution of the Cabildo of the Four *Ayllus* (local government) of the Province of Rafael Bustillos, Department of Potosí, Bolivia, November 28–29, 1996 (CEPROMIN database, La Paz).

15 Letter from the New Council for Defense of the Dignity and Interest of the *Ayllus* of the Province R. Bustillos, to the Lower and Upper House of the Parliament, Potosí, December 2, 1996. Ref.: Problem regarding mining and Territory of the *Ayllus* of Northern Potosí, Registry No. 002322, December 5, 1996 (CEPROMIN database).

16 See Núñez and Jungwiry (1997: 36).

17 Letter from Teddy Cuentas Bascopi, Mining National Secretary, to Dr. Carlos Sánchez Berzain, Minister of Government (Cite N.01040), La Paz, October 24, 1996 (CEPROMIN database, La Paz).

18 Report about the Participation of the Mining National Secretary in the conflict between the enterprise Da Capo Resources and the Amayapampa and Capasirca Workers' Union. Sent by Dr. Teddy Cuentas Bascope, Mining National Secretary, to Dr. Jaime Villalobos, Minister of Economic Development, January 10, 1997 (CEPROMIN database, La Paz).

19 Legal document from the Mining Company Da Capo Resources, Ltd., addressed to the Fiscal Agent of the Capital "Oruro," No. 7340416. Oruro, December 3, 1996 (CEPROMIN database, La Paz).

20 Letter From Yerko Kukoc del Carpio, Prefect and General Commander of the Department of Potosí, Bolivia, to Dr. Teddy Cuentas Bascope, Mining National Secretary, Potosi, December 10, 1996. Enclosed: Resolution of the Civic Committee of Llallagua, December 1996 (CEPROMIN database, La Paz).
21 Legal document signed by the Provincial Police and sent by Vista Gold to Mining National Secretary, December 20, 1996 (CEPROMIN database, La Paz).
22 Letter from Ing. David O'Connor to Dr. Teddy Cuentas Bascope, Mining National Secretary, Ministry of Economic Development. August 26, 1996 (DCB/73/96 Registry N.001857, 28 AGO 1996) (CEPROMIN database, La Paz); letter from Ing. David O'Connor and Dr. Raquel Portillo M., Legal Assistant to Dr. Teddy Cuentas Bascope, Mining Sub-secretary; copy of the letter sent to the Ministers of Labour and Mining and to the Sindicato Mixto de Trabajadores de Capasirca (Mixed Labour Union of Capasirca) to the TMC, September 16, 1996 (Registry N.001964, September 16, 1996) (CEPROMIN database, La Paz); letter from David O'Connor to Lic. Gonzalo Sánchez de Lozada, Constitutional President of the Republic of Bolivia, November 19, 1996 (vgc/005/96) (CEPROMIN database, La Paz).
23 Letter from David O'Connor to Lic. Gonzalo Sánchez de Lozada, Constitutional President of the Republic of Bolivia, November 19, 1996 (vgc/005/96) (CEPROMIN database, La Paz).
24 Aillón Gómez 1999: 85, 65; *Mining Magazine* 184, 5 (May 2001), p. 19; *The Economist* 336, 7930 (September 2, 1995), p. 59; *Mining Journal* 337, 8652 (September 21, 2001), p. 226; Apex Silver Mines (www.apexsilver.com).
25 Testimony of Yolanda Antezana, APDH-SIGLO XX activist. In APDHB 1998: 53–54.
26 Testimony of Silvia Rojas, APDH-SIGLO XX activist. In APDHB 1998: 40.
27 Testimony of Yolanda Antezana, APDH-SIGLO XX activist. In APDHB 1998: 58.
28 International Labour Organization (1989) *Convention No. 169*, Article 7, Concerning Indigenous and Tribal Peoples in Independent Countries. Adopted on June 27, 1989 by the General Conference of the International Labour Organization, seventy-sixth session, entry into force September 5, 1991.
29 On Vista Gold's webpage, the company states, "Our strategy is to acquire quality gold projects. We are in no hurry to take any of these projects into production, we feel that production at today's gold prices would prematurely deplete our valuable gold resources." www.vistagold.com/corp-profile.php (accessed June 5, 2003). Information here also comes from letters received from the Amayapampa community, March 2003.
30 Letter of Intentions between Empresa Minera Amayapampa S.A. (EMASA) and Minera Nueva Vista S.A. (MNV), signed by Ronald McGregor, Legal Advisor, Minera Nueva Vista S.A. La Paz, December 12, 2002.

6 Multilateralism, population displacement and resettlement in San Cristóbal silver mines

1 Apex owns twelve properties. In Bolivia, the San Cristóbal District (silver-zinc-lead), Cobrizos (silver-copper) and Rincón del Tigre (platinum-palladium). In Mexico, San Luis del Cordero (silver-zinc-copper), San Juan del Cordero (silver-zinc-lead), Platosa (silver-zinc-lead), El Aguila (gold-silver), Zacatecas (MMS/X silver-zinc-lead). In Peru, Aguila (silver-zinc-lead), Aventura III (gold-silver), Jehuamarca (silver-gold). In Kyrgyzstan, Jamgyr (gold) (Apex Silver Mines, October 27th, 2000 (www.apexsilver.com)).
2 Personal interview.
3 Apex Silver Mines, October 27, 2000 (www.apexsilver.com) also cited in *Presencia*, September 9, 1999 (a Bolivian newspaper).
4 Apex Silver Mines, October 27, 2000 (www.apexsilver.com).

5 Apex Silver Mines, May 10, 2000 (www.apexsilver.com).
6 Personal interview.
7 "The International Finance Corporation is a member of the World Bank Group and is the largest multilateral source of loans ... for private sector projects in the developing world." The Andean Corporation for Promotion, also a multilateral financial institution, has the task of supporting sustainable development and integration within the Andean Region by providing funding to both public and private sectors. "The principal shareholders are the five member countries of the Andean Region: Bolivia, Colombia, Ecuador, Peru and Venezuela. Other extraregional shareholders include the governments of Chile and Brazil, as well as 22 regional private commercial banks" (Apex Silver Mines, May 10, 2000) (www.apexsilver.com).
8 Personal interview.
9 Information provided by the Minister for Economic Development, José Luis Lupo, to *Ultima Hora*, August 21, 1999.
10 Information provided by the *Alcalde de Potosí*, René Joaquino, to *El Deber*, September 12, 1999.
11 Information provided by the Minister for Economic Development, José Luis Lupo, to *Ultima Hora*, August 21, 1999.
12 The major stakeholder of COMSUR is Gonzalo Sánchez de Lozada (Sanabria 1999: 65). As noted in the previous chapter he was the architect of the neo-liberal project and president of the country from 1993 to 1997, and again from August 2002 to October 2003, when he was obliged by a massive popular movement to abandon the country.
13 *La Prensa*, September 14, 1999.
14 Information given by the Minister for Economic Development, José Luis Lupo, to *Ultima Hora*, August 21, 1999.
15 President Hugo Banzer to *Ultima Hora*, August 21, 1999.
16 President Hugo Banzer to *Ultima Hora*, August 21, 1999.
17 *El Deber*, September 12, 1999.
18 *El Diario*, September 3, 1999 and *La Razón*, August 21, 1999.
19 *El Diario*, September 3, 1999.
20 *La Razón*, August 21, 1999.
21 Personal interview in New San Cristóbal.
22 www.tbpnewsletter.com.
23 Sikkink (1995: 5) argues that there is a tremendous social, economic and occupational diversity in the region.
24 Albó (Albó *et al.* 1990: 43) claims that pre-Hispanic *ayllus* that subsisted until today are located at the southwest and south of the *Desaguadero* river and in Northern Potosí, with some minor enclaves in other regions. These still maintain strong ancestral characteristics, even though they were modified during colonial and republican times.
25 Masculinity in the Andes is associated with what is positive, good and stronger; femininity is associated with what is negative, bad and weaker (Harris 2000: 178). Yet, both men and women living in the left side of a town are considered to have feminine characteristics and, vice versa, men and women living in the right side of a town are considered to have masculine qualities. To a degree, having male and feminine qualities is independent of being male or female.
26 Andean communities are both individualistic and collective at the same time. In fact, Albó *et al.* mention that one of the main problems between the communities and development organizations concerns elaborate individualistic programs and others collective ones. In the end, both programs hurt the communities because the communities are both things at the same time (Albó *et al.*1990: 76–77).
27 Anonymous interview conducted in August 2000.
28 On account of life expectancy being very low for the miners in the *puna* or highlands, at 40 years old people are considered elders.

7 President Evo Morales Ayma's *Pachakutik*. Re-founding Bolivia as an indigenous nation

1 El Nuevo Herald, February 22, 2005 from AFP.
2 Evo Morales web page, www.evomorales.org/ (accessed July 12, 2006).
3 Wikinoticias, June 7, 2005. Renuncia de Nuevo Carlos Mesa, http://es.wikinews.org/wiki/Renuncia_de_nuevo_Carlos_Mesa (accessed July 12, 2006); Espacio USA Vanguardia Latina: Lic. Carlos Mesa Gisbert, Expresidente de Bolivia, www.esmas.com/vanguardialatina/progact/532135.html (accessed July 12, 2006).
4 Evo Morales web page, op. cit.
5 The Supreme Decree's name "Heroes of Chaco" aims to honor those 50,000 Bolivian soldiers, many of them indigenous peoples, who died during the Chaco War against Paraguay (1932–1935) to defend Bolivia's oil reserves in El Chaco.
6 Morales' selection of the San Alberto oilfield to give his speech was not arbitrary. In fact, as one analyst, Raúl Zibechi, has mentioned, Morales accused Petrobras, the second largest company in the El Chaco region, of operating illegally and of blackmailing Bolivia by stating that it would defend its American investors – who represent 60 percent of the company – and would take the nationalization case to the New York Courts. In the first trimester of 2006, Petrobras' revenues amounted to US$3 billion, 33 percent more than in 2005. This is way more than the low US$300,000 million that Bolivia expects to gain with this nationalization. Raúl Zibechi, "Después de la nacionalización en Bolivia-Hacia un nuevo mapa regional." Translated by Nick Henry as "After Bolivia's Gas Nationalization –Toward a New Regional Map." IRC Americas Program Policy Report http://americas.irc-online.org/am/3290 (accessed July 10, 2006).
7 Foreign Policy Association, May 4, 2006: Bolivia and Energy Nationalization www.fpa.org/topics_info2414/topics_info_show.htm?doc_id=371644 (accessed July 11, 2006).
8 "Upside Down World," speech given by Evo Morales on May 1. Written by Evo Morales, translated by Rachel Eckersley on June 5, 2006 www.globalexchange.org/countries/americas/bolivia/3958.html (accessed July 11, 2006).
9 Evo Morales, "Upside Down World," op. cit.
10 BBC News, "Bolivia Gas Under State Control. Bolivia's President Evo Morales has Signed a Decree Placing his Country's Energy Industry Under State Control," May 2, 2006, http://news.bbc.co.uk/2/hi/americas/4963348.stm BBC news (accessed July 10, 2006). See also Whitney Jr., op. cit.
11 Mabel Azcui (La Paz), "Morales anuncia que todos los recursos naturales pasarán a manos del Estado. El presidente de Bolivia defiende la nacionalizacón del petróleo y el gas como un acto de valentía," published by El País (Spain), March 5, 2006, www.elpais.es/articulo/internacional/Morales/anuncia/todos/recursos/naturales/pasaran/manos/estado/elpporint/20060503elpepiint_2/Tes/ (accessed July 10, 2006.
12 World Views, "Nationalizing Natural Resources: In Bolivia, It's a Gas," http://sfgate.com/cgi-bin/blogs/sfgate/detail?blogid=15&entry_id=4905 (accessed July 10, 2006).
13 Raúl Zibechi, op. cit.
14 Raúl Zibechi, op. cit.
15 World Views, op. cit.
16 Walter Mignolo is the William H. Wannamaker Professor of Literature and Romance Studies at Duke University and writes about the coloniality of power and subaltern knowledges.
17 Walter Mignolo, "Beyond Populism: Decolonizing the Economy. Nationalization of Natural Gas in Bolivia." Counterpounch, May 9, 2006, http://counterpounch.org/mignolo05082006.html (accessed July 10, 2006).
18 Morales said that foreign gas or oil companies that accept Bolivia's new nationalization "will be welcome," and "their investment[s] will be respected." In World Views, op. cit.

19 Whitney Jr., op. cit.
20 Cited by Mabel Azcui, op. cit.
21 Mabel Azcui, op. cit.
22 La Jornada, January 26, 2009. Section Mundo, "Gana el sí a la Constitución; proclama Evo Morales la refundación de Bolivia" (www.jornada.unam.mx).
23 Mentioned by W.T. Whitney Jr., "Bolivia Joins New Alliance, Nationalizes Gas." People's Weekly World newspaper, May 11, 2006, www.pww.org/article/articleview/9115/1/321/ (accessed July 10, 2006). Note that by referring to the "Axis of Good," Morales is counteracting the discourse of the American New Right, which in the 1980s referred to the Soviet Union and Cuba as the "Axis of Evil," and in the new millennium they see Venezuela and Bolivia as joining this diabolic alliance.
24 Whitney Jr., op. cit.
25 IRC Americas Program Policy Report, May 30, 2006, "After Bolivia's Gas Nationalization – Toward a New Regional Map," http://americas.irc-online.org/am/3290 (accessed July 11, 2006).
26 "Cumbre extraordinaria de la Unión de Naciones Suramericanas (UNASUR). Los presidents suramericanos apoyan a Evo Morales y piden el fin de la violencia," El Mundo, España, September 16, 2008 (http:www.elmundo.es/elmundo/2008/09/16/internacional).
27 Declaration of Quito, Ecuador, Indigenous Alliance of the Americas on 500 Years of Resistance. July 1990. http://cumbrecontinentalindigena.org/quito_en.php (accessed May 10, 2010).
28 This section is based on a presentation given by the author at the Canadian Association for International Development Studies (CASID) that took place on May 31 to June 2, 2010 in Montréal. The presentation was entitled "The Fourth Moment of the New World Order: Obama, The Environment and a Shift in Capitalist Accumulation."
29 http://pwccc.wordpress.com/2010/04/29/final-conclusions-working-group13-intercultural-dialogue-to-share-knowledge-skills-and-technologies/ (accessed May 10, 2010).
30 http://pwccc.wordpress.com/2010/04/30/final-conclusions-working-group-n%C2%BA-8-climate-debt/ (accessed May 10, 2010).
31 People's Agreement of Cochabamba, April 24, 2010, http://pwccc.wordpress.com/2010/04/24/peoples-agreement/#more-1584 (accessed May 10, 2010).
32 People's Agreement of Cochabamba, April 24, 2010, http://pwccc.wordpress.com/2010/04/24/peoples-agreement/#more-1584 (accessed May 10, 2010).
33 http://pwccc.wordpress.com/2010/04/29/final-conclusions-working-group-14-forests/ (accessed May 10, 2010).
34 http://pwccc.wordpress.com/2010/04/29/final-conclusions-working-group-15-dangers-of-the-carbon-market/ (accessed May 10, 2010).
35 "ABI: Morales: Bolivia was not alone in Cancun, it stood with the people in defense of life" by Adalid Cabrera Lemuz in News, UN climate change negotiations, December 20, 2010.

References

"Monetarism." *TheFreeDictionary.com*: Farlex www.thefreedictionary.com/monetarism. (1998). Fascist Monetarism. *National Review*. November 23.

Abrahamsen, R. (1997). "The Victory of Popular Forces or Passive Revolution? A Neo-Gramscian Perspective on Democratisation." *Journal of Modern African Studies* 35(1, March): 129–152.

Absi, P. (1997). "The Treasure of the Cerro Rico." *UNESCO Courier* (December): 36(4).

AFP (2011). "Argentina, US in Diplomatic Spat after Cargo Seized," February 15. Available at: www.activistpost.com/2011/02/argentina-us-in-diplomatic-spat-after.html.

Aguilar, L. A. (1996). "El Tío de los Mineros. Resistencia y Solidaridad en la Mina." *Eco Andino, Revista del Centro de Ecología y Pueblos Andinos (CEPA)*. Año 1, No. 2. Oruro, Bolivia, CEPA.

Aillón Gomez, T. (1999). "Un Balance de la Política Neoliberal de Recuperación del Sector Minero en Bolivia. Cochabamba: Búsqueda." *Instituto de Estudios Sociales y Económicos (IESE)* Año 9(14, Julio): 75–90.

Albó, X., A. Godínez *et al.* (1990). *Para Comprender las Culturas Rurales en Bolivia*. La Paz: Ministerio de Educación de Bolivia, CIPCA, UNICEF.

Alda, S. (2007). "The Alliance between the People and the Armed Forces in Evo Morales' Social Transformation Project." Real Instituto Elcano de Estudios Internacionales y Estratégicos, 6pp.

Álvarez, S. E. (1999). "Advocating Feminism: The Latin American Feminist NGO 'Boom'." *International Feminist Journal of Politics* 1(2): 181–209.

Álvarez, S. E., E. Dagnino *et al.* (eds). (1998). *Cultures of Politics, Politics of Culture. Re-visioning Latin American Social Movements*. Boulder, CO: Westview Press.

Anonymous. (2009). "Oil Linked to US Move Toward Thaw with Cuba." *Oil & Gas Journal [Tulsa]* 107(17): 30–2.

Aparicio, J. (2006). *Briefing on the New Bolivian Administration*. Hudson Institute, Inc., 26pp.

Appadurai, A. (1998). "Dead Certainty: Ethnic Violence in the Era of Globalization." *Development and Change* 29(winter): 905–925.

APDHB. (1998). Report of the Permanent Assembly for Human Rights of Bolivia: Amayapampa, Capasirca y Llallagua: "La Masacre de Navidad." UNITAS.

Arthurs, H. (2001). "The Re-constitution of the Public Domain." In *The Market or the Public Domain: Global Governance and the Asymmetry of Power*, ed. D. Drache and R. Higgott. London: Routledge, pp. 85–110.

Arthurs, H. (2002). "Governance after the Washington Consensus: The Public Domain, The State and the Microphysics of Power." *Man and Development* 29: 85–112.

Arthurs, H. W. (1997). "Globalization of the Mind: Canadian Elites and the Restructuring of Legal Fields." *Canadian Journal of Legal Studies* 12(2, fall): 219–246.

Arthurs, H. W. (2001). "The World Turned Upside Down: Are Changes in Political Economy and Legal Practice Transforming Legal Education and Scholarship, or Vice-Versa?" *International Journal of the Legal Profession* 8(1): 11–21.

Assies, W. (2003). "David versus Goliath in Cochabamba: Water Rights, Neoliberalism, and the Revival of Social Protest in Bolivia." *Latin American Perspectives* 30(3, May): 14–36.

Astvaldsson, A. (2000). "The Dynamics of Aymara Duality: Change and Continuity in Sociopolitical Structures in the Bolivian Andes." *Journal of Latin American Studies* 32(1, February): 145–174.

Ayres, J. M. (2004). "Political Economy, Civil Society and the Deep Integration Debate in Canada." *American Review of Canadian Studies* 34.

Baber, Z. (2001). "Modernization Theory and the Cold War." *Journal of Contemporary Asia* 31(1): 71–85.

Baines, E. K. (2003). "Body Politics and the Rwandan Crisis." *Third World Quarterly* 24(3): 479–493.

Bakker, I. (1999). "Neoliberal Governance and the New Gender Order." *Working Papers* 1(1): 49–59.

Bakker, I. (2003). "Neo-liberal Governance and the Reprivatization of Social Reproduction: Social Provisioning and Shifting Gender Orders." In *Power, Production and Social Reproduction. Human In/security in the Global Political Economy*, ed. I. Bakker and S. Gill. New York: Palgrave Macmillan, pp. 66–82.

Bakker, I. and S. Gill. (2003). "Ontology, Method, and Hypotheses. Global Political Economy and Social Reproduction." In *Power, Production and Social Reproduction. Human In/security in the Global Political Economy*, ed. I. Bakker and S. Gill. New York: Palgrave Macmillan, pp. 17–41.

Bakker, I. and S. Gill (eds). (2003). *Power, Production and Social Reproduction. Human In/security in the Global Political Economy*. New York: Palgrave Macmillan.

Baldéz, L. (2006). "The Pros and Cons of Gender Quota Laws: What Happens When You Kick Men Out and Let Women In?" *Politics & Gender* 2: 102–109.

Bayes, J. H., M. E. Hawkesworth *et al.* (2001). "Globalization, Democratization, and Gender Regimes." In *Gender, Globalization, and Democratization*, ed. R. M. Kelly, J. H. Bayes, M. Hawkesworth and B. Young. Lanham, MD: Rowman & Littlefield, pp. 1–14.

Bayes, J. H. and R. M. Kelly. (2001). "Political Spaces, Gender, and NAFTA." In *Gender, Globalization, and Democratization*, ed. R. M. Kelly, J. H. Bayes, M. Hawkesworth and B. Young. Lanham, MD: Rowman & Littlefield, pp. 147–170.

Bearden, T. (2011) Press Release: *New Guantánamo Papers Released – A Massive Egg on the Face of the United States*. Washington, D.C.: Council on Hemispheric Affairs (COHA), May 4. Available at: http://cohaforum.blogspot.com/2011/05/tim-bearden-press-releasenew-guantanamo.html.

Bendaña, A. (2004). "'Good Governance' and the MDGs: Contradictory or Complementary?" In: Global Policy Forum. Available at: www.globalpolicy.org/socecon/develop/2004/1012goodgovernance.htm (accessed April 17, 2005).

Benería, L. (1999). "Globalization, Gender and the Davos Man." *Feminist Economics* 5(3, November): 61–83.

Berdal, M. and D. Keen. (1997). "Violence and Economic Agendas in Civil Wars: Some Policy Implications." *Millennium: Journal of International Studies* 26(3): 795–818.

Bieler, A. and A. D. Morton. (2001). "The Gordian Knot of Agency-Structure in International Relations: A Neo-Gramscian Perspective." *European Journal of International Relations* 7(1): 5–35.

Birdsall, N. and J. Williamson. (2002). *Delivering on Debt Relief: From IMF Gold to a New Aid Architecture* (with Brian Deese). Washington, D.C.: Center for Global Development; Washington, D.C.: Institute for International Economics.

Blaney, D. L. and N. Inayatullah. (2002). "Neo-modernization? IR and the Inner Life of Modernization Theory." *European Journal of International Relations* 8(1, March): 103–137.

Blondet, C. (2002). "The 'Devil's Deal': Women's Political Participation and Authoritarianism in Peru – Cecilia Blondet." In *Gender Justice, Development, and Rights*, ed. M. Molyneux and S. Razavi. Oxford: Oxford University Press and UNRISD, pp. 277–306.

Boge, V. (1998). "Mining, Environmental Degradation and War: The Bougainville Case." In *Ecology, Politics and Violent Conflict*, ed. M. Sulliman. London: Zed Books, pp 211–228.

Bolivia. (1997). "Código de Minería. Ley 1777."

Bond, P. (2004). "Fighting Globalization.Should the World Bank and IMF Be 'Fixed' or 'Nixed'? Reformist Posturing and Popular Resistance." *Capitalism, Nature, Socialism* 15(2, June): 85–105.

Borón, A. (2009). "Bolivia: Why did Evo Morales win?" *LINKS, International Journal of Socialist Renewal*. Available at: http://links.org.au/taxonomy/term/102?page=3.

Bouchey, F. L., R. W. Fontaine *et al.* (1979). "Documento Santa Fé I. Las Relaciones Interamericanas: Escudo de la Seguridad del Nuevo Mundo y Espada de la Proyección del Poder Global de Estados Unidos." Council for Inter-American Security. Available at: www.geocities.com/proyectoemancipacion/documentossantafe/santafei.doc (accessed September 18, 2005).

Bouchey, F. L., R. W. Fontaine *et al.* (1988). "Documento Santa Fé II. Una Estrategia para América Latina en la Década de 1990." Council for Inter-American Security. Available at: www.geocities.com/proyectoemancipacion/documentossantafe/santafeii.doc (accessed September 18, 2005).

Bourdieu, P. (1998). *On Television*. New York: The New Press.

Bourdieu, P. (2002). *Distinction. A Social Critique of the Judgement of Taste*. Cambridge, MA: Harvard University Press.

Briceño Ruiz, J. (2007). "Strategic Regionalism and Regional Social Policy in the FTAA Process." *Global Social Policy* 7(3): 294–315.

Briceño Ruiz, J. (2010). "La iniciativa del Arco del Pacífico Latinoamericano. Un nuevo actor en el escenario de la integración regional." *Nueva Sociedad* 228: 44–59.

Bright, J. (2008). *Bolivia: A National Clash over Multiple Worlds*. Madrid: Fundación para las Relaciones Internacionales y el Diálogo Exterior, 10pp.

Brohman, J. (1995). "Economism and Critical Silences in Development Studies: a Theoretical Critique of Neoliberalism." *Third World Quarterly* 16(2): 297–318.

Buerbach (2010). "Communitarian Socialism in Bolivia." *Global Alternatives* (April 10): 4. Available at: http://globalalternatives.org/node/113.

Buitrago, M. A. (2006). "El significado de la llegada de Evo Morales al poder en la República de Bolivia." *Iberoamericana: América Latina, España, Portugal* 6(22, June): 159–164.

Buitrago, M. A. (2007). "Bolivia's New Constitution – A Nation Faces the Acid Test." *GIGA Focus* 12: 1.

Buitrago, S. R. d. and M. A. Buitrago. (2008). "Intensifying Confrontation: The Communication Patterns of the Morales Government on Autonomy in Bolivia." *Lateinamerika Analysen* 3: 155–174.

Bullard, N. (December 2003). The Millennium Development Goals and the Poverty Reduction Strategy Paper: "Two Wrongs Don't Make a Right." In *Anti Poverty or Anti Poor? Millennium Development Goals and the Eradication of Extreme Poverty and Hunger*. Bangkok: Focus on the Global South, pp. 15–16.

Bumpus, A. G. and Liverman, D. M. (2008). "Accumulation by Decarbonization and the Governance of Carbon Offsets." *Economic Geography* 84 (2, April): 127–155.

Burbach, R. (2009). "Treating Bolivia as a Sovereign Partner." *NACLA Report on the Americas* 42(1, January–February): 33–35.

Bureau of International Narcotics and Law Enforcement Affairs (BINLEA). U.S. Department of State. Available http: www.state.gov/p/inl/rls/fs/122397.htm (accessed June 26, 2010).

Burfisher, M., S. Robinson *et al.* (2003). Regionalism: Old and New, Theory and Practice. International Agricultural Trade Research Consortium (IATRC). Paper Presented at the International Conference Agricultural Policy Reform and the WTO, "Where Are We Heading?" Capri, Italy, June 23–26.

Cámara, A. and M. Vernengo. (2001). "The German Balance of Payment School and the Latin American Neo-Structuralists." In *Credit, Interest Rates and the Open Economy*, ed. L. P. Rochon and M. Vernengo. Cheltenham: Edward Elgar.

Campbell, B. (2005). "The Case Against Continental Deep Integration www.carleton.ca/ ctpl/documents/TheCaseAgainstContinentalDeepIntegration-BruceCampbell.pdf."

Carlsen, L. (2011a). *Obama's Mexicogate? U.S. Gov't Agents Ran Guns to Mexican Drug Cartels*. Mexico City: Americas Program, Center for International Policy, April 23. Available at: http://axisoflogic.com/artman/publish/Article_62853.shtml.

Carlsen, L. (2011b). *Javier Sicilia: "The United States Imposed This War on Us, It Should Change the Strategy."* Mexico City: Americas Program, Center for International Policy, June 7. Available at: www.cipamericas.org/archives/4759.

Cassen, B. (2006). "Une nouvelle Amerique latine a Vienne." *Le Monde Diplomatique* 53(627, June): 20.

CEPROMIN. "Data Base. Correspondence between the Da Capo Resources/Vista Gold, Government and Labour Unions, La Paz."

Cernea, M. M. (1995a). "Understanding and Preventing Impoverishment from Displacement: Reflections on the State of Knowledge." *Journal of Refugee Studies* 8(3): 245–264.

Cernea, M. M. (1995b). "Social Integration and Population Displacement: The Contribution of Social Science." *International Social Science Journal* 47(1, 143, March): 91–112.

Cernea, M. (1997). "The Risks and Reconstruction Model for Resettling Displaced Populations." *World Development* 25: 1569–1587.

Cerny, P. G. (1997). "Paradoxes of the Competition State: The Dynamics of Political Globalization (A Tribute to the Work of Ghita Ionescu)." *Government and Opposition* 31(2, spring): 250–275.

Charmaz, K. (2005). "Grounded Theory in the 21st Century: Applications for Advancing Social Justice Research."In *The SAGE Handbook of Qualitative Research*, ed. N. K. Denzin and Y. S. Lincoln. Thousand Oaks, CA: Sage, pp. 507–536.

Chávez-Malaluan, J. J. and S. Guttal. (2003). "Poverty Reduction Strategy Papers: A Poor Package for Poverty Reduction. Bangkok, Focus on the Global South." In *Anti Poverty or Anti Poor? The Millennium Development Goals and the Eradication of Extreme Poverty and Hunger*, pp. 17–32.

Chilcote, R. H. (1994). *Theories of Comparative Politics.The Search for a Paradigm Reconsidered*. Boulder, CO; San Francisco, CA; Oxford: Westview Press.

Chomsky, N. (2009) "Obama Recycles George W. Bush Plans. Marina Portnoya Interviewing Political Activist Noam Chomsky." *Russia Today*, May 11. Available at: www.youtube.com/watch?v=63HNuL2tfNc.

Christensen, J. (2011). "The Looting Continues: Tax Havens and Corruption." *Critical Perspectives on International Business* 7(2): 177–196.

Clémençon, R. (2008). "The Bali Road Map: A First Step on the Difficult Journey to a Post-Kyoto Protocol Agreement." *The Journal of Environment and Development* 17(1, March): 70–94.

CODHES (2010). "Consultoria para los Derechos Humanos y el Desplazamiento." Colombia. Available at: www.codhes.org/.

Coleman, K. M. and G. C. Herring. (1991). *The Central American Crisis*. Wilmington, DE: Scholarly Resources.

Concheiro-Bórquez, L., R. D. Quintana *et al.* (2000). *Derechos Territoriales y Agrarios, Movilidad y Mercado de Tierras a 18 Años de Política Neoliberal en México*. Hands Across the Hemisphere in the New Millennium, Latin American Studies Association, twenty-second International Congress, Miami, Florida, March 16–18.

Connell, R. W. (2001). "The Social Organization of Masculinity." In *The Masculinities Reader*, ed. S. M. Whitehead and F. J. Barrett. Cambridge: Polity Press, pp. 30–50.

Conway, D. and B. F. Timms. (2010). "Re-branding Alternative Tourism in the Caribbean: The Case for Slow Tourism." *Tourism and Hospitality Research* 10(4): 329–344.

Correa, R. (2008). "Ecuador: 21st Century Socialism." *Politique Internationale* 121(autumn): 419–434.

Cox, R. W. (1981). "Social Forces, States and World Orders: Beyond International Relations Theory." *Millennium* 12(2): 116–155.

Cox, R. W. (1993). "Gramsci, Hegemony and International Relations: An Essay in Method." In *Gramsci, Historical Materialism and International Relations*, ed. S. Gill. Cambridge: Cambridge University Press, pp. 49–66.

Cox, R. W. (ed.). (1996). *Approaches to World Order*. Cambridge: Cambridge University Press.

Cox, R. W. ([1977]1996). "Labour and Hegemony." In *Approaches to World Order*, ed. R. W. Cox. Cambridge: Cambridge University Press, pp. 420–470.

Cox, R. W. ([1983]1996). "Gramsci, Hegemony, and International Relations: An Essay in Method." In *Approaches to World Order*, ed. R. W. Cox and T. J. Sinclair. Cambridge: Cambridge University Press, pp. 124–143.

Cox, R. W. ([1992] 1996). "Towards a Posthegemonic Conceptualization of World Order: Reflections on the Relevancy of Ibn Khaldun." In *Approaches to World Order*, ed. R. Cox and T. J. Sinclair. Cambridge: Cambridge University Press, pp. 144–190.

C-PROBOL. (1998). *Bolivia Guarantees your Investment. Information for the Investor*. La Paz: Centro de Promoción Bolivia.

Craske, N. and M. Molyneux (eds). (2002). *Gender and the Politics of Rights and Democracy in Latin America*. New York: Palgrave Macmillan.

Curtin, C. (2011). "Infelicitous 40: The Anniversary of the U.S.'s War on Drugs." COHA, June 29. Available at: www.coha.org/the-anniversary-of-the-us-war-on-drugs/.

Dalton, G. (ed.). (1969). *Primitive, Archaic, and Modern Economies. Essays of Karl Polanyi*. Boston, MA: Beacon Press.

Da Silva, L. I. (2010). "The BRIC Countries Come into Their Own as Global Players." Available at: www.huffingtonpost.com/luiz-inacio-lula-da-silva/the-bric-countries-come-i_b_539541.html.

Delatorre, R. (2012). "Todos los caminos de salida conducen a Beijing." *Página 12*, June 26: 2–3.

del Granado, H. (2007). *Energy in Bolivia*. Real Instituto Elcano de Estudios Internacionales y Estratégicos, 6pp.

de Soysa, I. (2000). "The Resource Curse: Are Civil Wars Driven by Rapacity or Paucity?" In *Greed and Grievance: Economic Agendas in Civil Wars*, ed. M. Berdal and D. Malone. Boulder, CO: Lynne Rienner.

Dembele, D. M. (2004). "PRSPs: Poverty Reduction or Poverty Reinforcement?" *Economic Justice News* 7 (January, 1). Available at: www.50years.org/cms/ejn/story/40. Dakar, Senegal: Forum for African Alternatives & 50 Years is Enough Network South Council.

Denzin, N. K. and Y. S. Lincoln. (eds). (2003). *The Landscape of Qualitative Research: Theories and Issues*. Thousand Oaks, CA: Sage, 2nd edn.

Denzin, N. K. and Y. S. Lincoln. (eds). (2005). *The SAGE Handbook of Qualitative Research*. Thousand Oaks, CA: Sage, 3rd edn.

Desai, V. and R. Imrie. (1998). "The New Managerialism in Local Governance: North–South Dimensions." *Third World Quarterly* 19(4): 635–650.

Devlin, R. and A. Estevadeordal. (2001). *What's New in the New Regionalism in the Americas?* Working Paper No.6, Inter-American Development Bank, INTAL, ITD & STA.

Devlin, R. and Ricardo Ffrench Davis. (1999). "Towards an Evaluation of Regional Integration in Latin America in the 1990s." *The World Economy* 22(2): 261–290.

Donaldson, M. (1993). "What Is Hegemonic Masculinity?" *Theory and Society* 22(5, October): 643–657.

Duffield, M. (1998). "Post-modern Conflict: Warlords, Post-adjustment States and Private Protection." *Civil Wars* 1(1): 66–102.

Duncan, L. E., B. E. Peterson *et al.* (2003). "Authoritarianism as an Agent of Status Quo Maintenance: Implications for Women's Careers and Family Lives." *Sex Roles: A Journal of Research* 49(11/12, December): 619–630.

Dunkerley, J. (1985). *The Long War. Dictatorship and Revolution in El Salvador*. London: Verso, 2nd edn.

Dunkerley, J. (1990). "Reflections on the Nicaraguan Elections." *New Left Review* 182(July/August).

Dunkerley, J. (1994). *The Pacification of Central America. Political Change in the Isthmus, 1987–93*. London: Verso.

Dunkerley, J. and V. Bulmer-Thomas. (1999). *The United States and Latin America. The New Agenda*. ILAS, The David Rockefeller Center for Latin American Studies, and Harvard University Press.

Dunkerley, J. and R. Sieder. (1996). "The Military in Central America: The Challenge of Transition." In *Central America: Fragile Transition*, ed. R. Sieder. Basingstoke: Macmillan.

Eisenstein, H. (2009). "Some Strategies for Left Feminists (and Their Male Allies) in the Age of Obama." *Socialism and Democracy* 23 (2, July): 21–46.

Eriksoson-Baaz, M. and M. Stern. (2009). "Why Do Soldiers Rape? Masculinity, Violence, and Sexuality in the Armed Forces in the Congo (DRC)." *International Studies Quarterly* 53(2, June): 495–518.

Escobar, A. (1995). *Encountering Development. The Making and Unmaking of the Third World*. Princeton, NJ: Princeton University Press.

Escobar, A. (2003). "Displacement, Development, and Modernity in the Colombian Pacific." *UNESCO*: 157–167.

Estellano, W. (1994). "From Populism to the Coca Economy in Bolivia." *Latin American Perspectives* 21(4): 34–45.

Esteradeordal, A., J. Goto *et al.* (2001). "The New Regionalism in the Americas: The Case of Mercosur." *Journal of Economic Integration* 16(2, June): 180–202.

Fairhead, J. (2000). "The Conflict over Natural and Environmental Resources." In *The Origins of Humanitarian Emergencies: War and Displacement in Developing Countries*, ed. E. W. Wayne, F. Stewart and R. Vayrynen. Oxford: Oxford University Press.

Farthing, L. and B. Kohl. (2001). "Bolivia's New Wave of Protest." *NACLA Report on the Americas* 34 (5, March/April): 8–11.

Fernández-Kelly, M. P. (1984). *For We Are Sold, I and My People*. Albany, NY: SUNY Press.

Fishel, J. T., J. Graf *et al.* (2006). "Bolivia's Future: The Government of Evo Morales." *Security and Defense Studies Review* 6(3, winter): 263–284.

Fix-Fierro, H. and S. López-Ayllo. (1997). "The Impact of Globalization on the Reform of the State and the Law in Latin America (International Law in the Americas: Rethinking National Sovereignty in an Age of Regional Integration)." *Houston Journal of International Law* 19(3, spring): 785–805.

Fontaine, R., L. A.Tambs *et al.* (1999). Documento Santa Fé IV. "Latinoamérica Hoy." Council for Inter-American Security. Available at www.geocities.com/proyectoemancipacion/documentossantafe/santafeiv.doc (accessed September 18, 2005).

Freire, P. (2000). *Pedagogy of the Oppressed*. New York: Continuum.

Freud, S. (1989). *Civilization and Its Discontents*. New York, London: W.W. Norton.

Fuentes, F. (2007). "The Struggle for Bolivia's Future." *Monthly Review* 59(July–August): 95–109.

Furtado, C. (1987). "Transnationalization and Monetarism." *International Journal of Political Economy* 17(1): 15–44.

Gall, N. (2006). *Gas in Bolivia: Conflicts and Contracts*. Real Instituto Elcano de Estudios Internacionales y Estratégicos, 7pp.

Gamarra, E. A. (2007a). *Bolivia on the Brink*. New York: Brookings Institution Press.

Gamarra, E. A. (2007b). *Working with Evo Morales: Building Constructive US–Bolivia Relations*. New York: Brookings Institution Press.

García Linera, A. (2006). "Neo-liberalism and the New Socialism." Speech, October 29.

Gavin, E. (2010). *Guantanamo Bay: Change We Can't Believe In*. Washington, DC: Council on Hemispheric Affairs (COHA). Available at: www.coha.org/guantanamo-bay-change-we-can%E2%80%99t-believe-in/.

Gay-Stolberg, S. (2009) "In Mexico, Obama Seeks Curbs on Arms Sales", *New York Times*, April 17. Available at: www.nytimes.com/2009/04/17/world/americas/17prexy.html?pagewanted=print (accessed June 28, 2011).

Gedda, G. (2006). "Pressure Grows for Change in the Americas." *Foreign Service Journal* 83(4, April): 20–26.

Geldard, R. (2000). *Remember Heraclitus*. Lindisfarne Books.

Gelles, P. H. (1995). "Equilibrium and Extraction: Dual Organization in the Andes." *American Ethnologist* 22: 710–742.

Gherardi, S. and B. Poggio. (2001). "Creating and Recreating Gender Order in Organizations." *Journal of World Business* 36(3, fall): 245–259.

Gill, L. (1997). "Relocating Class: Ex-miners and Neoliberalism in Bolivia." *Critique of Anthropology* 17(3, September): 293–312.

Gill, L. (2004). *The School of the Americas: Military Training and Political Violence in the Americas*. Durham, NC: Duke University Press.

Gill, S. (1990). *American Hegemony and the Trilateral Commission.* Cambridge: Cambridge University Press.

Gill, S. (1995). "The Global Panopticon? The Neoliberal State, Economic Life, and Democratic Surveillance." *Alternatives: Social Transformation and Humane Governance* 20(1, January–March): 1–49.

Gill, S. (ed.). (1997). *Globalization, Democratization, and Multilateralism.* New York: St. Martin's Press.

Gill, S. (2000). "The Constitution of Global Capitalism." *Global Site*: Paper presented to a Panel: The Capitalist World, Past and Present at the International Studies Association Annual Convention, Los Angeles. Available at: www.theglobalsite.ac.uk/press/.

Gill, S. (2003). *Power and Resistance in the New World Order.* Basingstoke: Palgrave Macmillan.

Ginzburg, C. (1992). *The Cheese and the Worms. The Cosmos of a Sixteenth-century Miller.* Baltimore, MD: The Johns Hopkins University Press.

Ginzburg, C. (2002). *The Judge and the Historian.* London. New York: Verso.

Golinger, E. (2009). "USAID's Silent Invasion in Bolivia." *NACLA Report on the Americas.* Available at: http://nacla.org/node/5832.

Gómez Rocabado, P. (2006). "Mining Companies must Respect not Just the Law but the People." In *Community Rights and Corporate Responsibility. Canadian Mining and Oil Companies in Latin America*, ed. L. North, T. D. Clark and V. Patroni. Toronto: Between the Lines, pp. 87–89.

Gramsci, A. (1997). *Selections from the Prison Notebooks*, ed. Q. Hoare and G. Nowell Smith. New York: International Publishers.

Gratius, S. (2007). *The "Third Populist Wave" of Latin America.* Madrid: Fundación para las Relaciones Internacionales y el Diálogo Exterior.

Gratius, S. and L. Tedesco. (2009). *Bolivia y Venezuela: Caminos políticos cada vez más diferentes.* Fundación para las Relaciones Internacionales y el Diálogo Exterior (FRIDE), 5pp.

Grebe López, H. (2006). *Uncertainties in the Bolivian Process.* Real Instituto Elcano de Estudios Internacionales y Estratégicos, 5pp.

Greenhill, R. (2002). "New World Bank Reports Confirm that the HIPC Initiative is Failing." www.jubileeplus.org/analysis/articles/hipc290402.htm: Jubilee Research (accessed April 27, 2005).

Grimson, A. and E. P. Soldán. (2000). *Migrantes Bolivianos en la Argentina y los Estados Unidos.* La Paz, Bolivia: Programa de Naciones Unidas para el Desarrollo (PNUD).

Guevara, E. (1996a). *Ernesto "Che" Guevara: Obras Completas.* Buenos Aires: Legasa.

Guevara, E. (1996b). "La Alianza fracasará (Discurso pronunciado el 17 de agosto de 1961, Universidad de la República del Uruguay)." In *Ernesto "Che" Guevara: Obras Completas.* Buenos Aires: Legasa, pp. 281–294.

Guevara, E. (1996c). "Quieren hacernos pagar muy alto el precio de la paz (Discurso pronunciado el 16 de agosto de 1961, reunión del CIES, Punta del Este, Uruguay)." In *Ernesto "Che" Guevara: Obras Completas.* Buenos Aires: Legasa, pp. 267–277.

Guevara, E. (1996d). "Si la Alianza para el Progreso fracasa (Discurso pronunciado el 8 de agosto de 1961, reunión del CIES, Punta del Este, Uruguay)." In *Ernesto "Che" Guevara: Obras Completas.* Buenos Aires: Legasa, pp. 219–254.

Gupta, A. (2010). "Haiti: A New U.S. Occupation Disguised as Disaster Relief?" *Z Magazine* 23 (3): 6.

Gutiérrez, R. and D. Mokrani. (2006). "Nationalization without Expropriation?" *Foreign Policy In Focus* (June 12): 6.

Guttal, S. (2002). "Poverty Reduction? or PRSP?" Presentation at the Seminar on the Participation of Civil Society in PRSPs, Brussels, September 16, 2002. Available at: www.cadtm.org/imprimer.php3?id_article=265 (accessed April 27, 2005), Focus on the Global South.

Guttal, S. (2003). "Missing the Mark, or Deliberately Misleading? The World Bank's Assessments of Absolute Poverty and Hunger." Bangkok: Focus on the Global South. In *Anti Poverty or Anti Poor? The Millennium Development Goals and the Eradication of Extreme Poverty and Hunger*, pp. 37–42.

Guzmán Rada Cusicanqui, V. R. (1999). *El Llanto de la Razón.Obra de Teatro en un Acto por Viraguracu*. La Paz, Bolivia: CEPROMIN.

Hackenberg, R. A. (1999). "Victims of Globalization: Is Economics the Instrument Needed to Provide Them a Share of the Wealth?" *Human Organization* 58(4, winter): 439–442.

Hahn, D. R. (1996). "The Use and Abuse of Ethnicity: The Case of the Bolivian CSUTCB." *Latin American Perspectives* 23: 91–106.

Hampton, M. P. and J. Christensen (2002). "Offshore Pariahs? Small Island Economies, Tax Havens, and the Re-configuration of Global Finance." *World Development* 30(9): 1657–1673.

Hampton, M. P. and J. Christensen. (2007). "Competing Industries in Islands. A New Tourism Approach." *Annals of Tourism Research* 34(4):998–1020.

Harootunian, H. (2002). "Quartering the Millennium." *Radical Philosophy* 116(November–December): 21–29.

Harris, O. (2000). *To Make the Earth Bear Fruit: Ethnographic Essays on Fertility, Work and Gender in Highland Bolivia*. London: Institute of Latin American Studies, University of London.

Harvey, D. (1988). "The Geographical and Geopolitical Consequences of the Transition from Fordist to Flexible Accumulation." In *America's New Market Geography*, ed. G. Sternlieb and J. W. Hughes. New Jersey: Rutgers.

Harvey, D. (1990). *The Condition of Postmodernity*. Oxford: Blackwell.

Harvey, N. (1998). *The Chiapas Rebellion: The Struggle for Land and Democracy*. Durnham, DC: Duke University Press.

Hasenclever, Mayer *et al.* (1997). *Theories of International Regimes*. Cambridge: Cambridge University Press.

Henry, J. S. (2004). "Brazil's 1964 Military Coup. The Political Foundations of Regressive Development." *Submerging Markets*: 1–14.

Heraclitus. (2003). *Heraclitus, Fragments*. Foreword by James Hillman, translated by Brooks Haxton. New York: Penguin Books.

Hershberg, E. (2005). "The Political Economy of Development." *LASA Forum* 36(3, fall): 11–12.

Hobsbawm, E. (2010). "Interview: World Distempers." *New Left Review* 61 (January–February): 133–150.

Hopton, J. (1999). "Militarism, Masculinism and Managerialisation in the British Public Sector." *Journal of Gender Studies* 8(1, March): 71–82.

Htun, M. N. (2003). "Why Identity Groups Get Represented in Politics." *Draft*. Available at: newschool.edu: www.newschool.edu/gf/polsci/seminar/Htun9–25–03.pdf (accessed July 1, 2006).

Htun, M. N. (2004). "Is Gender like Ethnicity? The Political Representation of Identity Groups." *Perspectives on Politics* 2(3): 439–458.

Htun, M. N. (2006). "Women, Political Parties and Electoral Systems in Latin America.": www.idea.int/publications/wip2/upload/Latin_America.pdf (accessed July 1, 2006).

Htun, M. N. and M. P. Jones. (2002). "Engendering the Right to Participate in Decision-making: Electoral Quotas and Women's Leadership in Latin America." *Gender and the Politics of Rights and Democracy in Latin America*, ed. N. Craske and M. Molyneux. New York: Palgrave MacMillan, pp. 32–56.

Huntington, S. (1968). *Political Order in Changing Societies*. New Haven, CT: Yale University Press.

Hursthouse, G. and T. Ayuso. (2010). *Cambio? The Obama Administration in Latin America: A Disappointing Year in Retrospective*. Washington, D.C.: Council on Hemispheric Affairs (COHA) (January 26), 8pp.

Inayatullah, N. and D. L. Blaney. (1999). "Towards an Ethnological IPE: Karl Polanyi's Double Critique of Capitalism." *Millennium: Journal of International Studies* 28(2): 311.

International Labour Organization. (1989). Convention No. 169 Concerning Indigenous and Tribal Peoples in Independent Countries, Available at: www.usask.ca/nativelaw/ILO169.html (accessed May 2002).

Isacson, A. (2005). "Closing the "Seams": U.S. Security Policy in the Americas." *NACLA Report on the Americas* 38(6, May/June): 13–17.

Jaquette, J. (2000). "Women and Democracy, Regional Differences and Contrasting Views." *Journal of Democracy* 12(3): 111–125.

Jenkins, R. (2002). *Pierre Bourdieu (Revised Edition)*. London: Routledge.

Joas, H. (1999). "The Modernity of War. Modernization Theory and the Problem of Violence." *International Sociology* 14(4, December): 457–472.

Jones, M. P. (2004). "Quota Legislation and the Election of Women: Learning from the Costa Rican Experience." *Journal of Politics* 66(4): 1203–1223.

Jones, M. P. (2005). "The Desirability of Gender Quotas: Considering Context and Design." *Politics & Gender* (1): 645–652.

Jones, T. and P. Hardstaff. (May 2005). *Denying Democracy: How the IMF and World Bank Take Power from People*. London: World Development Movement. Available at: www.wdm.org.uk/democracy/democracy.doc (accessed February 24, 2006): 1–39.

Jost, S. (2006). "Bolivia after the Political Landslide." *GIGA Focus* 2(February): 1–15.

Jost, S. (2008). "Bolivia: Political Refoundation in a Deadlock." *GIGA Focus* 7.

Kaldor, M. (1999). *New and Old Wars. Organized Violence in a Global Era*. Cambridge: Polity Press.

Kalima, B. (2001). "PRSPs – SAPs in Disguise?": Harare, Zimbabwe: African Forum and Network on Debt and Development (AFRODAD). Available at: www.afrodad.org/prsp/prsp-sap.htm (accessed April 27, 2005).

Kanchan, C. (2005). "Ethnic Parties and Democratic Stability." *Perspectives on Politics* 3(2, June): 235–252.

Kaplan, S. (2006). "Making Democracy Work in Bolivia." *Orbis* 50(3, summer): 501–517.

Karl, T. L. (1997). *The Paradox of Plenty: Oil Booms, Venezuela, and other Petro-States*. Berkeley, CA: University of California Press.

Keeley, J. (1990). "Toward a Foucauldian Analysis of International Regimes." *International Organization* 44: 83–105.

Keen, D. (1998). *The Economic Functions of Violence in Civil Wars*. Oxford: Oxford University Press.

Klare, M. (2002). *Resource Wars: The New Landscape of Global Conflict*. London: Owl Books, reprint edn.

Klein, H. S. (1992). *Bolivia: The Evolution of a Multi-ethnic Society*. New York and Oxford: Oxford University Press.

Klein, N. (2008). *Naomi Klein on Obama, the Real News, Paul Jay Interviewing Naomi Klein*, August 26. Available at http: www.youtube.com/watch?v=_e4daR54iIQ.

Kohl, B. (2003). "Democratizing Decentralization in Bolivia: The Law of Popular Participation." *Journal of Planning Education and Research* 23(2): 153–164.

Kohl, B. and R. Bresnahan. (2010). "Bolivia under Morales: Consolidating Power, Initiating Decolonization." *Latin American Perspectives* 37(3, May): 5–17.

Kornbluh, P. (1999). "Declassifying U.S. Intervention in Chile." *NACLA Report on the Americas* 32(6, May/June).

Kornbluh, P. (2003). "Opening Up the Files: Chile Declassified." *NACLA Report on the Americas* 37(1, July/August).

Krasner, S. (1983). "Structural Causes and Regime Consequences: Regimes as Intervening Variables." In *International Regimes*, ed. S. D. Krasner. Ithaca, NY, and London: Cornell University Press, pp. 1–21.

Krook, M. L. (2004). "Reforming Representation: The Diffusion of Candidate Gender Quotas Worldwide." Annual International Studies Association Convention, Montréal, Canada, March 2004. Available at: columbia.edu www.columbia.edu/~mlk22/isa_proceeding_14671.pdf.

Krook, M. L. (2006). "Gender Quotas, Norms, and Politics." *Politics & Gender*(2): 110–118.

Kuczynski, P. P. and J. Williamson (eds). (2003). *After the Washington Consensus: Restarting Growth and Reform in Latin America*. Washington, D.C.: Institute for International Economics.

La Feber, W. (1993). *Inevitable Revolutions. The United States in Central America*. New York and London: W.W. Norton.

La Jornada. (2009). "Gana el sí a la Constitución; proclama Evo Morales la refundación de Bolivia." Available at: www.jornada.unam.mx2009/01/26. México.

Lantos, N. (2011). "El Gobierno presentará una queja a Estados Unidos por el 'material camuflado' hallado en un avión oficial. Una protesta formal por la valija." *Página 12*, February 14. Available at: www.pagina12.com.ar/diario/elpais/1–162332–2011–02–14.html.

Lantos, N. (2012a). "El nacimiento de la 'quinta potencia mundial." *Página 12*, August 1: 2–3.

Lantos, N. (2012b). "Hay que igualar para crecer." Interview with Alicia Barcena, Executive Secretary of CEPAL. *Página 12*, July 1:16.

LASA Forum. (fall 2005). 36(3).

Latham, R. (n.d.). Available at: www.yorku.ca/robarts/projects/canada-watch/obama/pdfs/Latham.pdf.

LatinoAméricAhora. (2009a). "En Cumbre de Unasur se desnudó pacto militar entre Colombia y EEUU." *Darío Vive, Portal latinoamericano de pensamiento crítico y plebeyo*, August 29. Available at: www.dariovive.org/p=163 (accessed September 2, 2009).

LatinoAméricAhora. (2009b). "Unasur: Uribe, Correa, Morales, Chávez y Lula". *Darío Vive, Portal latinoamericano de pensamiento crítico y plebeyo*. Available at: www.dariovive.org/?p=161.

La Vía Campesina. (2010). "Haitian Peasants March against Monsanto Company for Food and Seed Sovereignty." Available at: http://viacampesina.org/en/index.php?option=com_content&view=article&id=930:haitian-peasants-march-against-monsanto-company-for-food-and-seed-sovereignty&catid=49:stop-transnational-corporations&Itemid=76.

Lawrence, R. Z. (1996). *Regionalism, Multilateralism, and Deeper Integration.* Washington, D.C.: Brookings Institution Press.

Le Billon, P. (2001). "The Political Ecology of War: Natural Resources and Armed Conflicts." *Political Geography* 20: 561–584.

Lefebvre, H. (2008). *The Production of Space.* Oxford: Blackwell.

Lehoucq, F. (2008). "Bolivia's Constitutional Breakdown." *Journal of Democracy* 19(4): 110–124.

Leite, C. and J. Weidmann. (1999). "Does Mother Nature Corrupt? Natural Resources, Corruption, and Economic Growth." *IMF Working Paper WP/99/85*, Washington, D.C.

Leitner, H., E. Sheppard and K. M. Sziarto (2008). "The Spatialities of Contentious Politics." *Transactions of the Institute of British Geographers* 33(2): 157–172.

Levy, D. L., M. Alvesson *et al.* (2003). "Critical Approaches to Strategic Management." In *Studying Management Critically*, ed. M. Alvesson and H. Willmott. Newbury Park, CA: Sage.

Lewis, L. (2007). "Man Talk, Masculinity, and a Changing Social Environment." *Caribbean Review of Gender Studies* (1, April): 1–20.

Lins-Ribeiro, G. (1998). "Cybercultural Politics: Political Activism at a Distance in a Transnational World." In *Cultures of Politics. Politics of Cultures. Re-visioning Latin American Social Movements*, ed. S. E. Álvarez, E. Dagnino and A. Escobar. Boulder, CO: Westview Press, pp. 325–352.

López San Miguel, M. (2012). "La conspiración se instaló hace mucho. Entrevista a Domingo Laíno, líder histórico del Partido Liberal paraguayo." *Página 12*, June 29: 22.

Lowenthal, A. F. (2010). "Obama and the Americas: Promise, Disappointment, Opportunity." *Foreign Affairs* 89 (4, July–August): 110–124.

Lowy, M., E. Sader *et al.* (1985). "The Militarization of the State in Latin America." *Latin American Perspectives* 12(4): 7–40.

Luoma, A. and G. Gordon. (2006). "Turning Gas into Development in Bolivia." *Dollars and Sense* 268(November–December): 22–29.

Madrid Lara, E. (1999). *Del Abrigo de los Mallkus al Frío del Cemento: Negociaciones entre Apex Silver Limited y la Comunidad San Cristóbal de Nor Lípez (Bolivia).* Oruro: Centro de Ecología y Pueblos Andinos, y Santiago de Chile: Observatorio Latinoamericano de Conflictos Ambientales.

Malamud, C. (2006). *Venezuela's Withdrawal from the CAN (Andean Community of Nations) and the Consequences for Regional Integration (Part 3): The Nationalization of Bolivian Hydrocarbons.* Real Instituto Elcano de Estudios Internacionales y Estratégicos, 10pp.

Marchand, M. H. (2005). "Contesting the Free Trade Area of the Americas: Invoking a Bolivarian Imagination to Construct an Alternative Regional Project and Identity." In *Critical Theories, International Relations and "The Anti-globalisation Movement": The Politics of Global Resistance*, ed. C. Eschle and B. Maiguashca. London, New York: Routledge, pp. 103–116.

Matsunaga, F. (2009). *Amid UNASUR Summit, Brazil Likely to Emerge a Winner, With Colombia a Questionable Beneficiary.* Washington, D.C.: Council on Hemispheric Affairs, September 2. Available at: www.coha.org/amid-unasur-summit-brazil-likely-to-emerge-a-winner/.

McFarren, W. (1992). "The Politics of Bolivia's Economic Crisis: Survival Strategies of Displaced Tin-Mining Households." In *Unequal Burden: Economic Crises, Persistent Poverty, and Women's Work*, ed. L. Benería and S. Feldman. Boulder, CO, and Oxford: Westview Press, pp. 131–158.

McMichael, P. (1996). *Development and Social Change: A Global Perspective*. Thousand Oaks, CA: Pine Forge Press.

McSherry, J. P. (2000). "Argentina: Dismantling an Authoritarian Legacy." *NACLA Report on the Americas* 33(5, March/April).

Medinacelli-Monrroy. (1999). *El Actual Sistema Tributario en la Minería. Análisis Económico*. La Paz, Bolivia: Ministerio de Hacienda, Unidad de Análisis de Políticas Sociales y Económicas (UDAPE), pp. 147–168.

Meyer, M. K. and E. Prügl. (1999). *Gender Politics in Global Governance*. Lanham, MD: Rowman & Littlefield.

Mignolo, W. D. and M. V. Tlostanova. (2006). "Theorizing from the Borders: Shifting to Geo- and Body-Politics of Knowledge." *European Journal of Social Theory* 9(2, May): 205–221.

Miranda, C. (1990). *Tyranny and Longevity: Stroessner's Paraguay*. Boulder, CO: Westview Press.

Molinié Fioravanti, A. (1986). "The Andean Community Today." In *Anthropological History of Andean Polities*, ed. J. V. Murra, N. Wachtel and J. Revel. Cambridge and Paris: Cambridge University Press and Editions de la Maison des Sciences de l'Homme, pp. 342–360.

Molyneux, M. (2001). "Ethnography and Global Processes." *Ethnography* 2(2).

Molyneux, M. and N. Craske. (2002). "The Local, the Regional and the Global: Transforming the Politics of Rights." In *Gender and the Politics of Rights and Democracy in Latin America*, ed. N. Craske and M. Molyneux. New York: Palgrave Macmillan, pp. 1–31.

Monasterios, P. K. (2007). "Bolivian Women's Organizations in the MAS Era." *NACLA Report on the Americas* 40(2, March–April): 33–37.

Montes Ruiz, F. (1999). *La Máscara de Piedra: Simbolismo y Personalidad Aymaras en la Historia*. La Paz, Bolivia: Editorial Armonía, 2nd edn.

Morales, E. (2006). "Return of the Rising Son: Evo Morales and Bolivia's Revolution." *Political Affairs* 85(4, April): 38–41.

Morales, E. (2008). "Bolivia: A Revolution in Progress." *Politique Internationale* 119(spring): 49–67.

Morales, E. (2009). "Discurso del Presidente Constitucional de la Republica, Evo Morales, en ocasión de la promulgación de la nueva CPE." *Mariátegui, la revista de las ideas*, February 7, 2009. Available at: www.nodo50.org/mariategui/boliviadiscursodelpresidenteconstitucionaldelarepublica.htm (accessed March 6, 201)1.

Moraña, M. (2008). "Negotiating the Local: The Latin American 'Pink Tide' or What's Left for the Left?" *Canadian Journal of Latin American & Caribbean Studies* 33(66): 31–41.

Murphy, R. (2011). "Tax Havens, Secrecy Jurisdictions and the Breakdown of Corporation Tax." *Real-world Economics Review* 57.

Murra, J. (1980). *Research in Economic Anthropology, The Economic Organization of the Inka State*. Greenwich, CT: Jai Press.

Mushakoji, K. (2004). *Introduction to Human Security Sudies: In Face of Global Fascism*. Tokyo: Kokusai Shoin.

Nash, J. (1993). *We Eat the Mines and the Mines Eat Us. Dependency and Exploitation in Bolivian Tin Mines*. New York: Columbia University Press.

Nash, J. and M. P. Fernández-Kelly (eds). (1983). *Women, Men, and the International Division of Labor*. Albany, NY: SUNY Press.

Nef, J. (2005). "Globalization and Insecurity in the Americas." In *Latin America. Its*

Problems and its Promise. A Multidisciplinary Introduction, ed. J. Black. Boulder, CO: Westview Press, pp. 207–229.

Nef, J. (2006). "Human Security and Insecurity: A Perspective from the Other America." In *Protecting Human Security in a Post 9/11 World: Critical and Global Insights*, ed. G. Shani, M. Sato and M. K. Pasha. Basingstoke: Palgrave/Macmillan.

Nobel Prize Laureates. Available at: http://nobelprize.org/nobel_prizes/peace/laureates/2009.

North, L., T. D. Clark and V. Patroni. (2006). *Community Rights and Corporate Responsibility, Canadian Mining and Oil Companies in Latin America*. Toronto: Between the Lines.

North, L. and T. Korovkin. (1981). *The Peruvian Revolution and the Officers in Power 1967–1976*. Montréal: Centre for Developing Area Studies, McGill University.

Núñez M. R. and C. Jungwiry. (1997). *Oro y Sangre de Amayapampa y Capasirca*. Oruro: Santiago de Chile, Centro de Ecología y Pueblos Andinos; Observatorio Latinoamericano de Conflictos Ambientales.

Nuñes Lins, H. (2009). "State and Social Territorial Conflicts in Bolivia in the 21st Century." *Revista de Economía Política* 29(2): 228–244.

Obama, B. (2007). "Renewing American Leadership." *Foreign Affairs* 86(4): 2.

Obama, B. (2008). "A New Partnership for the Americas." Available at: BarackObama. com. http://obama.3cdn.net/f579b3802a3d35c8d5_9aymvyqpo.pdf.

Ocampo, J. A. (2009). "Latin America and the Global Financial Crisis." *Cambridge Journal of Economics* 33(4): 703–724.

Ocheje, P. (1997). "Legalizing Displacement: the Legal Order in the Political Economy of Nigeria." *Journal of Asian and African Studies* 32: 120–133.

O'Donnell, G. A. (1988). *Bureaucratic Authoritarianism*. Berkeley and Los Angeles, CA: University of California Press.

O'Donnell, G. A. (1994). "Delegative Democracy?" *Journal of Democracy* 5(1): 55–69.

O'Donnell, G. A. (1996). "Illusions About Consolidation." *Journal of Democracy* 7(2): 34–51.

Ong, A. (1990). "State versus Islam: Malay Families, Women's Bodies, and the Body Politic in Malaysia." *American Ethnologist* 17(2): 258–276.

Ossio, J. M. (1997). "Cosmologies." *International Social Science Journal* 49: 549–562.

Oualalou, L. (2009). "Les bases US en Colombie suscitent une crise régionale," Le Figaro, August 7. Available at: www.coha.org/2009/08/les-bases-us-en-colombie-suscitent-une-crise-regionale/.

Página 12. (2009a). "Opacidad de las finanzas mundiales." April 4.

Página 12. (2009b). "El arte de la evasión." April 4.

Página 12. (2009c). "Uruguay abre una ventana para compartir secretos." April 4.

Página 12. (2012). "Unidos hacia afuera, abiertos hacia adentro." June 30: 5.

Palan, R. (1996). "The Parasites: Tax Havens and Off-shore Finance." In *State Strategies in the Global Political Economy*, ed. R. Palan and J. Abbott. London: Pinter, pp. 166–183.

Palan, R. (1998). "Trying to Have your Cake and Eating it: How and Why the State System has Created Offshore." *International Studies Quarterly* 42: 625–644.

Palan, R. (2002). "Tax Havens and the Commercialisation of State Sovereignty." *International Organization* 56(1): 153–178.

Palan, R. (2003). *The Offshore World: Virtual Spaces and the Commercialisation of Sovereignty*. Ithaca, NY: Cornell University Press.

Palan, R. (2010). "The History of Tax Havens." *History & Policy*, available at: www.historyandpolicy.org/papers/policy-paper-92.html.

Palan, R. and C. Chavagneux. (2006). *Paradis Fiscaux*. Paris: La Decouverte.

Panizza, F. and R. Miorelli. (2009). "Populism and Democracy in Latin America." *Ethics & International Affairs* 23(1, spring): 39–46.

Patel, R. and P. McMichael. (2004). "Third Worldism and the Lineages of Global Fascism: The Regrouping of the Global South in the Neoliberal Era." *Third World Quarterly* 25(1): 231–254.

Paulson, S. and P. Calla. (2000). "Gender and Ethnicity in Bolivian Politics: Transformation or Paternalism?" *The Journal of Latin American Anthropology* 52: 112–149.

Pauwels, G. (1996). "Vetas y Venas (Editorial)." *Eco Andino, Oruro: Revista del Centro de Ecología y Pueblos Andinos (CEPA)* Año 1(2): 5–6.

Pearce, J. (1999). "Peace-building in the Periphery: Lessons from Central America." *Third World Quarterly* 20(1, February): 51–68.

Pearson, H. W. (ed.). (1977). *The Livelihood of Man. Karl Polanyi*. New York; San Francisco, CA; London: Academic Press.

Peterson, V. S. (1997). "Whose Crisis? Early and Post-modern Masculinism." In *Innovation and Transformation in International Studies*, ed. S. Gill and J. H. Mittelman. Cambridge: Cambridge University Press, pp. 185–202.

Pettman, J. J. (1997). "Body Politics: International Sex Tourism." *Third World Quarterly* 18(1): 93–108.

Pettman, N. J. (1996). "Women and Gender in the International Political Economy." In *Worlding Women. A Feminist International Politics*. London: Routledge, pp. 112–132.

Phillips, N. (2001). "Regionalist Governance in the New Political Economy of Development: 'Relaunching' the Mercosur." *Third World Quarterly* 22(4).

Phillips, N. (2003a). "Hemispheric Integration and Subregionalism in the Americas." *International Affairs* 79(2).

Phillips, N. (2003b). "The Rise and Fall of Open Regionalism? Comparative Perspectives on Regional Governance in the Southern Cone of Latin America." *Third World Quarterly* 24(2).

Phillips, N. (2004a). *The Southern Cone Model: The Political Economy of Regional Capitalist Development in Latin America*. Abingdon: Routledge.

Phillips, N. (2004b). The Americas. *The New Regional Politics of Development*. Basingstoke: Palgrave.

Phillips, N. (2005). "US Power and the Politics of Economic Governance in the Americas." *Latin American Politics and Society* 47(4): 4.

Phillips, N., S. Breslin *et al.* (2002). *New Regionalisms in the Global Political Economy: Theories and Cases*. Abingdon: Routledge.

Pickard, M. (August 24, 2005). "Trinational Elites Map North American Future in 'NAFTA Plus'." *Americas Program, International Relations Center (IRC)*. Available at: http://americas.irc-online.org/am/386 (accessed September 8, 2005).

Pieterse, J. N. (1991). "Dilemmas of Development Discourse: The Crisis of Developmentalism and the Comparative Method." *Development and Change* 22(1, January): 5–29.

Piette, C. (2009). "Leaders to Tackle US–Colombia Deal". BBC, August 28. Available at: www.coha.org/2009/08/bbc-leaders-to-tackle-us-colombia-deal/.

Pilger, J. (2008a). "John Pilger on Obama and US Foreign Policy, Democracy Now, Amy Goodman Interviewing John Pilger." November 7. Available at: www.youtube.com/watch?v=J1sFJVnw1bI.

Pilger, J. (2008b). "Obama is a Truly Democratic Expansionist." *New Statesman* 137 (4901): 22.

Platt, T. (1986). *El Rol del Ayllu Andino en la Reproducción del Régimen Mercantil*

Simple en el Norte de Potosí (Bolivia). Identidades Andinas y Lógica del Campesinado. Lima-Geneva, Editorial Mosca Azul and Institut universitaire d'études du développement.

Polanyi, K. (1944). *The Great Transformation: The Political and Economic Origins of Our Time.* Boston, MA: Beacon Press.

Polanyi, K., C. M. Arensberg *et al.* (eds). (1957). *Trade and Market in the Early Empires. Economies in History and Theory.* Glencoe, IL: The Free Press and the Falcon's Wing Press.

Polanyi-Levitt, K. (1985). "The Origins and Implications of the Caribbean Basin Initiative: Mortgaging Sovereignty?" *International Journal* 40(2): 229–281.

Poppe, R. (1977). *Compañeros del Tío. Cuentos Mineros.* La Paz, Bolivia: Centro de Información para el Desarrollo (CID).

Raby, D. (2008). "Latin America's Leftward Turn." *Global Dialogue* 10(1): 1–10.

Radcliffe, S. A. (2001). "Development, the State and Transnational Political Connections: State Formation and Networks in Latin America." *Global Networks* 1(1): 19–36.

Radio Pío XII. (1997). "La Masacre de Navidad (The Christmas Massacre) Amayapampa – Capasirca (Norte de Potosí)." *Eco Andino, Oruro: Revista del Centro de Ecología y Pueblos Andinos (CEPA)* Año 2(3).

Ramsaran, R. (1982). "The US Caribbean Basin Initiative." *The World Today* 38(11): 430–436.

Rapoport, M. and R. Laufer. (2000). "Los Estados Unidos ante el Brasil y la Argentina – los Golpes Militares de la Década del 60." *Estudios Interdisciplinarios de América Latina y el Caribe (EIAL)* 11(2, July–December). Available at: www.tau.ac.il/eial/ XI_2/rapoport.html.

Reiss, S. (2010). "Beyond Supply and Demand: Obama's Drug Wars in Latin America." *NACLA Report on the Americas* 43 (1, January–February): 27–31.

Remón, C., M. Powers *et al.* (January 26, 2005). Special Edition – The Impact of Mining. *Latin America Press* 37: 1–37.

Renner, M. (1996). *Fighting for Survival: Environmental Decline, Social Conflict, and the New Age of Insecurity.* New York: Norton.

Renner, M. (2002). *The Anatomy of Resource Wars.* Washington, D.C.: World Watch Institute.

Reno, W. (2000). "Foreign Firms, Natural Resources, and Violent Political Economies." *Social Science Forum.* Available at: www.social-science-forum.org.

Rist, G. (2002). *The History of Development.* London and New York: Zed Books.

Robin, P. (2000). "The Rotten Institution: Corruption in Natural Resource Management." *Political Geography* 19: 423–443.

Robinson, W. I. (1996). *Promoting Polyarchy. Globalization, US Intervention, and Hegemony.* Cambridge: Cambridge University Press.

Rodríguez, K. (2010). "Cuba–U.S. Rhetoric Timeline: Hope for a Basic Shift in Policy Disintegrates into Continued Polarization." *Council on Hemispheric Affairs* (March 17): 5.

Rogers, H. (2010). "The Greening of Capitalism?" *International Socialist Review* 70 (March–April). Available at: www.isreview.org/issues/70/feat-greencapitalism.shtml.

Roncallo, A. (2006). "Bolivia's Amayapampa and Capasirca Mines: Social Resistance and State Repression." In *Community Rights and Corporate Responsibility.Canadian Mining and Oil Companies in Latin America*, ed. L. North, T. Clark and V. Patroni. Toronto: Between the Lines, pp. 63–86.

Roncallo, A. (2010a). "The Cochabamba People's Accord as a Response to Obama's Market Approach to the Environment." Panel: Sustainable Development in the

Post-Copenhagen Era. Presented at the CASID Conference: Development in a New World Order, May 31–June 2 at Concordia University, Montréal, Québec, Canada.

Roncallo, A. (2010b). "The Post-Cold War: Cosmologies and Regionalisms from 'Above' & 'Below' in the Americas. A Polanyian Approach." Panel: Race, Ethnicity, Indigenous Peoples and Politics: Law, Territoriality and the Environment. Presented at the Canadian Political Science Association (CPSA), June 1–3 at Concordia University, Montréal, Québec, Canada.

Ross, M. L. (1999). "The Political Economy of the Resource Curse." *World Politics* 51: 297–322.

Rupert, M. (1993). "Alientation, Capitalism and the Inter-state System: Toward a Marxian/Gramscian Critique." *Gramsci, Historical Materialism and International Relations*, ed. S. Gill. New York; Melbourne: Cambridge University Press, pp. 67–92.

Ryan, J. J. (2004). "Decentralization and Democratic Instability: The Case of Costa Rica." *Public Administration Review* 64(1): 81–91.

Sachs, J. (1995). "Consolidating Capitalism." *Foreign Policy* 98(spring): 50–64.

Sachs, J. D. (2005). "The End of Poverty." *Time Magazine*, March 14: 41–52.

Safa, H. (1993). "The Social and Economic Consequences of Export Led Industrialization in the Caribbean Basin." In *Comparative Development Experiences*, ed. S. Kim, C. Kim and Y. Gong. Korea: Ajou University Press.

Safa, H. (1994). "Export Manufacturing, State Policy, and Women Workers in the Dominican Republic." In *Global Production: The Apparel Industry in the Pacific Rim*, ed. E. Bonacich, L. Cheng, N.Chinchilla, N. Hamilton and P. Ong. Philadelphia, PA: Temple University Press.

Safa, H. (1995a). "Economic Restructuring and Gender Subordination." *Latin American Perspectives* 22(2): 32–50.

Safa, H. (1995b). "Gender Implications of Export-led Industrialization in the Caribbean Basin." In *Engendering Wealth and Well-being*, ed. R. Blumberg, C. Rakowski, I. Tinker and M. Monteón. Boulder, CO: Westview Press.

Sanabria, H. (1999). "Consolidating States, Restructuring Economies, and Confronting Workers and Peasants: The Antinomies of Bolivian Neoliberalism." *Comparative Studies in Society and History* 41(3, July): 535–562.

Sassen, S. (2000). "Women's Burden: Counter-geographies of Globalization and the Feminization of Survival." *Journal of International Affairs* 53(2, spring): 503–524.

Saurin, J. (2001). "Global Environmental Crisis as the 'Disaster Triumphant': The Private Capture of Public Goods." *Environmental Politics* 10(4, winter): 63–84.

Schild, V. (1998). "Beyond the 'Passive State' and Other Globalism Myths: Nation States, Social Movements and Gendered Market Citizens." *Development* 41(2): 33–37.

Schinke, W. and P. Stricker. (2003). "Popular Participation Against Neoliberalism." *Latin American Perspectives* 30(3): 12–101.

Schneiderman, D. (1996). "NAFTA's Takings Rule: American Constitutionalism Comes to Canada." *University of Toronto Law Journal* 46(499).

Schneiderman, D. (2000a). "Constitutional Approaches to Privatization: An Inquiry into the Magnitude of Neo-liberal Constitutionalism." *Law and Contemporary Problems* 83: 83–107.

Schneiderman, D. (2000b). "Investment Rules and the New Constitutionalism." *Law and Social Inquiry* 25(3): 757–787.

Serbin, A. (2010). "Regionalismo y soberanía nacional en América Latina: los nuevos desafíos." *Nueva Sociedad*: 1–21.

Shettima, K. A. (1997). "Ecology, Identity, Developmentalism and Displacement in Northern Nigeria." *Journal of Asian and African Studies* 32: 66–80.

Shifter, M. (2010). "Obama and Latin America: New Beginnings, Old Frictions." *Current History* 109(724): 67–73.

Shultz, J. (2010). "'Evonomics' Gets a Second Term in Bolivia." *NACLA Report on the Americas* 43(1, January/February): 4–5.

Sukkink, L. (1995). "The Household as the Locus of Difference: Gender, Occupational Multiplicity and Marketing Practices in the Bolivian Andes." *Anthropology of Work Review* 16(1–2, March/June): 5–10.

Sikkink, L. and M. B. Choque. (1999). "Landscape, Gender and Community: Andean Mountain Stories." *Anthropological Quarterly* 72: 167–182.

Sinclair, T. J. (1999). "Synchronic Global Governance and the International Political Economy of the Commonplace." In *Approaches to Global Governance Theory*, ed. M. Hewson and T. J. Sinclair. New York: State University of New York, pp. 157–171.

Sklair, L. (1995). *Sociology of the Global System*. Baltimore, MD: Johns Hopkins University Press.

Slater, D. (1998). "The Spatialities of Democratization in Global Times." *Development* 41(2): 22–29.

Smith, A. (2010). "Haiti After the Quake. Imperialism with a Human Face", *International Socialist Review* 70 (March–April): 29.

Smith, P. H. (1996). *Talons of the Eagle. Dynamics of U.S –Latin American Relations*. New York; Oxford: Oxford University Press.

Smith, P. H. (2002). "From NAFTA to FTAA? Paths toward Hemispheric Integration." In *NAFTA in the New Millennium*, ed. E. J. Chambers and P. H. Smith. Edmonton and La Jolla: University of Alberta Press and Center for U.S.–Mexican Studies, University of California, San Diego, pp. 471–496.

Soederberg, S. (2004). "American Empire and 'Excluded States': The Millennium Challenge Account and the Shift to Pre-emptive Development." *Third World Quarterly* 25(2): 279–302.

Soltis, K. (2011). *Mexican Drug Violence Fueled by U.S. Guns*. Washington, D.C.: Council on Hemispheric Affairs (COHA), June 27. Available at: www.coha.org/mexican-drug-violence-fueled-by-u-s-guns/.

Stewart, F. and M. Wang. (n.d.). "Do PRSPs Empower Poor Countries and Disempower the World Bank, or is it the Other Way Around?" Yale University. Available at: www.yale.edu/ycias/globalization/stewart.pdf (accessed April 26, 2005).

St. John, R. B. (2006). "Peru's Humala is Washington's next 'Worst Nightmare'." *Foreign Policy In Focus* (April 25): 6.

Stern, S. J. (2010). "Filming the Fractured Soul of Chile: Guzmán's Epic and Elegy of Revolution." *NACLA Report on the Americas* 43(2, March–April): 40–44.

Strange, S. (1982). "Cave! Hic Dragones: A Critique of Regime Analysis." *International Organization* 36: 479–496.

Strange, S. (1998). *Mad Money: When Markets Outgrow Governments*. Ann Arbor: University of Michigan Press.

Suarez Montoya, A. (2011). "A Decade of Plan Colombia." *Pravda*, Russia, January 27. Available at: http://english.pravda.ru/hotspots/conflicts/27–01–2011/116693-A_decade_of_Plan_Colombia-0/.

Swords, A. and R. L. Mize. (2008). "Beyond Tourist Gazes and Performances. U.S. Consumption of Land and Labor in Puerto Rican and Mexican Destinations." *Latin American Perspectives* 35(3, May): 53–69.

Tedesco, L. (2008). *State Crisis and the Social Pact in Bolivia*. Madrid: Fundación para las Relaciones Internacionales y el Diálogo Exterior.

Theberge, A. (1999). *The Latin American Debt Crisis of the 1980s and its Historical Precursors*. Columbia University, Mimeo, pp. 1–17.

The Economist. (2006a). "Bolivia: Morales the Bountiful." 381(8508): 35–36, December 16–22.

The Economist. (2006b). "Bolivia: Now it's the People's Gas." 379(8476, May 6–12): 37–38.

The Economist. (2006c). "A Revolution Faces the Voters." 380(8484, July 1–7): 33–34.

Thiele, G. (1995). "The Displacement of Peasant Settlers in the Amazon: the Case of Santa Cruz, Bolivia." *Human Organization* 54(3, fall): 273–283.

Thompson, S. (2009). "Bull Horns and Dynamite: Echoes of Revolution in Bolivia." *NACLA Report on the Americas* 42(2 April 21–27.

Tiano, S. (1994). *Patriarchy on the Line: Gender, Labor, and Ideology in the Mexican Maquila Industry*. Philadelphia, PA: Temple University Press.

Tinsman, H. and S. Shukla. (2005). "Interdisciplinarity and Historical Encounter of the Americas." *LASA Forum* 36(3, fall): 17–19.

Torres, C. A. and D. Schugurensky. (2002). "The Political Economy of Higher Education in the Era of Neoliberal Globalization: Latin America in Comparative Perspective." *Higher Education* 43: 429–455.

Torres Rivas, E. (2010) "Las democracias malas de centroamérica. Para entender lo de Honduras, una introducción a Centroamérica", *Nueva Sociedad*, 226(March–April): 52–66.

Valenzuela, A. (1997). "Paraguay: The Coup That Didn't Happen." *Journal of Democracy* 8(1): 43–55.

Van Auken, B. (2012). "Paraguay's President Ousted in Parliamentary Coup." World Socialist Website. Available at: www.wsws.org/articles/2012/jun2012/lugo-j25.shtml (accessed July 2012).

Van Der Pijl, K. (1998). *Transnational Classes and International Relations*. London: Routledge.

Van Der Pijl, K. (2005). "Gramsci and Left Managerialism." *Critical Review of International Social and Political Philosophy* 8(4, December): 499–511.

Vanden Berg, T. M. (1999). "We are not Compensating Rocks: Resettlement and Traditional Religious Systems." *World Development* 27(2): 271–283.

Vanden, H. E. (1997). "Democracy Derailed: The 1990 Elections and After." In *The Undermining of the Sandinista Revolution*, ed. H. E. Vanden and G. Prevost. London: Macmillan.

Vanden, H. E. and G. Prevost. (1993). *Democracy and Socialism in Sandinista Nicaragua*. Boulder, CO: Lynne Rienner.

Vanden, H. E. and G. Prevost. (1999). *The Undermining of the Sandinista Revolution*. London: Macmillan; New York: St. Martin's Press.

Van Schaick, A. (2008). "Morales Remakes Bolivia. A New Constitution Grants Indigenous People Unprecedented Rights." In These Times, December 16. Available at: www.inthesetimes.com/main/article/4097/.

Velarde, M. (2007). "The Mexican Connection: Opening the Bonds of Drug Cartels in the Andean Region." *Security and Defense Studies Review* 7(2, fall): 245–265.

Von der Heydt-Coca, M. (1999). "When Worlds Collide: The Incorporation of the Andean World into the Emerging World Economy in the Colonial Period." *Dialectical Anthropology* 24(1, March): 1–43.

Von der Heydt-Coca, M. (2009). "Neoliberal Agenda in Bolivia and its Aftermath." *Perspectives on Global Development and Technology* 8(2–3): 347–371.

Walker, T. (1991). *Revolution and Counterrrevolution in Nicaragua: 1979 Through 1989*. Boulder, CO: Westview Press.

Waterfield, B. (2010). "Haiti Earthquake: US Ships Blockade Coast to Thwart Exodus to America." *Telegraph*, January 19. Available at: www.globalresearch.ca/haiti-earthquake-us-ships-blockade-coast-to-thwart-exodus-to-america/17116.

Watson, H. (1985). "The Caribbean Basin Initiative and Caribbean Development: A Critical Analysis." *Contemporary Marxism* 10: 1–37.

Waylen, G. (1998). "Gender and Governance: Democratic Consolidation and Economic Reform." *Journal of International Development* 10(7): 957–967.

Weber, H. (2004). "Reconstituting the 'Third World'? Poverty Reduction and Territoriality in the Global Politics of Development." *Third World Quarterly* 25(1): 187–206.

Weber, H. (2006). "A Political Analysis of the PRSP Initiative: Social Struggles and the Organization of Persistent Relations of Inequality." *Globalizations* 3(2): 187–206.

Wickham-Crowley, T. (1989). "Understanding Failed Revolution in El Salvador: A Comparative Analysis of Regime Types and Social Structures." *Politics and Society* 17(4, December): 511–537.

Wickham-Crowley, T. (1998). "Guerrilla Warfare" and "Latin American Popular and Guerrilla Revolts: 1960–1996." *Encyclopedia of Political Revolutions*. Washington, D.C.: Congressional Quarterly: 209–211 and 307–309.

Williamson, J. (2002). "Did the Washington Consensus Fail? www.iie.com/publications/papers/williamson1102.htm Washington, Institute for International Economics": Speeches, Testimony, Papers. Outline of remarks at the Center for Strategic & International Studies, November 6, 2002 (accessed April 20, 2005).

Winn, P. (2006). *Americas: The Changing Face of Latin America and the Caribbean*. Berkeley: University of California Press.

Witness for Peace. (2011). Available at: www.witnessforpeace.org/downloads/Col_FTA_factsheet.pdf (accessed July 4, 2011).

Wolfensohn, J. P. (2001). Memorandum to the Executive Directors, Operational Policy on Involuntary Resettlement, Draft OP/BP 4.12 (September 18). The World Bank, Washington, D.C.

Wolff, J. (2008). "Bolivia after the Constituyente: Contention In and About Democracy." *Lateinamerika Analysen* 2: 165–180.

World Bank Industry, A. E. D. (1996). *A Mining Strategy for Latin America and the Caribbean*. Washington, D.C.: World Bank.

World Bank PRSP Sourcebook. Available at: http://web.worldbank.org/WBSITE/EXTERNAL/TOPICS/EXTPOVERTY/0,,menuPK:336998~pagePK:149018~piPK:149093~theSitePK:336992,00.html (accessed February 24, 2006).

Xinhua Agencies. (2012). "Bolivian Government Condems Coup Attempt of Striking Police." June 25. Available at: www.globaltimes.cn/NEWS/tabid/99/ID/716906/Bolivian-govt-condems-coup-attempt-of-striking-police.aspx (accessed June 2012).

Yashar, D. J. (1998). "Contesting Citizenship. Indigenous Movements and Democracy in Latin America." *Comparative Politics* 31(1, October): 23–42.

Yashar, D. J. (1999). "Democracy, Indigenous Movements, and the Postliberal Challenge in Latin America." *World Politics* 52(1): 76–104.

Young, B. (2001). "Globalization and Gender: A European Perspective." *Gender, Globalization, and Democratization*, ed. R. M. Kelly, J. H. Bayes, M. Hawkesworth and B. Young. Lanham, MD: Rowman & Littlefield, pp. 27–47.

Young, O. R. (1982). *Resource Regimes. Natural Resources and Social Institutions*. Berkeley; Los Angeles; London: University of California Press.

Young, O. R. (1989). *International Cooperation: Building Regimes for Natural Resources and the Environment*. Ithaca, NY: Cornell University Press.

Yúdice, G. (1998). "The Globalization of Culture and the New Civil Society." In *Cultures of Politics. Politics of Cultures. Re-visioning Latin American Social Movements*, ed. S. E. Álvarez, E. Dagnino and A. Escobar. Boulder,CO: Westview Press, pp. 353–379.

Zibechi, R. (2009). *Massacre in the Amazon: The U.S.–Peru Free Trade Agreement Sparks a Battle Over Land and Resources*. Posted on CIP Americas June 15, 2009. Available at: www.cipamericas.org/archives/1748.

Zibechi, R. (2010). "Bolivia and Ecuador: The State against the Indigenous People." *Cipamericas*: www.cipamericas.org/archives/2810.

Zissis, C. (2006). "Bolivia's Nationalization of Oil and Gas." *Council on Foreign Relations, Inc.* May 12.

Index

For Product Safety Concerns and Information please contact our EU
representative GPSR@taylorandfrancis.com
Taylor & Francis Verlag GmbH, Kaufingerstraße 24, 80331 München, Germany

www.ingramcontent.com/pod-product-compliance
Lightning Source LLC
Chambersburg PA
CBHW070410270326
41926CB00014B/2773